Motivation in Language Planning and Language Policy

MULTILINGUAL MATTERS SERIES
Series Editor: Professor John Edwards, *St. Francis Xavier University, Antigonish, Nova Scotia, Canada*

Other Books in the Series
Beyond Bilingualism: Multilingualism and Multilingual Education
  Jasone Cenoz and Fred Genesee (eds)
Can Threatened Languages be Saved?
  Joshua Fishman (ed.)
Community and Communication
  Sue Wright
Identity, Insecurity and Image: France and Language
  Dennis Ager
Language and Society in a Changing Italy
  Arturo Tosi
Language Attitudes in Sub-Saharan Africa
  Efurosibina Adegbija
Language, Ethnicity and Education
  Peter Broeder and Guus Extra
Language Planning in Malawi, Mozambique and the Philippines
  Robert B. Kaplan and Richard B. Baldauf, Jr (eds)
Language Planning in Nepal, Taiwan and Sweden
  Richard B. Baldauf, Jr and Robert B. Kaplan (eds)
Language Planning: From Practice to Theory
  Robert B. Kaplan and Richard B. Baldauf, Jr (eds)
Language Reclamation
  Hubisi Nwenmely
Linguistic Minorities in Central and Eastern Europe
  Christina Bratt Paulston and Donald Peckham (eds)
Multilingualism in Spain
  M. Teresa Turell (ed.)
Quebec's Aboriginal Languages
  Jacques Maurais (ed.)
The Other Languages of Europe
  Guus Extra and Durk Gorter (eds)
The Step-Tongue: Children's English in Singapore
  Anthea Fraser Gupta
A Three Generations – Two Languages – One Family
  Li Wei
Other Books of Interest
At War With Diversity: US Language Policy in an Age of Anxiety
  James Crawford
The Languages of Israel: Policy, Ideology and Practice
  Bernard Spolsky and Elana Shohamy
A Reader in French Sociolinguistics
  Malcolm Offord (ed.)

Please contact us for the latest book information:
Multilingual Matters, Frankfurt Lodge, Clevedon Hall,
Victoria Road, Clevedon, BS21 7HH, England
http://www.multilingual-matters.com

MULTILINGUAL MATTERS 119
Series Editor: John Edwards

Motivation in Language Planning and Language Policy

Dennis Ager

MULTILINGUAL MATTERS LTD
Clevedon • Buffalo • Toronto • Sydney

Library of Congress Cataloging in Publication Data

A catalog record for this book is available from the Library of Congress.

British Library Cataloguing in Publication Data

A catalogue entry for this book is available from the British Library.

ISBN 1-85359-529-2 (hbk)
ISBN 1-85359-528-4 (pbk)

Multilingual Matters Ltd

UK: Frankfurt Lodge, Clevedon Hall, Victoria Road, Clevedon BS21 7HH.
USA: UTP, 2250 Military Road, Tonawanda, NY 14150, USA.
Canada: UTP, 5201 Dufferin Street, North York, Ontario M3H 5T8, Canada.
Australia: P.O. Box 586, Artarmon, NSW, Australia.

Printed and bound in Great Britain by the Cromwell Press Ltd.

Contents

Table and Figures

Introduction

During the last quarter of the twentieth century a number of major political changes have taken place in the world. Some have been drastic, violent and bloody, like the break-up of Yugoslavia. Others have been less so: Czechoslovakia became two Republics, devolution in the UK created a Scottish Parliament and a Welsh Assembly, a close-run vote nearly separated Quebec from Canada. Germany reunited and the European Union brought increasing numbers of countries together in formal organisations. Aboriginal land rights were more or less recognised in Australia. Immigration from South to North and East to West has increased to the stage where ethnic and linguistic minorities are present, although often unwelcome, in every major European country.

Many of these changes have been accompanied by new, draconian language policies or by major changes in old ones. France has passed laws making it a criminal offence to use some English words; Belgium has divided along linguistic lines; provision for teaching Roma has disappeared from Slovakia; anti-Hispanic feeling in the USA has led to some States declaring English their official language and barring welfare provision for illegal immigrants speaking other languages. At the same time, the European Charter for Regional and Minority Languages has been approved by more and more governments; there have been increased subsidies for Scottish Gaelic; British primary schools have a compulsory 'literacy hour' for all; both civil servants and citizens, now sometimes transformed into 'customers' of civil services, have gone to law to protect their linguistic human rights to use one language rather than another.

Behind all these examples of language planning or language policy lies the issue of motivation. Why should communities and governments wish to influence language behaviour? Is governmental language policy simply a selfish pursuit of elitist advantage? What exactly are the conscious or unconscious motives planners and policy-makers have for carrying out language-related actions, where the benefits, if indeed there are any, are likely to be long-term? Are motives for public policy related to the goals that ethnic, religious and linguistic communities adopt for their own language behaviour? Is there a similarity between public policies and plans, the deliberate plans groups adopt for language use, and the ways individuals manage their own language behaviour? If so, what is it?

In earlier publications we have investigated language policies typical of contemporary France and Britain, concluding that motives such as identity, insecurity and the creation of an image for the external world were important for each country (Ager, 1996b: 1999). Are these the only motives that matter? How far are the language planning motives of communities and states unique to such human groups? It is to explore questions such as these that we intend to consider and compare the motives and language behaviour of individuals, of language, ethnic or social communities, and of politically independent states and their governments and political parties. To do this we need to consider briefly the relevance of established theories about language and language behaviour; about language planning; and about motivation.

Language and Language Behaviour

Language can be studied as an abstract system, divorced from its users, rather like a computer language or set of mathematical notations, or as a system of signs and symbols, written as well as spoken, enabling human beings to interact with each other within a social setting. We are concerned here with the latter approach, with studying a form of human behaviour and with relevant approaches as outlined for example in sociolinguistics or the sociology of language (see Chambers, 1995; Halliday, 1978). At the same time we need to examine how the users themselves behave in relation to language and how it is used, whether their own or somebody else's. Hence, as well as looking at language-as-instrument, as a device used by human beings to communicate, we shall be considering language-as-object, as something about which people, communities and states have opinions and feelings. Language behaviour means both how humans behave when they use language and also how they behave towards others using language, or even towards the communication system being used.

Language-as-instrument

Language, as used by human beings within particular settings, has basically the three functions of expression, interaction and reference long since discussed by the Prague School of linguistics and its followers (Bühler, 1934; Halliday, 1978: 48). Speech and writing enable individuals and groups to express themselves, to give vent to feelings and thoughts. Sometimes they do this whether or not they are aware of any recipient for what they have to express, and whether or not they take much notice of their immediate setting or environment. Great poets and authors may write for posterity rather than for an immediate audience, and some care little about anything other than expressing themselves. In its second function, language enables interactive communication between one or many 'senders' and one or many 'receivers'. Language and the associated behaviour is intended to influence the recipient, to persuade, inform, give messages to, and receive them from, an interlocutor. Interaction is by definition two-way, and the most obvious example is spoken conversational interchange where the participants face each other and jointly construct the meaning of what is being said through constant adjustment depending on feedback.   The third function of language is to enable speakers and writers to refer to and describe objects, individuals, thoughts and ideas, whether or not these have ever existed in the past, exist now or might exist at some point in the future. Biography, scientific description, financial analysis are, at least on the surface, examples of dispassionate referential language use.

A speaker or sender intending to communicate in a specific 'speech event' does so from within a setting of which he or she is consciously aware to a greater or lesser extent. Senders understand, and in their message make more or less deliberate use of, environmental characteristics like time, geography or setting each of which has possible effects on the form as well as the content of the message. The sender has available a communicative mechanism which includes the language but also such paralinguistic techniques as the influence of vocal variation (breathing, timbre...), facial expression and gesture, or the effect on the message of using a particular typeface or handwriting style. The sender, too, can call on a range of alternative mechanisms, other ways of saying the same thing, including sometimes other languages or language varieties, and 'knows' how to vary these in ways that are appropriate to the circumstances. Usually, and certainly when the purpose of communication is interaction, the sender is aware of the intended recipient and their environment. The speech event itself takes place in response to some sort of stimulus, but is provoked, and its contents, the speech acts and the individual messages, are constantly adjusted by the sender's own communicative intent or purpose, which itself changes in response to ongoing analysis of the environment, the progress and success of the act itself, and feedback, if any, from the recipient.

Individual human beings must learn to use these functions of language in a particular society. Then, as they communicate in specific settings, they must 'plan' their use of language to produce the effect they seek. Even though the planning involved may be extremely rapid, the use of language is not simply an automatic reaction to the environment. Any parent who watches and listens to the youngest baby listening, analysing and creating his or her own means of communication can observe the planning process in action. Adults continuously select the language elements most appropriate to their intent, but also often try to 'improve' their own manner of speech, their own use of their own language in speech events. Many, for a variety of reasons, also learn a foreign language, learn a different variety of their own language for use in situations they wish to enter, learn how to persuade, or how to speak in public. The purpose of this is firstly to acquire or to improve their own linguistic, paralinguistic and social skills in order to achieve communicative competence: the ability to communicate successfully. But secondly adults aim to use language as a weapon by selecting communicative mechanisms to reflect their own personality, to influence others and to help them better understand their environment. The discourse speakers employ tells us much about who they are. Similarly, politicians, governments, advertisers and lawyers are adept at putting a spin on facts, at presenting their actions within a discourse they construct. Planning for language behaviour in these senses is planning for behaviour using language-as-instrument, and it is reasonable for motives for particular types of discourse use to be investigated (see e.g. Fairclough, 1989).

Language-as-object

In addition to finding out how to express oneself, influence others and make reference to visible, tangible and intangible objects and thoughts individuals also plan for, and in some cases, plan, the language behaviour of others. Young babies soon learn that they delight their parents by smiling and babbling and can delight themselves by provoking parents to talk to them; older children ask their parents and siblings to repeat sounds, to say one thing rather than another. Children manipulate, or plan, the language behaviour of their parents. Like children, adults too plan to influence the linguistic instruments others use: they encourage speakers to use particular ways of speaking, and respond to the discourse elements they wish to hear used. As a political audience, they construct the meaning of a political event such as a rally or protest march by encouraging or forcing the speakers to articulate some, and not other, political sentiments. Adults also try to 'correct' the speech patterns of others, particularly their offspring and those they consider to be in some ways inferior to themselves. Many, including those in authority, try to tell their co-citizens how to express themselves: which words to use, which pronunciations to adopt, which terms, languages and language varieties to use and which to reject. Many people go farther, and try to plan the communicative system itself. They express their pride in their own language, while denigrating other languages for a variety of reasons. Many people go as far as maintaining that a specific language has many unique characteristics: it is a sublime creation of the human spirit, it uniquely represents human cultural, intellectual and social achievement, and should be defended or used more widely for these reasons. It is usually the case that people praising a language know it well; it is often their own; and they tend to apply the same positive attitude towards its speakers. Other languages, or language varieties, are condemned for being sloppy, barbaric noises barely able to convey more than the most basic emotions, mere grunts. Typically, people condemning a language or language variety are, or profess to be, unaware of it in detail, and tend, too, to get 'poor' speakers to give up 'bad' habits and adopt 'proper' language. Many people thus try to influence language behaviour as though language behaviour were somehow divorced from its users. Although people thus go beyond language to try to influence social behaviour as well, often seeing the two as indissolubly linked, planning for language behaviour in these senses is planning language-as-object.

Language Planning

It is in this second sense of 'language behaviour' that the terms 'language planning' or 'language policy' have usually been used (cf. Kaplan and Baldauf, 1997). They have usually been used, too, when considering the language behaviour of communities or states rather than individuals. Language planning has thus come to mean the ways in which organised communities, united by religious, ethnic or political ties, consciously attempt to influence the language(s) their members use, the languages used in education, or the ways in which Academies, publishers or journalists make the language change. Language policy is official planning, carried out by those in political authority, and has clear similarities with any other form of public policy. As such, language policy represents the exercise of political power, and like any other policy, may be successful or not in achieving its aims.

Language planning is usually divided into three fields of application: status, corpus and acquisition planning. Status planning modifies the status, and hence the prestige, of languages or language varieties within society, often by modifying the way the language codes groups or individuals use are perceived ('deliberate efforts to influence the allocation of functions among a community's languages'). Corpus planning in the traditional sense is what communities do to the forms of the language ('graphization, standardisation, modernisation and renovation'), but is sometimes also subdivided into codification of the existing language together with its elaboration and modernisation by adding new terms or styles and controlling neologisms. Acquisition planning affects the 'acquisition, reacquisition or maintenance of first, second or foreign languages' (quotations from Cooper, 1989).

Cooper (1989: 89) developed an 'accounting scheme' to make it clear that analysing language planning of these three types means tracking eight components.

> What _actors_ attempt to influence what _behaviours_ of which _people_ for what _ends_, under what _conditions_, by what _means_, through what _decision-making process_, with what _effect_?

Three types of actors are usually distinguished as relevant to language issues: individuals, communities and states, although with the increasing complexity of modern society a number of organisms do not altogether fit this neat division. Global multinationals behave in many ways as though they were political states; supra-national groupings like the Commonwealth or the European Commission have their own planning and policy departments. While 'planning' is usually kept to the two definitions of 'influence' we have used - planning one's own use and planning (or manipulating) that of others - the word 'policy' is also loosely used, although it should be kept strictly to apply to the political actions of governments or states. Our usage here, in examining motives and motivation, keeps the word 'planning' for the unofficial influence exercised by individuals and communities, and 'policy' for official influence; and concentrates on the traditional three actors: individuals, politically dependent communities, and states or governments which have, to a greater or lesser extent, political control over a politically defined society. How different or how similar, in practical terms, the behaviour of these three actors is in relation to language-as-instrument or language-as-object remains to be seen.

Motivation: Goals, Attitudes and Motives

The component we are mainly concerned with in studying motivation is Cooper's 'ends'. Others use words like 'goals', 'aims' or 'purposes'. The motives for language planning are not always clear, nor openly stated, nor always understandable. Is there a general theory of motivation which might apply to human beings and to human groups, and which might help to illuminate planning and behavioural purposes? Psychology and social psychology do not lack theories of motivation. Most are directed towards understanding why people make choices, and most are aimed at reducing the complexity of the human situation by trying to identify key variables. A recent summary expresses the range thus:

> Expectancy-value theories assume two factors: expectancy of success in a task and the value attached to success in it. Sub-theories include: attribution theory, how one processes past achievement; self-efficacy theory, people's judgment of their capability of carrying out tasks; and self-worth theory, that the highest human priority is self-acceptance and the maintenance of positive face.
> Goal theories require that goals be set and pursued; key variables concern goal properties.
> Self-determination theory suggests that the essence of motivated action is a sense of autonomy.
> The key tenet in social psychology is that attitudes exert directive influence on behaviour.
> In addition to these four broad approaches, other factors have been seen as central to motivation: instincts, volition, psychical energy, stimulus and reinforcement, basic human needs. (Adapted from Dörnyei and Otto, 1998: 44)

Although we shall consider the appropriateness of many theories at different points, two of the broad approaches to motivation seem immediately relevant and have frequently occurred in the language planning literature. These two are goal theory and the study of attitudes, central to social psychology.

Goal theory and the satisfaction of needs provides the most obvious, and most direct entry point for studying specific acts of language behaviour, particularly those of individuals. Goals, ends, or purposes, as these may be variously called, may be immediate and short-term or long-range. They may be concrete and identifiable or vaguer and more idealistic. One possible set of distinctions between types of goal may thus be as follows, and as far as possible we shall maintain these terminological distinctions from this point, reserving the word 'goal' for the overall purpose and the overall theory.

An <u>ideal</u> (vision, intention) is an idealistic future state, unlikely to be achieved but essential as an end-point towards which planning is ultimately directed. An example would be peace and harmony between all conflicting ethnic groups, or an individual's perfect happiness.

An <u>objective</u> (mission, purpose) is a way of achieving the vision, or at least a realisable 'end' on the way towards it. An example might be the creation of a harmonious nation-state within which no ethnic community would feel threatened, or an individual's assimilation with a target ethnic group. Such an objective, although realisable, may not be easily attained. It is essentially long-term and future-oriented, and it may not be altogether clear when it is attained.

A <u>target</u> is a precise, achievable, identifiable point on the way towards the objective. Achievement of the target is measurable and often quantifiable. An example might be the cessation of hostilities in 1999 between two ethnic groups in the Balkans, or the introduction in the year 2003 of a new syllabus for foreign languages in education in France.

Consider nonetheless the following motives, each of which has been shown to explain the success of some individuals in one type of language behaviour, foreign language learning (Young, 1994). Not all of these are easily explained by goal theory:

- peer and parental pressure and expectation, as when a target-language group provides support for language learners, when competition spurs on individuals to greater achievement or when parents encourage young people to acquire career-relevant skills ;
- own achievement and the experience of success: high achieving language learners are positively motivated to greater efforts. Conversely, those who experience little success are often inclined to do less;
- imitation: an individual can often so admire a leader that he or she aspires to similar language behaviour;
- self-esteem: the wish to improve one's own skills, to be or appear to be competent;
- personality variables: extroversion, for example, can have positive motivating effect on those who wish to show their own level of expertise, while facilitating anxiety can motivate language users to a higher level of personal achievement in language.

Some of these motivations seem closer to needs than to goals. Maslow (1954) proposed a hierarchy of human needs which developed from basic physiological requirements like shelter, food and warmth to psychological ones like affection and belonging, to the highest levels of self-respect, esteem and self-actualisation. He considered that all needs have obvious motivational consequences on the actions of individuals and possibly also of groups, and at the higher levels led into the concept of goals and goal fulfilment. Communication through language has a role in the satisfaction of most such needs and goals. The need for affection, for example, betrays a feeling of insecurity. Self-realisation means that the concepts of personal and group identity become important. Spiritual fulfilment, likewise, depends on the types of belief one has, the ideology or set of beliefs one pursues. Goal theory, then, leads to concern with motives of instrumentality and integration, identity, ideology and insecurity.

How does the study of attitudes in social psychology clarify the motivation issue? There is a difference to be noted between the attitudinal theories developed to account for the behaviour of individuals, and those developed in social psychology aimed at unravelling the motives of groups. While goal theory, including the satisfaction of identified needs, is of obvious importance for the linguistic behaviour of individuals, particularly when considering language-as-instrument, the language attitudes developed in a particular community or state could be important in understanding the motives of groups in planning for language-as-object. Indeed attitudes towards different types of language behaviour have often been seen as central to understanding community language policies (cf. Baker, 1992). Attitudes also represent the emotion behind the specification of ideals, objectives and goals, explaining why a specific course of action is undertaken. Attitudes, in social psychology, are regarded as having three components, although emotion is central and for some the only element of importance: knowledge about the object or person, an emotion such as liking or hatred, and a tendency towards action of some sort in relation to the object or person.

In this book we start from an assumption that there exist about seven motives for language planning and policy actions: identity, ideology, image creation, insecurity, inequality, integration with a group, and instrumental motives for advancement. These derive in the first place from observation of the language planning literature, and their origins can be briefly summarised as follows. Larsen-Freeman and Long (1991: 172-93) reported that Gardner and Lambert (1959) grouped language-learning motives into two main tendencies, particularly relevant for their study of adult foreign language learning in officially bilingual Canada. Basing their views on the individual's quest for identity they made a distinction between integrative and instrumental motives. The former essentially social motive led individuals to learn a language so that they could associate with a particular community. The second set of reasons, essentially economic, related simply to career and self-advancement.

Ryan and Giles (1982) proposed two main 'motivating attitudes' for much of the language behaviour of communities. They called these status and solidarity. A search for (an improved) status for one's own language or language variety, and sometimes for a language not one's own, seems to be a main cause for much action aimed at improving the relative social position of the relevant community. The improvement of status goes hand-in-hand with an affirmation of the separate identity of the relevant social group, and indeed this term has been much used since to explain the motive of those minority communities seeking to improve their relative position in society. Solidarity, too, has often been redefined as a search for integration and fellow-feeling, and hence a matter of correcting social inequality between groups and communities in society. The motives of identity, essentially political, and the essentially social one of correcting inequality, as with the instrumentalism and integration pair proposed for individuals, have constantly recurred since in discussions of the reasons why communities take the actions they do.

On a more practical level Kaplan and Baldauf give a long list of what they call the goals of formal language planning (1997: 61). This list is derived mainly from the activities of language planning agencies working on behalf of states or communities and contains a number of goals of varying degrees of specificity. Some, in our terminology, are ideals (language reform) or objectives (stylistic simplification); others are much more specific targets (spelling standardisation). Others, again, like language maintenance, language spread or educational equity, seem to approach four of the motives we have noted so far: instrumentalism, integration, identity, inequality. The authors add others: the creation of a favourable image; issues of ideology, like social equity or the maintenance of a dominant language; and awareness of insecurity, as in issues of language rights. The authors did not attempt to hierarchise or systematise the list, which they developed from Nahir (1984). Indeed, while some goals seem like our motives and others like our goals, others such as language purification or (teaching languages of) international communication seem more like strategies to achieve goals which are not stated or to satisfy deeper motives. All could be thought of as essentially political, economic or social. In considering their list, the authors make three provisos (Kaplan and Baldauf, 1997: 59):

- language planning is seldom done with a single goal in mind;
- it may be based on contradictory goals;
- many of these goals are carried out to reach rather abstract purposes, which may be related to national policy goals.

Macro level	Alternative formulations	Examples
Language purification		
External purification		
Internal purification		French
Language revival		Hebrew
	restoration	
	transformation	
	regenesis	
	revitalisation	
	reversal	
Language reform		Turkish
Language standardisation	spelling and script standardisation	Swahili
Language spread		
Lexical modernisation	term planning	Swedish
Terminological unification	discourse planning	
Stylistic simplification		
Interlingual communication		
World-wide IC		
English LWC (language of wider communication)		
Regional IC	Regional identity	
Regional LWC	National identity	
Cognate languages IC		
Language maintenance		
Dominant LM		
Ethnic LM		
Auxiliary code standardisation		
Meso level planning for		
Administration: training and certification of officials and professionals		
Administration: legal provisions for use		
The legal domain		

The legal domain
Education equity: pedagogical issues
Education equity: language rights/identity
Education elite formation/control
Mass communication
Educational equity: language handicap
Social equity: minority language access
Interlanguage translation: training for professions, business, law etc.

The discussion so far implies that motivation is complex, consisting of three main elements. These are the seven motives for a specific plan or policy at a general level; the attitudes of policy-makers or planners towards a particular language or variety; and the more specific goals which their action aims to achieve, together perhaps with needs they hope to satisfy. In achieving such goals and satisfying such needs, we shall probably need also to consider the strategies planners and policy-makers adopt, as these are likely to modify the goals. Chapters 1 to 6 explore a number of cases of language planning or policy with the intention of looking at these three main aspects in further detail. Chapters 7 to 9 return to the discussion of motives, attitudes and goals. In summary, our three proposed components of motivation are:

Motive	Attitude	Goal
Identity	Knowledge of language	Ideal
Ideology	Emotion towards language	Objective
Image	Desire to take action	Target
Insecurity		Needs
Inequality		Physiological
Integration		Psychological
Instrumentality		Strategies to achieve these

Chapter 1

Identity

The politics of identity have marked the last quarter of the twentieth century with a degree of violence and horror which is unprecedented. They have been particularly vicious in the resurgence of ethnic nationalism. Ethnic nationalism, often symbolised by language or religion, has been the root cause of many murders, crimes, attacks on neighbours and outright wars in different parts of the world. Examples of the negative effects of nationalism abound in the former Yugoslavia and in the chaos following the disintegration of the Soviet state, where redefining boundaries, new legal restraints on citizenship, attacks on ethnic groups and forced evictions are matched by the continuing exclusion of immigrants and strenuous attempts at keeping foreigners out. Xenophobia has often been the defining principle for the identity of those 'within'. Opposition and conflict have seemed to be essential components of nationalism. But at the same time nationalism and the associated discovery or rediscovery of the links which unite human groups, including ethnicity, have occasionally brought people together, have reversed decades and even centuries of denigration and denial of human rights, and have given renewed pride and confidence to the oppressed. The affective component, the emotional and lyrical feeling of togetherness has gained strength in regions, countries and states of all sizes and in many parts of the world.

Although our identity motive is not exclusively realised in and through nationalism, it is in the desire of groups to become or to remain nations, and preferably nation-states, that the identity motive can be explored most clearly. What are the constitutive elements of nationalism, according to such representative theorists as Kedourie, 1961; Fishman, 1972; Anderson, 1983; Gellner, 1983; Smith, 1991; Williams, C. H. 1994? Space and territory: a geographical location limits the terrain, necessarily ensuring that the group is regarded as separate from the universal brotherhood of man. Time is significant, in that the

13

development from traditional cultures to modern societies has brought in its train changes in modes of production and consumption which require large(r) groups to work together in new economic relationships. Indeed for some analysts, the modernisation of societies through the rejection of such societal organisations as feudalism is the only feature which defines the nation as such.   Culture is important, in that the social norms of society express the habits and traditions, the way of life, of the group. Family patterns, modes of dress, taboos, cuisine, educational norms and patterns of politeness all form part of the socio-cultural practice of particular societies. So too does the (literary or musical) culture of the group. The artistic production of the group determines its own definitions of greatness, and great literature is by no means necessarily felt as universal. Any American list of the hundred best books of the century is certain to be quite different from any such English, French or Brazilian list. Language is an essential component for smaller national groups, in that it enables the group to maintain daily communication, to express its wishes and desires, and reflects the nature of its world view. Religion, too, often forms a major component, particularly if it has a history of oppression and persecution which it shares with the actual or potential nation. Language and religion in particular often become symbols of nationalism. The (myth of a) common origin and a shared history, particularly if this shows periods of oppression, suffering, conflict contrasting with times of freedom and liberty, is for many a fundamental component of national sentiment and fellow-feeling. Part of the shared history is a desire for gaining or regaining liberty and control of affairs, so the political is very frequently close to the affective. The key to the strength of nationalism and the sense of identity in many cases is the presence of the outsider, of 'them', against whom struggle takes place and whose domination or potential threat stresses the necessity of collective endeavour. Other boundaries of the ethnic relationship, realised through physical markers like skin colour, nose shape, colour of hair, are equally fundamental: indeed, it seems important to some that outsiders rather than insiders decide who is or is not a member of a particular ethnic or national group. For most theorists, there is little difference between the integrative feelings which maintain ethnicity and those which support nationalism: both reflect attraction and allegiance to a defined or definable human group, even though the specific ties may differ. The precise definition of nationalism, of ethnic and nationalist feeling and its relationship to language is the subject of continuing discussion, and each new example makes close definition even more difficult.

This chapter reviews the language policies of five parts of the world, policies which seem to find their motivation in beliefs about the specific identity of communities, and about the link between linguistic and political communities. Each exemplifies a different factor in the definition of identity. We deal first with France, since the French Revolution of 1789 and the nation-state theories it developed have influenced so many countries since.   Algeria has created itself by contrast to the former colonial power. Catalonia is developing political and cultural autonomy as a region within Spain. Indian language policy shows the effect of practical   reality and sheer necessity on political dreams centred on the concept of identity. The recent history of Wales and Welsh examines the   relationship between politics, culture, economics and language in the definition of identity.

Territorial Integrity: France and Regional Languages 1539-1950

France is usually thought of as the country which invented the concept of the nation-state, and which has most consistently followed a policy based on bringing together the geographical, the political, the social, the cultural and the linguistic. The state, in terms of a political organisation, and the nation, in terms of a contract binding together people who have an affinity for each other, have, in the French conception, the same values and a common origin. They are rooted in a physical location, symbolised as the geometrical hexagon formed by the frontiers of metropolitan France. This mental image of the six-sided figure is imprinted on French citizens through the wide use of the word in education and the media, and the equally wide-spread use of the image, usually with splashes of blue, white and red, on items ranging from official publications to luxury products. It is this myth of the perfect hexagon that inspired the French language policy of oppression of regional languages from the sixteenth century until 1950 (Girardet, 1983; Grillo, 1989; Ager, 1996b; Ager, 1999).

French can be said to trace its origin to 842, when the Serments de Strasbourg given in 'French' and 'German' by two sons of Charlemagne before each other's troops, established each 'language' as different from the other. At this time, and indeed for many centuries afterwards, what had been Roman Gaul contained many languages and dialects. Feudalism strengthened their local nature and not even the centralising political power of the Paris-based royal dynasties saw much need for a single language. If there was a need, as in church services or the collection of taxes, Latin (of a sort) still served. It is generally said, not altogether accurately, (see Ager, 1996b; Ayres-Bennet, 1996; de Certeau et al., 1975; Lodge, 1993; Sanders, 1993; Walter, 1988) that the first piece of linguistic legislation in France aimed at imposing one form of a 'national' language over the many regional languages and dialects spoken in what was gradually becoming modern France is clauses 110 and 111 of the Edicts of Villers-Cotterêts, agreed by François Premier in 1539. These simply instructed lawyers that in order to make clear the purpose and meaning of decisions, they should be written in such a way that there should be 'no ambiguity or uncertainty, nor need to require interpretation', and, since 'such things have often arisen on the understanding of Latin contained in such decisions', no language other than French was to be used in the law courts and tribunals. Although the aim might have been to eliminate Latin, the effect was to remove all other languages as well in these written, legal settings. In a very few years there was little trace, in formal writing, of regional languages even in the many parts of France where (Parisian) French was little understood by the local population and certainly not used in the spoken form.

Under Royalty, before the Revolution of 1789, language policy mirrored the political aim of reducing regional power bases. The social attack on regional languages was not simply represented by legal acts. Just as effectively those who could not manipulate French well got left behind in the aristocratic world, and the dictates of Court grammarians, the salons where courtiers met, and the Academy set up in 1635 (its first dictionary was published in 1694) had the effect of confirming the high status of 'Royal' French. It was nevertheless not until the Revolution that such language policy became identified with the idea of nationhood. Much of the country at that point in time simply did not understand French and had little use for it. Regional languages and dialects, many of them significantly different from the language of the Revolutionary Assembly in Paris, were the normal means of communication. Commerce was conducted in 'patois', which term subsumed languages like Basque, Breton, Catalan, Corsican, German, Occitan, and Flemish as well as a range of regional and social dialects of both northern French and Occitan. Except for matters directly affecting the conduct of royal business, the feudal authorities saw little need to bother themselves with the ways in which the peasants communicated.

The 1789 Revolution saw things differently: the people inhabiting France became the repository of sovereignty, and they had both the rights and the duties of citizens, among which the most important was to give their assent to the creation of the Nation-State. The Revolution rejected particularisms and communities, and their languages, in defining the Rights of Man and in regarding its values as universal. It followed that its advantages and freedoms should be available to all, expressed in the language of freedom and enlightenment, rather than lost in the obfuscations of little-used dialects and the languages used by the enemies of freedom. Indeed, the period of the Alsace language terror confirmed the belief that foreign languages (including regional languages) had to be suppressed, mainly because they might themselves attack what French represented.

Nationhood, associated with the Republicanism of the revolutionaries, was under actual or potential attack from two main sources: neighbouring countries which were fearful that Republicanism would destroy their own monarchies, and, internally, from regions of the country where local loyalties, to Church or to local leaders, opposed the centre. In some of the border areas, particularly in Alsace, the local language was close to that of a neighbouring country and the frontiers were potentially fluid. In others, notably Brittany and the Vendée, local priests opposed to the secular Revolution encouraged opposition and led revolt in the local language. By 1794, the language policy of the government associated Breton with federalism and superstition, German with emigration and hatred for the Republic, Italian with counterrevolution, and Basque with fanaticism. French, the 'finest language in Europe, which first freely expressed the Rights of Man and Citizen', had the duty of transmitting the most profound thoughts of liberty and politics. It was around and through the use of French, therefore, that the regions could be brought under control and that the national territory could be both identified as such and preserved from such attacks. In consequence, a linguistic terror was imposed on parts of the country, notably Alsace, and those who spoke other languages or could not understand the decrees of the revolutionary government were punished.

But it was the educational policy of the late nineteenth century that effectively ensured the destruction of the regional languages. Primary education was made secular, obligatory and free in 1881, and from then until after the second World War a consistent policy of using French, banning regional languages from the school itself, and both punishing and ridiculing any child caught speaking a language other than French led to the practical disappearance of local languages and dialects from public life. Although there were sporadic attempts at reversing the trend, ranging from the romantic revival of Provençal in the nineteenth century under the influence of the major poet Frédéric Mistral, to violent political protests aimed at bringing about the autonomy of Alsace in the 1920s, these came to nothing. The formation of a Breton battalion in the Nazi Army in the 1940s did little to help the cause of the regionalists. Such indications show that although the regional languages might have gone from official domains, they were still there: in parts of the country such as Brittany, Alsace and large stretches of the south, they were the normal first language of what was usually the bilingual family. Although regionalism as a force had little political power after the end of the second World War, politicians were never altogether sure that there might not be a residual threat to the state. In 1951 Parliament adopted a permissive Act (the Loi Deixonne) enabling four regional languages to be taught in schools. Either by design or by lack of general interest, it took a further 18 years before this law was implemented in any real sense. Violent protests on behalf of the regionalists continue: the Breton Revolutionary Army (_Armée Révolutionnaire Bretonne_) detonated a bomb in Cintegabelle near Toulouse, chosen because it was the electoral base of Prime Minister Jospin, in June 1999, eight months after a similar explosion in the constituency of Chevènement, then _Ministre de l'Intérieur_. Attempts to ensure that the increasing need for regionalisation and decentralisation were balanced by strong central control had already led to the resignation of de Gaulle in 1969 and were one of the main policies of the incoming Mitterrand government in 1981, which in 1983 openly declared its refusal to 'support the break-up of France' by giving greater independence to regional languages as symbols of regional independence. It took until the 7th May 1999 for the French government to sign the European Charter for Regional and Minority Languages, and its ratification posed problems for the Constitutional Council. Language is one of the central issues in the Corsican situation, and attempts by Jospin to solve this by Constitutional changes and by awarding practical autonomy to the regionalists in 2000 achieved only minimal success. The centre-periphery battle is still an important constituent of French political thinking today.

France had no problems in applying the same centralised linguistic policy even when its territory expanded beyond the Hexagon. During the height of the colonial period between 1880 and 1960, the same education was provided for (some) children in Africa as for those in Lille: the same textbooks were used, the same cultural references employed, the same insistence that the territory of France should be preserved. Indeed, the Constitution requires that one of the President's duties be to preserve the integrity of the territory. Even today, when France's former Empire is reduced to a small number of Overseas

Departments,, regarded as constituent parts of the Republic, and Overseas Territories, these retain the educational principle that education is conducted in French. From Guadeloupe to Tahiti, from French Guyana to New Caledonia, the language of the Republic is French and there is little or no provision for the maintenance and use of local languages. The point was reinforced in 1992 in the light of the creation of a new unified Europe: French was the language of the Republic, although this formula was changed to 'The language of the Republic is French' when French-speaking Canadians, Belgians, Swiss and others made clear their disapproval.

French nationalism and national identity are apparently based on the principles of the Revolution and the ideas of the Republic. All French political parties would subscribe to Renan's definition of nationalism: the belief that the Republic is a voluntary union of all citizens, that it is one and indivisible, is secular, and that its founding principles, Liberty, Equality and Fraternity and the Rights of Man and the Citizen, are of universal validity. But there are two different underlying conceptions of nationalism: territory and residence, the _jus soli_, contrasts with ethnic Frenchness and the myth of the common origin, the _jus sanguinis_. Territory, centrality and universality are traditionally the Left-wing position, while origin, ethnicity and specificity are traditionally that of the Right. The French tradition of a democratic gift of power to a strong man, Bonaparte, de Gaulle, uniting the forces of universality, ethnicity and individuality, confuses the picture further. Most French citizens nonetheless agree that the only way of maintaining the nation-state is through a process of assimilation to the Republic and its values, and that 'Anglo-Saxon' multiculturalism is racist, divisive and objectionable. The identity of France hence becomes all-embracing: one language, one culture, one territory, one political conception. There is no room for the 'particularism' of other identities, whether regional or immigrant, and certainly not for any language other than that which unites.

Attitudinally, the superiority of France, French culture and the French language is justified by and justifies the creation of the nation-state. The language has to be the symbolic centre. It must be used in every facet of life, be better, more vital, more attractive, than any other spoken in the territory to ensure the continuance of the state itself.

The Nationalist Imperative: Arabic in Algeria from 1962 to 1990

Algeria gained its independence from France in 1962, after a long and bitter fight, and the Provisional Government of the Algerian Republic made its triumphant entry to Algiers on 3rd July (Stora, 1994; Benrabah, 1995). By September 1963, Algeria had a one-party system and a Presidential Government; the Constitution incorporated socialism and the Front National de Libération (FLN). In 1989, other political parties were legitimised. The Front Islamique du Salut (FIS) won the municipal elections in June 1990 and the majority of Parliamentary seats in December 1991. After the army reversed this democratic decision and took power in January 1992, Mohammed Boudiaf, who had been exiled in 1962, was appointed President on 14th January, and assassinated on 29th June. During those thirty years three Presidents had ruled with the Front National de Libération (FLN) and the aid of the army: Ahmed Ben Bella from 1962 to 1965, Houari Boumedienne from then until 1978, Chedli Benjeddid until 1991 and the recall of Boudiaf. But during that time the population had grown from ten million to twenty-seven million; three quarters of the population had no recollection of French colonialism; vast oil revenues had been obtained, and spent; the Islamic religion had grown from a tightly controlled symbol to a powerful, independent force.

The Constitution of 1963, together with all those that have followed it, imposed Classical Arabic as the sole official and national language. The decision in fact antedated the take-over of power by the FLN. Messali Hadj, leader of the national movement, had decided in 1949 that only one definition of nationhood would be followed. This was based on the idea that Algeria had only existed after the arrival of the Arabs and of Islam, and that its identity could only be defined by them. The alternative conception, that of an Algeria which recognised the forms of Algerian Arabic together with the Berber languages and others (including French) as constituting 'Algerian Algeria', was condemned and outlawed.

The language policy defining identity as based on Classical Arabic, firmly kept to although it defied and defies the reality of language use in Algeria, is paradoxically yet fundamentally marked by the experience of colonisation. It may be that the disastrous situation of contemporary Algeria, torn by internal war, atrocities and vicious opposition, is as much the result of what came after colonisation as of colonisation itself. The hatred for the colonisers of those who threw them out led to a rigid, austere regime unable, subsequently, to cope with the population explosion, the gradual loss of the memory of colonial days, the lack of oil revenues and the desire of the population for better things. In any case, the nature of the regime in power for thirty years has been military, socialist and dedicated to reversing colonialism, but confusingly tied to the same mode of thinking as the French in many respects. Among these is the belief in a single, unifying language, a language of high quality and internal perfection which does not accept social or regional variation. Because France had defined Classical Arabic as a foreign language in 1938, rejecting it for internal use, it became the sole official and national language in 1963. Algerian Arabic and the Berber languages were accused of having been used by the French the better to divide and rule the country. The pressure to use only Classical Arabic in official life including education was only modified in 1977 when it became clear that the complete lack of Arabic-speaking civil servants and teachers, which had led to the massive import of Egyptian staff thought to be able to implement the policy, was 'suicidal' for the creation of a properly Algerian state and nation.

Algeria today is the second largest French-speaking country in the world after France. Yet it does not officially recognise French and plays no part in the international Francophone movement. It defines its identity against French, but uses the same arguments as the colonisers to decry its own version of Arabic and to deny separate existence to the Berber languages. The FLN aim to create a centralised, unified nation-state was based on one language, one religion, and one political party. Other aspects of Algerian language and educational policy similarly reflect this monolingual and monocultural concept of identity. Official dictionaries of Maghreb Arabic usage in fact sometimes prefer forms which are closer to Classical and to Egyptian (central) Arabic. The official histories for use in school prioritise Arab influence rather than the Roman influence whose physical remains lie all over the country. The refusal to accept French, Algerian Arabic or the Berber languages has even meant that English terms are used in preference in the Press, that scientific education at University level finds English of greater use than French, and that English has been introduced as the preferred language of education. Indeed English, here, finds itself in the strange situation of being a language without connotations of domination, without a political past and, as in Belgium and elsewhere, a convenient way of getting the job done.

The Algerian attitude towards identity is based on the political integrity of the territory, even though in practice internal groups have rarely questioned this. It prioritises conflict and opposition to any internal dissent, added to rejection of the language of the coloniser. The search for identity fastened on a particular language and a particular religion as the bases for a recreation of the culture destroyed by the denigration of the Algerian way of life, language and social structure which had existed before 1830. But the thinking which led to such decisions was itself constrained and moulded by the thinking of the coloniser: such a language, and cultural, policy is only conceivable within the French beliefs about their importance and their centrality in the construction of the nation. Despite the unreality of using a written classical language for anything other than religious and ceremonial purposes, the symbol is all-important. Classical Arabic may be thought to be attractive and immensely superior; in use it is restricted to very few domains. Nationalism requires action to ensure its symbolic role, while at the same time the real linguistic situation is officially practically ignored.

Regional Autonomy: Catalan 1978 to 1998

Catalonia, as a region of Spain, is particularly notable in this discussion of identity because it typifies the situation where speakers of one language form a minority within the state, with all that implies, and yet form a majority of speakers within a region. Because language has formed a central element in the pursuance of autonomy and independence by Catalan politicians, the region and its language policy have been extensively studied (Massana, 1992 and 1993; Hoffmann, 1995; Guibernau, 1997 give initial bibliographies). The situation is not by any means unique: most European states have similar regional or provincial minorities within their borders. Spain now recognises seventeen autonomous Communities and three languages in addition to Castilian: Basque, Catalan and Galician, although Valencian is also given separate status to Catalan in some publications. Catalan is spoken in Spanish regions outside Catalonia: Valencia and the Balearic islands, in particular, and in France, but here we shall concentrate on Catalonia, where, at the beginning of the 21st century, more than half the population has Catalan as mother tongue and only ten per cent or so of the population do not understand it.

From the seventeenth century the policy of the Castilian-speaking kings of Spain had been to centralise and to assimilate. Public documents had to have at least a Castilian version, although Catalan remained the normal language for local and domestic use. The territory was recognised as a separate administrative region between 1914 and 1925. After 1923 and the seizure of power by General Primo de Rivera the previous centralisation policy returned and was strengthened since the new government saw Catalan regionalism as an attempt to gain political independence. Between 1931 and 1939, political autonomy was to a certain degree achieved: both Catalan and Castilian could be used as official languages within the Generalitat, and by private citizens in their dealings either with the regional or the central government. The regional government legislated in Catalan. But outright centralisation returned with the Franco regime, which restored the primacy of Castilian and did not tolerate regional aspirations of any sort.

Forty years of Franco's centralised Spain ended with a new Constitution in 1978. At this time it was estimated that no more than 25% of school entrants had a knowledge of Catalan. The new Constitution required all Spaniards to know Castilian as the official language of Spain, but declared other languages to be official within their respective autonomous communities. The 1979 Catalan Statute of Autonomy was followed by elections in 1980, and the Convergence and Unity Party (CiU) under its leader Jordi Pujol obtained and retained power during the whole of the period under examination here. Catalan legislation on language dates from 1983 and 1994 and is aimed at supporting the growth of Catalan, beyond bilingualism and into a position where it becomes the sole official language. 'Official', in this context, now means that Catalan must be used in most public contexts: speakers have the right to use it, and, after 1994, administrations must reply in kind. Since Spanish citizens are however supposed to know Castilian, Catalan-Castilian interpreters are not always provided in some state organisations, and conflict continues between those who would see Catalonia as a monolingual region using only Catalan and those who wish to retain and use Castilian as well. The role of Castilian as official language of the Spanish state has to be preserved, although the 1994 Law of Linguistic Normalisation makes it clear, as indeed did the 1983 legislation, that the aim is to reduce its role as much as possible. The laws have insisted that only Catalan must be used in regional government. Catalan must be taught in schools, used as a medium of instruction, and the school leaving certificate will not be not issued to those with no Catalan. Teachers must be bilingual, although parents do not have the right to insist on the total use of one language at all times. By 1998, generations of children had in effect followed monolingual Catalan education, and the consequences of this were affecting the labour market.

The Catalan approach to the question of language rights has been to press for political rights for the community, the Generalitat, rather than for individual rights of expression and service: the territorial principle has been supreme. In this context the term used for language policy, 'normalisation', means both language recovery and language spread: restoring to the language the right to be used in public domains and functions, and helping it to increase the range of settings within which it can and sometimes must be used. This policy hence implies a constant battle for more: it is difficult to see what would satisfy the activists, who certainly give the impression that they would like to see the role of Castilian reduced to the minimum. There is of course good reason for pride in Catalan:

- In terms of population numbers (about ten million), Catalan is nineteenth most popular European language, with more speakers than Bielorussian, Danish, Norwegian, Finnish, Albanian and others;
- Catalan is the majority language within its linguistic community;
- Catalonia is a highly developed region with a high income level per head;
- the language has a significant cultural history;
- it is used by all social classes, and notably by the middle classes as the preferred vehicle of social and cultural transmission;
- linguistically, Catalan is codified and standardised, with little dialectal variation.

Although widely used in television, Catalan has not conquered all public and private domains: the written Press, the law, private business are not always obliged to use it. Indeed the 1994 requirement to enforce minimum levels of Catalan in radio (50% of speech, 25% of songs), cinemas (50% of new films), and private business (labelling, advertising and information in Catalan), has provoked considerable opposition and elections are dominated by the language question.

For Catalonian identity, like that of Algeria, the symbolism of language has been central. The primacy of the symbolic language has in turn been founded on opposition to another language. By contrast to Algeria, pride in the everyday and widely used language, Catalan, has here played a major part, and the province (i.e. the political power in the province) has refused to accept the denigration as an inferior language which Castilian is said to have tried to impose on Catalan. This type of pride has two elements: awareness of a long history of independence, and the support for a prestigious yet practical role accorded by all social strata and particularly the middle classes. The severity of oppression which regional languages suffered under Franco led to a swing of the pendulum in 1978 and since, and the fight against domination by Castilian has been led by the regional government and significant politicians like the CiU leader from 1974, Jordi Pujol. There is close connection between linguistic and sociopolitical aims. But by contrast to both France and Algeria, where the territorial principle is paramount, here Catalan is widely spoken outside Catalonia and Castilian speakers live and work within the region. The ethnic factor is not present, either, because immigration to Catalonia has produced a situation where although ninety per cent of the population may understand Catalan, under half can trace Catalonian origins. The answer to the question of 'who is Catalan', in CiU discourse, is 'someone who lives and works in Catalonia and wants to be a Catalan' (quoted in Guibernau, 1997: 91). It is probably because of the double status of the Catalan-speaking population in the province, too, that the words 'minority' and 'majority' are little used: Catalan speakers are the majority in Catalonia, although a minority of all Spaniards, and thus feel themselves the equal of their opponents.

Catalonian identity is based on time, as Catalonians 'regained' democratic freedom in 1978; on the general will of all sections of the population and not just of the elite; on the physical presence of a majority of Catalan speakers within the territory, which itself is defined as that part of the Catalan-speaking area which lies within the borders of Spain; and on a particular interpretation of nationalism developed by Pujol and his movement. This latter, to some degree lyrical, mystical and messianist, bases identity on 'language, culture, social cohesion, collective consciousness, common project and country pride, opposing absorption and homogenizing policies' (quoted in Guibernau, 1997: 101). And yet Catalonian identity exists, as the Statute of Autonomy puts it, 'within a framework of free solidarity with the other nationalities and regions of Spain'. Politically, Catalonia seeks autonomy and not independence. The definition of precisely what this means in practice changes. But the ideal is in essence federalism with very weak central institutions, rather than a Spanish supranational state.

The Force of Necessity: Indian Language Policy

The identity issue in India shows considerable differences from the cases we have already considered (Brass, 1994; Basu, 1997; Kohli, 1997). Indian language policy is the result of bitter conflicts, both on the question of the language representing the state and on that of the proper role for the 1,625 languages, 33 of them with more than a million native speakers each, which are spoken in India. Despite this complexity and size, India is the world's largest democracy and by common consent the country in which community conflict, although ever-present, is by now managed as well as, if not better than, in any other part of the world.

Congress Party leaders assumed during the struggle for independence that India would adopt Hindi as its national and official language, and the Constitution called for that to be the case fifteen years after independence was declared. Hindustani, a common form of Hindi and Urdu and essentially a spoken language, was used by Mahatma Ghandi and the Indian National Congress during the years of opposition to colonial rule and in the struggle for liberation from British rule. The language had and has been little used for literature and high culture. The religious divisions between Hindus and Muslims which led to the creation of an independent Pakistan using Urdu and the Persian-Arabic script as its national language meant that Hindi, using the Devanagari script, became a more likely candidate as national and official language. But although Hindi was spoken by the majority of Indians and was widespread in the North, if it were used as the only national and official language it would become the passport to public-sector employment, and the consensus of non-Hindi-speaking states was that English had to be retained for interstate and official uses. The eventual compromise of the Official Languages Act as modified in 1967 after bitter conflicts, particularly in Tamil Nadu, provided for

> joint use of Hindi and English in Parliament, for the use of Hindi as the language of communication between the Centre and the Hindi-speaking states and the use of English for communication between the Centre and non-Hindi-speaking states. (Brass, 1994: 166)

The country is so vast, and contains so many different groups and communities, that the only practical solution to retaining its political unity, and particularly its administrative unity through the Indian Administrative Service bureaucracy was thus to accept the force majeure solution and continue to use the language of the colonial administrators, English. But the English used has been adapted, changed, modified, not by diktat but by daily use, so that Indian English is a recognisable variety of the language, different from its other forms in Australia, the United States or indeed Britain, and likely to change still further in the future. Far from the opposition to the former colonial language which has so marked Algeria, Indian English is widely accepted in India and indeed is a source of pride, even though knowledge of it is clearly still an elitist possession and a passport to riches in career terms. Indian identity can, to a certain extent, be expressed through this non-Indian language. Indeed, the continuing and constantly renewed contacts between Indians and the diaspora, whether in Britain or throughout the world, means that Indian identity itself is both modified by Indian English and itself modifies this symbol: one has only to read the world literature written by Indian authors to see how this has occurred. But at the same time English alone is not, and never can be, the basis of Indian identity. With the complexity of the linguistic situation there has to be some other solution.

Hindi is the most widespread language, with over three hundred million speakers of which it is first language for at least two hundred million. It is a lingua franca in the North and a regional language of northern and central states. But it is unlikely to displace English, partly because extreme Hindu nationalism can be offensive to those who share neither language nor religion and partly because the southern and eastern states remain opposed to an Indian identity based either on assimilation or on a composite but common nationalism. For the moment at least then, the Indian state has both Hindi and English as official languages, and since the educational system teaches English everywhere, it is to be expected that citizens will necessarily obtain at least one of these two languages, in some cases both.

Necessity has also driven language policy in relation to the many other languages with millions of speakers and with major claims to official and administrative, as well as cultural and religious use. During the Nehru period, states were reorganised on linguistic lines so that to a large extent language groups in particular states could expect that their language would become official in that state. Four principles guided the process to avoid secession and disintegration: firstly, that central government would not recognise groups making secessionist demands but would use force against them. The Indian Army has been involved in a number of in some cases continuing battles in pursuance of this principle, notably in Kashmir, Assam, the Punjab and the north-eastern region. Where the particular demand for secession has been dropped, the central government has conceded status and even statehood, as with Tamil in Tamil Nadu. Secondly, religion as a basis for regional demands is not tolerated. This is partly due to the consequences of the separation of Pakistan from the future India, but has also affected Sikh demands for a Sikh-majority political community. Thirdly, central authorities have only responded to demands based on both popular support and on political demands: in effect, power at the centre has responded only to sufficient demonstration of power in the periphery. Fourthly, reorganisation depended on action by all, or at least most, of the language groups involved in a particular region, so that Madras was reorganised early because both the main groups (Telugu and Tamil) wanted it, while the Punjab and the north-eastern regions are still not fully reorganised on language lines. The second layer of language policy hence ensures that regional languages are recognised as official in the linguistically reorganised states. These languages are then listed in the Eighth Schedule to the Constitution, and are in order of the number of native speakers Hindi (together with a number of 'variants', some very distant), Telugu, Bengali, Marathi, Tamil, Urdu, Gujarati, Kannada, Malayalam, Oriya, Punjabi, Kashmiri, Sindhi, Assamese, Konkani and Sanskrit. Sindhi and Sanskrit have official status, but Sindhi is the language of the province of Sindh now in Pakistan, while Sanskrit, although still used for learned works, is not a widespread mother tongue. Inclusion on the schedule gives language rights in education, in protection by the central and state authorities, in central government development committees, and is hence sought after by 'mother tongue' speakers (such as those of Maithili, a dialect of Hindi or a separate language according to who presents the issue) who have not yet been able to summon up sufficient pressure, while state authorities generally resist such demands because of the expense involved..

Hindi is now one of the two official languages of India, the state language of six states and the first language/mother tongue of at least two hundred million people in India and outside it. Urdu, a language closely related, is the state language of two Indian states, and the official language of Pakistan. It is spoken by over twenty-five million people. In both India and Pakistan English (the other Indian official language) is the practical means of communication at the highest political level, that at which the country's governing institutions work, and in relations with the outside world. This situation is not necessarily the choice of either country, but is the result of pure necessity. The same is true of the second layer of policy: necessity, in terms of the response of central authorities to regional demands, has ensured official status for some but not for all of India's languages. Insofar as language policy is concerned, the formula of 'three plus or minus one' summarises the position for citizens. A citizen of Rajasthan, where Hindi is official, must learn English as well if career opportunities are to be open; in Tamil Nadu the citizen must have Tamil in addition, while in Karnataka a Marathi speaker learns four languages: Marathi, Hindi, English and Kannada, the state language of Karnataka. Every Indian citizen needs from two to four languages, and most seem to accept this policy.

How then, has the nature of political and cultural identity been affected both by this adoption of the language of the former colonial administrator and by the complexity of the linguistic situation within a large multicultural democracy? The answer lies, insofar as English is concerned, on its conquest and successful use: on turning the tables on the previous administrators and making use of the 'war booty' constituted by language in a way that Algeria specifically refused to do. Although Indian English has retained sufficient interintelligibility to enable the language to be used internationally, it is quite different from standard British or American English in pronunciation, particularly intonation, in syntax, and in vocabulary. It is a recognisably different language which can hence form part of Indian identity.

But as an established multicultural democracy it is inevitable that ethnic and other conflicts should have arisen and continue to arise in India. Kohli (1997: 328) considers the Indian pattern is that of a 'centralizing, personalistic ruling elite (confronting) a variety of oppositional elites, who mobilize that which is most readily mobilizable, namely, community identities, and help transform them into rigid ethnic and group boundaries'. The separatist movements demanding a Dravidistan, a Punjabi Suba or a Khalistan have become stronger or waned over time, since the identity issue they raise has been stronger or weaker in relation to changes in the balance of power between the centre and the constituent communities. This analysis suggests that ethnic, and hence language, conflicts are not 'inevitable expressions of deep-rooted differences' but depend on the circumstances of the time; 'the strategies and counter-strategies may be amenable to a bargaining type of rationalist analysis'. Other political analysts such as Basu agree that community identities are varied, but note that the overall importance of the identity issue will depend firstly on the actions of the state and political leaders and secondly on the presence of and perception of other ethnic and linguistic groups within the polity, although they agree that such actions and such perceptions change. The main example is that of the centralisation and personalisation of power in the Congress Party which led to its collapse as an all-India force, and eventually to political, even jingoistic Hinduism. The second point is shown by the position in north-east India, where, when Assamese leaders 'equated the territorial identity of multiethnic Assam with the ethnolinguistic identity of the Assamese speakers of the Brahmaputra valley, other groups reacted by demanding autonomy' (Basu, 1997: 393).

In sum, the Indian experience closely affects the issue of identity. Despite the present growth of nationalist groups, the 3 + or - 1 language policy seems stable enough to mean that this variety of multilingualism is permanent. Indian identity overall is founded on (its form of) English plus Hindi, while there is room for many millions of Indians with other languages as well to feel comfortable with this form of nation-state identity, which both generally allows for education in the mother tongue and also allows career opportunities in languages other than the majority language of the Union. The identity of ethno-linguistic groups and indeed of the multi-nation-state as a whole is not however a fixed entity, immutable and inevitable, but a dynamic construct which gains much of its effectiveness from the possibility of its deliberate manipulation. While this is true of the cultural field it is particularly key to the political, where in any form of political analysis power struggles make use of whatever weapons lie to hand. Group identity is a potent weapon, but the effectiveness of its use at any one time depends on the overall political environment. The linguistic component of Indian identity is both stable and yet potentially explosive.

Politics, Culture and Economics: The Welsh Language Act of 1993

In the consultations which took place prior to the new Welsh Language Act of 1993, which followed on and extended the Act of the same title of 1967, opposition to the Welsh activists, themselves mainly educationists and intellectuals, came mainly from business and the economic sector. The motive for the Act's strengthening by the Conservative UK government of the day was the continuing poor showing of the party in Wales, where it had never achieved more than thirty per cent of the vote since the second World War. In terms of our discussion of identity therefore, the policy authority seems to have been giving way to a bottom-up definition of identity in the hope that it might be able to associate itself with community feeling and thus gain some credence in a region where otherwise, as in Scotland, its political future would practically disappear.

This explanation for the Act's existence is rarely acknowledged. It is more usual to ignore the UK government and track the nature of the Welsh struggle for the recognition of Wales as an autonomous region, following the different attitudinal strands which have gone to make up the movement. These can be seen as three, perhaps reflecting three types of internal elite (Kellas, 1991; Williams, C.H., 1994; Thomas, 1997). Firstly, the cultural imperative, stressing the independent past, the literary and cultural inheritance, and the fact that the language is still spoken by more than twenty percent of the population of the country, making it naturally an acceptable vehicle in all domains of life. The view that the Welsh situation represents internal colonialism by the English is the second strand, and its analysts have pointed to the core-periphery imbalance in economics, to Welsh mineral and industrial production as opposed to London financing and profit-taking. The language is used in few domains other than the domestic, and suffers from lack of prestige and stature. But such a 'colonial core-periphery exploiter-exploited interpretation is ideologically blinkered' (Williams, C. H., 1994: 117), marginalising both the economic strength of Wales and the fact that many Welshmen including a British Prime Minister (Lloyd George) have been and still are at the heart of UK political power. The third strand of explanation has concentrated on a similarly Marxist view that ethnicity or Welshness was less significant than the role of the Welsh in the class struggle, and built all opposition to the centre into a universalist conflict model whose positive outcome for Wales could only be subsequent to changes in the socioeconomic field. The revolutionary call to action, including action on language, was the inevitable attitudinal stance.

There is no doubt that all these factors - the cultural, the linguistic, the ethnic, the economic, the social and the political - have been present in the Welsh nationalist movements, particularly in the political party Plaid Cymru formed in 1925. Although Plaid Cymru prioritised language, it saw that Welsh as a medium of education from primary school to University, and as an official language of Wales, would never exist without control of the political apparatus. But, by contrast to Catalonia, Welsh speakers were not in a political majority within the country, although they are over twenty percent of the population, now number half a million (508,098 in the 1991 census) and have maintained the position of the language between the censuses of 1981 and 1991; indeed, there was a slight advance in the overall numbers and growth in language use among young people over these ten years. Plaid Cymru, and the Welsh language movement in both legal and illegal steps demanded equality of treatment with English, state education in and through Welsh, access to government services in Welsh, bilingual employment in the public sector, control of the media in Wales, and a continuing language body. To a certain extent, all these form part of the 1967 and to a greater extent the 1993 legislation.

The Welsh Language Act of 1993 established a Board to

> promote and facilitate the use of the Welsh language, to provide for the preparation by public bodies of schemes giving effect to the principle that in the conduct of public business and the administration of justice in Wales the English and Welsh languages should be treated on a basis of equality, to make further provision relating to the Welsh language... (Welsh Language Act, 1993, c. 38)

The approach therefore was to delegate language policy from the state firstly to the Welsh Language Board and thence to the local authorities and other public bodies, Health Authorities and Hospital Trusts, including (by agreement with them) some Crown agencies such as the Inland Revenue and the Benefits Agency. This typically British pragmatic approach meant that the details of language policy could be debated by the activists directly with the bodies which would have to implement them; it also enabled the central government to avoid entering into protracted and continuing fights over such 'details'. Language policy left the arena of grand policy statements and debates over rights to enter the mundane world of administrative detail and long, pernickety quibbles. For some, the move makes language policy immensely practical; for others, it merely means marginalising the issue, losing it among the detail and taking it out of the political arena.

The reception of the Act by activists was not particularly favourable (Wynne-Jones, 1993). Their main complaints were based on the question of individual rights:

- no general clause to guarantee an individual the right to use Welsh with any public body;
- a Welsh speaker may not demand a bilingual jury;
- parents do not have the right to demand Welsh medium education;
- the Act does not amend race relations legislation to permit employers to advertise (exclusively) for Welsh speakers;
- full, official status is not given to Welsh.

The Welsh Language Society, possibly the most extreme of the pressure groups, objected to the Act too but got little support. The National Language Forum, an association of 28 member organisations, although it rejected the legislation, did so more in sorrow than anger and in effect tolerated it. Significant opinion took a pragmatic approach, intending to make the legislation work in the detail.

In terms of the identity question, Wales presents some significant differences from the   Catalonian situation. There has been less of a history of violent and recent opposition between 'dominant' English and Welsh than has existed between Catalan and Castilian. Welsh is spoken only in Wales and in minor groups outside, although Celtic languages are obviously spoken elsewhere and Breton is very similar. Unlike many parts of other nations therefore (Belgium, Quebec, Alsace), but like Catalonia, Wales cannot look to major cultural centres abroad. Welsh speakers, like Breton and Basque speakers in France, are bilingual, and this is both a positive and a negative ability: it enables them to gain employment in any language, but prevents the development of a uniquely Welsh-language economy. It enables them to participate in wider political concerns than the purely local, but tends to ensure that the use of Welsh in public domains becomes a statement of ideology rather than a practical means of communication. In political terms, the 25-year 'reign' of Catalan regionalists cannot be matched in Wales. While the Welsh language's future remains dubious, the institutions protecting and maintaining it are in a dominant role while users find it difficult to reject linguistic purism, although Welsh language television and other media do reflect actual rather than idealised usage. The danger is that the ideology of the language pressure groups, whatever it may be, could end up by controlling the language users. The disappearance of Conservative party influence and the thinking that goes with Conservatism from language revivalist movements is thus paradoxically a danger to democracy. If the ideology of language maintenance is essentially left-wing, as it has been in Wales, then language maintenance becomes an indicator of left-wing allegiance and right-wing thinkers, automatically opposed, are rejected from the language support movement. Put another way, language maintenance has been a question for public bodies, for the media and for the cultural elite, and private industry, the nitty-gritty of the daily grind, feels itself not to be concerned. Put yet another way, language maintenance is an ideological question and not a practical one; individuals can pay lip-service to it but avoid actually doing anything about it. Similarly it is the local, not the central, political power that has dominated the language question and thus it is local interests that are at the forefront: 'The Welsh language lobby ... is unique to Wales and can be perceived by sections of the non-Welsh-speaking public as a powerful interest group - a 'taffia' (Thomas, 1997: 326). Migration, or the free movement of people, is another issue. The language activists would clearly prefer Welsh speakers to remain in Wales and prevent in-migration of non-Welsh speakers, particularly those with small children but who are not prepared to support Welsh-medium education. But such prevention of free movement is hardly democratic.

The cultural, traditional, literature-oriented definition of Welsh and Welshness has to a certain extent gained what it wanted. The institutionalisation of Welsh has taken place, particularly in the educational sphere and in the media with the specific language support role of the television channel S4C. There are language support grants, the Welsh Language Board, and the language activists have access to the Welsh Office within a policy community openly established to give them a forum. The future of Wales as a bilingual country which perhaps might put Welsh first, or which at least would establish 'natural bilingualism' for the total population, depends now on what happens to the political and economic strands. The point has been well recognised by language activists and by those aiming at constructing and changing Welsh identity. The Welsh Assembly may change the political situation, depending on how the interaction of central and Welsh government develops, and on the relationship between political ideologies and autonomy, although the Welsh situation is extremely unlikely ever to develop towards a Catalan solution. Creating a viable Welsh and Welsh-speaking economy to replace coal mining, the steel industry and other industries which helped to retain Welsh, assuming the non-democratic options are excluded, means both creating satisfactory careers at home, in order to retain existing Welsh-speakers, and also a satisfactory white collar bilingual career path. The former has been helped by the inward investment of assembly plants which has gone some way towards replacing the former mass employment outlets of steel-making and mining, although they have generally remained in the manufacturing sector and are hence sensitive to currency movements, to the nature of subsidies and to the global priorities of multinationals. The identity question here turns yet again towards the future of the public service, for private industry is necessarily turned towards UK-wide activity, towards Europe, or towards export unless it is very small. The public services, particularly in recent years in the UK, are very stretched in terms of the resources they have available and in terms of the constraints upon them. The additional resources made available through the Welsh Language Act certainly help in the provision of support for the language, but paradoxically it is at this point that the general European approach to the support of the languages of migrant workers imposes another burden. Indeed, if the Welsh labour force is insufficient for all tasks and if therefore in-migration takes place from within the European Union or from outside it, countries within the Union are expected to provide mother-tongue maintenance schemes. In some industrial areas providing such schemes could become quite a burden if it meant, for example, taking resources away from Welsh-language support and providing language classes for the children of the immigrant workers already present, who include speakers of Turkish, Dutch, Japanese, Italian, and Greek.

The European and international approach to such language situations has been to develop the issue of language rights. In this approach the identity of the individual and the community to which he/she belongs should be supported by the wider community in which he/she lives. Linguistic rights are hence both individual and collective; are inalienable and should be exercised in any situation. Article 3 of the draft Universal Declaration of Linguistic Rights spells them out (Argemi, 1996):

Inalienable personal rights
- the right to be recognised as a member of a language community;
- the right to use one's own language in private and in public;
- the right to interrelate and associate with other members of one's language community of origin;
- the right to maintain and develop one's own culture.

Collective rights of language groups
- the right for their own language and culture to be taught;
- the right of access to cultural services;
- the rights to an equitable presence of their language and culture in the communications media;
- the right to receive attention in their own language from government bodies and in socioeconomic relations.

These rights may not hinder in any way the interrelation of such persons or groups with the host language community or their integration into that community. Nor must they restrict the rights of the host community or its members to the full public use of the community's own language throughout its territorial space.

The European Charter for Regional or Minority Rights adopts the same approach, and plans have been made for the UK government formally to sign this in due course, although this is dependent on a resplution of the conflict situation in Northern Ireland.

How then does the Welsh case illuminate the definition of identity as a motive for language policy? The Welsh case is clearly a matter of reversing language shift, in Fishman's (1991) terms. Possibly it helps in three ways. Firstly by underlining the fact that the policy authority has here responded to the definition of identity presented to it by a minority, not in the sense of an attempt to correct inequality or put right a historic wrong, but in terms of recognising the logic of its own definition of identity. It helped the Conservative party in defining British identity that the UK is not a monolithic state, and does not pretend to the absolutism of the French model or the historic Spanish one. Paradoxically, while it was protesting against the multiculturalism of the trendy sixties and attempting to ensure the teaching of the standard language to all, the then government was accepting the logic of multiculturalism: the United Kingdom, the political community, is made up of a number of diverse communities each of which is entitled to its own definition of identity. But the central government did take the view that any such definition of a local, regional or community identity was the business of that community. Similarly, most of the Welsh pressure groups accepted that they were part of the UK: it was equal validity and bilingualism that the more moderate of them were requesting, with support for monolingualism in Welsh if that was what parts of the community wanted but without insisting that such an end-point was the only aim. The more moderate accepted the linguistic rights of the majority as well as those of the minority.

Second, identity is made up of a patchwork of factors: the cultural, traditional and linguistic are important, but the economic factor, which ensures the presence of people, is essential. This factor in particular fundamentally alters the definition of identity for Wales from that which Catalonia adopted. Without satisfactory economic conditions, identity is a pipe-dream. Similarly, identity is often thought of as an essentially political question: the aim of language activists is to ensure that political control is in the hands of the regional language speakers. But a political programme needs more than the one issue, and converting language manifestos into wider political statements can be a dangerous strategy. The 1992 manifesto of the Welsh Language Society 'sketched out an agenda that went far beyond specific demands for language bodies or acts of parliament. It set out a general critique of free market policies and expressed a belief that by their very nature they represent a threat to Welsh-speaking communities' (Thomas, 1997: 341). Nationalism is a political idea, but presenting it as part of a wider programme, socialist, fascist or other, can destroy the political consensus around it.

Third, people must be shown the advantages of the identity. There is little point in insisting on Welsh-medium schools if that merely leads to the unemployability of monolingual youth. The bodies with which the people communicate must be prepared to do so in the local language, and must demonstrate that they have the proper resources and systems in place to maintain the ability. It is pointless that politicians and intellectuals may be able to make speeches in the language; what matters is that people of all walks of life can file their tax returns, write cheques, draw their benefit payments in the language. Without the bottom-up advantages, without an identity in which all social categories can share, language policy will remain an empty, symbolic gesture, a plaything for the intellectuals. Whether this is a political, a social or an economic consideration is a moot point: the key element is that nationalism, and identity as a motive for it and for language policy, is multifaceted.

Identity as a Motive for Language Policy

Identity and its strong form for collectivities, nationalism, is a main motive for action on language. But the word covers a variety of different realities and reflects many goals and attitudes. First, we have the nationalism closely associated with national construction, nowadays often associated with the defence of national economic as well as territorial integrity against attacks from globalisation and the internationalisation of commerce and media. A strong feature is the national project: the driving idea based on making people aware of the issues and binding them together around the idea of dynamic construction. A second, equally strong, feature of the identity issue is the opposition many nations feel towards others. This xenophobia may derive from a history of domination, from a colonial past or from the presence of powerful neighbours. Thirdly, nationalism is strongly imbued with the ethos of rights, both of the collectivity and of the individual, and not merely language but political and economic rights too. Cynically, one might say that collective rights often hold sway over those of the individual, just as strongly within regional and minority language movements as in central authorities. The collective right to education is the most significant aspect of this, where the individual may wish the education of children to take place in a particular language but the collectivity, forming either the state majority or the regional majority/national minority, may prevent such rights and instead impose its own view of the primacy of the collective. It is at this point that the question arises as to whose nationalism we are considering. Often, the activists in nationalist movements are an elite, with safe careers in intellectual and cultural professions. The nationalist motive is a way of ensuring that they obtain the power they have not been able to gain in the larger community. To become 'maîtres chez nous' may simply imply, for the citizen, a change of master rather than any increase in democracy. Finally, nationalism and identity are not in themselves political ideas: both right-wing and left-wing policies, ideologies and parties call on nationalism as their inspiration. Some nationalists are Marxists before they are regionalists. Some nationalisms are almost fascist in their insistence on the state and on the mystical power of origins, particularly of ethnic origin, and such symbols of the imagined and mythical community as religion, the historical tradition, a common language.

Other nationalisms, at least apparently universal in their beliefs that freedom, equality and brotherhood are the inalienable rights of all human beings, nonetheless define their own identity against the necessity for their own economic development and modify their emotive belief in the collectivity in the light of practicality. This is particularly true where the nation is not the state; where autonomy is not independence.

Language policy is obviously motivated by attitudes towards the identity issue and the goal of its most acute form, the nation-state. But the analyses of nationalism that we have reviewed here, whether they are based on elitist theory, on rationalist approaches or on the analysis of leadership have shown that the three aspects of identity, culture, economics and politics, are interrelated. Cultural nationalism, without the economic factor, is often condemned to remain lyrical and myth-based folklore. Without the lyricism, without the collective myths, nationalism can often just be another name for protectionist economics. But without the political and power struggles, whether between groups or individuals, identity is simply a background and a decor. Identity is dynamic, too. The politics of accommodation, 'consociational democracy', is an important constitutive element in what happens to the identity issue in power struggles whether between communities or between their leaders. As Kohli noted (1997: 343), 'leaders - especially national leaders, but also leaders of ethnic movements - who persistently choose to be unaccommodating will channel normal power conflicts down a destructive path'. The identity of a political community is precious to it: language is generally believed to be its symbol and as such its own identity is created in and through the language which symbolises it, and whose use it aims to control. But language conflict motivated by the identity issue can be accommodated, or can become a flashpoint, depending on the interaction between the relevant community and those it sees as its opponents. Nationalist attitudes generally consider the language superior to others and attractive. Sometimes they accept that it is lacking in vitality and is not used in all the spheres of life which it should rightly occupy. Nationalists are often linguistic activists, and most linguistic activists are nationalists in the broader sense.

The goal of language policy deriving from the identity motive can be a form of simple assimilation to a nationalist ideal as in the French model. Such a policy may be successful, but as in France it may need centuries of brutal domination over rivals or minorities to be effective and to result in that ideal, rare situation, a practically monolingual nation-state. The larger the territory, the more difficult this becomes. Policy can erect a language into a national symbol, in the process rejecting another language because of its associations of domination, as in the case of Algeria. Such a policy may work, but the economic cost may be high. More subtly, ex-colonies may use the colonists' language for their own purposes, and (re-)construct their own identity through reconstructing the previously dominating language, as in India. The realities of multilingual states show that political power is still the driving force behind the realisation of group identity, however. In Catalonia, time, consistent pressure over at least one generation and careful use of the emotive myths in support first of limited targets in education, then of the more extensive objective of autonomy, and finally perhaps of the ideal of independence, has shown that a language policy of recovery and spread is possible despite the presence of equally powerful rivals both within the relevant territory and at state level. But India's experience of developing a seemingly stable language policy on the basis of a subtle interweaving of identities at a number of levels, despite the continuing conflicts, shows a form of identity motivation which is not necessarily based solely in opposition to one ex-colonial power or one linguistic group, but sits in opposition or in collaboration within a multicultural entity. The Welsh situation shows, again, the essential coexistence of the cultural, political and economic factors in the nature of identity. Lyrical, emotive, myth-based appeals to cultural identity need political power to put the relevant policy into place, and the relevant policy must demonstrate economic advantages if it is to stick.

Chapter 2

Ideology

The debate over the standard language issue in the UK has gone on for centuries (Crowley, 1989; Milroy and Milroy, 1985; Bailey, 1991; Honey, 1997). The point at issue has been to determine what the codified form of the standard language is, and, particularly in education, whether it, and it alone, should be taught in schools. The debate has demonstrated many times the extent of the confusion in people's minds about language questions, and the nature of the motives for language policy in education which different groups have held from time to time. During the 1980s, the issue arose as a significant element in the Conservative Party's successful attempt to reform British educational practice in order to ensure greater central control over the nature of the education provided in schools and to establish a different process for measuring educational outputs. The specific aim for this part of the process, following the ideology of the party, was to ensure that all children were taught standard English as part of a traditional curriculum, and that the social and economic role of the standard was fully understood.

Standard English in the UK from 1988 to 1995

The underlying political ideology of the Conservative Party's Radical Right which ousted Edward Heath as leader of the party and won the general election in 1979 rested on a desire for change, particularly concerning the role of the state, and the need to conduct change as radical reform. On the 'positive' side, a coherent political philosophy was propounded based on competition, efficiency, profit, and individualism. The key thinker in the UK was Keith Joseph, and the key to the implementation of the policies the succession of electoral victories achieved by Mrs, later Lady, Thatcher as party leader and Prime Minister. The influence of the ideology of free market thinkers such as

Hayek was profound (Marsh and Rhodes, 1992). On the 'negative' side, New Right ideology gave the impression of belligerent opposition to its enemies. It challenged corporatism, organised interests and the Establishment, particularly experts and established thinking, and 'even the concept of society' (Smith, 1993: 83). The rejection of Keynesianism and of full employment, together with the goal of reducing the role of the state and cutting taxation led to direct challenges to the power of special interest groups, particularly the trade unions. Since the prized values included individualism and cherished the free market and its values, the state was seen as at least neutral and at best as the instrument and servant of policy-makers. The role of government was to determine policy in pursuance of its ideological agenda. State administrative and managerial functions were to be reduced as far as possible, through privatisation of any commercial or pseudo-commercial functions. Hence the sale of utilities like gas, electricity, water. Government involvement in policy networks increased, or it simply abolished them. Debate and discussion on policy outside party networks was reduced. Economic policy prioritised the free market, and limited capitalism as little as possible. Social policy was determined by government and was to concentrate on the 'customer', while 'providers' - teachers, social workers, trade unions - were to be excluded from developing it. The ideological aim was to reject socialism, however defined, to reduce or remove state involvement in welfare and to change ways of thinking so that the individual should face his or her responsibilities (Marsh and Rhodes, 1992).

Much of the thinking in the Conservative party of the time was led by 'think-tanks' and internal pressure groups, ranging from the 'No Turning Back' group of Tory MPs to longer-established groups such as the Conservative Political Centre, the Centre for Policy Studies (the CPS, founded in 1974 by Keith Joseph and Margaret Thatcher), the Institute of Economic Affairs, and the National Council for Educational Standards. Pamphlets, leaflets and research studies were published in considerable numbers in attempts to influence Government thinking. Individuals concerned in language matters over this period included Dr J. Honey, Dr Sheila Lawlor, Dr John Marenbon, Mr Oliver Letwin, all of whom contributed pamphlets, letters or articles to discussion of the standard language issue.

The question of English in the National Curriculum for secondary schools, and its relationship to the question of national identity, formed a key part of the new policies for education. The whole idea of a national curriculum itself was a new departure for British governments.

The curriculum had been a 'secret garden', controlled only by Local Authorities, individual headmasters and the needs for pupils to pass the General Certificate of Education at Ordinary or Advanced level, introduced shortly after the second World War. To achieve the Certificate pupils had to pass in any subject, with a minimum of one subject, an unlimited maximum and no requirement for any specific mix of subjects. The language policy issue hence needs to be seen as part of an overall, radical restructuring of education policy followed after 1979 (Knight, 1990; Baker, 1993; Lawton, 1994).

Lawton (1994: 146), no friend of the Conservative Party, identified six 'value positions' underlying the policy changes introduced in education:

- a desire for more selection;
- a wish to return to traditional curricula and teaching methods;
- a desire to reduce the influence of experts and educational theory;
- an appeal to parental choice to encourage market forces;
- a wish to reduce educational expenditure;
- a process of increased centralisation (and reducing LEA power/influence).

These attitudes were developed during the period of Opposition from 1964 to 1970, but achieved their high point in the period from 1979 to 1986, characterised by Lawton as 'the attack on education'. Educational providers were regarded as 'an unholy alliance of socialists, bureaucrats, planners and Directors of Education acting against the true wishes of the nation's children and parents by their imposition on the schools of an ideology' (Knight, 1990: 155). The vision of 'vested education interests', including the Civil Servants ('the guardians of this culture') and the Inspectors ('its priesthood') (Baker, 1993: 164, 168) as the enemy consistently marked Conservative education policy and attitudes until the appointment of Gillian Shephard as Secretary of State for Education in 1994. It lies behind the downgrading of the education Inspectorate run by the Ministry of Education to keep itself informed of what the education system was doing, and which worked essentially as an information network for civil servants. The Inspectorate role was much sharpened by the Office for Standards in Education (OFSTED), whose role was to show up poor standards through a public process, later to be known as 'naming and shaming'.

Kenneth Baker, as Minister from 1986 to 1989, introduced the consolidating Education Reform Act of 1988. This implemented most of the free market and individualistic values of New Right Conservatism: it reduced, for example, the role of Local Education Authorities, enabling schools to 'opt out'; it enabled open enrolment, giving parents 'free' choice of where to send their children. It imposed a National Curriculum, with testing against stated standards in order to give parents measures of quality to implement their market choice. Yet the 1988 Act also centralised, and in this rejected some of the key tenets of New Right philosophy. It imposed a broad National Curriculum, whereas the idealised free-market approach only wanted a minimalist one; it tried to require a quality education for all, rather than accepting that choice would imply different standards; it centralised (financial and academic) control of Higher Education and removed the autonomy of the universities, making them subject to the political will of ministers.

The influence of Margaret Thatcher was strong, and she is on record as noting her disappointment with the planned content of the curriculum, particularly in history and English. In both these subjects her preference was for traditional approaches: in history, where memorising dates and events was for her the essence of the subject, and in English, where knowledge of standard English, and 'the traditional learning of grammar and learning by heart' were her preferences.

Conservative beliefs and values, the proposals of some pressure groups, and the personal preferences of Mrs Thatcher thus directly affected British education and language policy in the 1980s and 1990s, and the debates surrounding it. There was a major Education Act every year between 1979 and 1994, with the exception of 1982, 1985 and 1991. Language matters generally were at the forefront of the discussion: 'language becomes a crucial focus of tension and debate at critical historical moments, serving as the site upon which political opinions are contested' (Crowley, 1989: 258). The debate was conducted in the political forum, and although much of the opposition came from educationalists, particularly teachers, it quickly became political in tone and content. Professional and academic linguists who attempted to remain dispassionate and objective found that facts were simply treated as ammunition for one side or the other. Some were recruited as supporters or opponents of the changes, usually opponents; others tried to distinguish their academic and their citizenship roles. A newspaper article in The Observer in 1982, for example, complained of a general decline in literacy since 1960, associating 'the overthrow of grammar' with a general decline in moral standards. Academic linguists Milroy and Milroy (1985: 50), attempting a 'rational' reply, pointed to lack of clarity over what is meant by 'grammar', doubted whether there had been a decline in literacy, identified the author's confusion between 'grammar' and 'effective writing', and noted that children who wanted to acquire standard English and 'get on' had to 'opt for status and reject solidarity', leaving behind the social identity of their community. But Milroy and Milroy conceded that the issue was social and, in the end, political, rather than linguistic.

The Kingman Report

The 1988 Education Reform Act, which required the Secretary of State to make orders specifying the content of the National Curriculum, followed the March 1988 report of the Kingman Committee. This had been established in 1987 (although the Secretary of State announced its formation on 7 November 1986) to recommend a model of the English language as a basis for teacher training and professional discussion. The introduction to the Report summarises what provoked it: 'widespread concern that pressures on time and energy, together with inadequacies in the professional education and training of teachers and a misunderstanding of the nature of children's learning, are causing important areas of language teaching to be neglected, to the detriment of children's facility with words' (Kingman, 1988: 1). The 'progressive' assumptions widely held in education at the time and which the report was required to probe were that children should be exposed (only) to varieties of language, that conscious knowledge of structure of the language was unnecessary, that attempting to teach structure (i.e. 'grammar') was unsuccessful in developing the capacity to use language effectively, and that imposing an authoritarian view of the standard was unacceptable to many communities in society. The view that these progressive assumptions were responsible for the poor performance of Britain's children was particularly evident in a pamphlet for the CPS (Marenbon, 1987), but had been part of Conservative thinking before.

Kingman located the Report in a sequence of attempts to solve what he defined as this same problem: the Bullock report of 1975, the speech by the then (Labour) Prime Minister James Callaghan at Ruskin College, Oxford in 1976, the 1984 White Paper 'Better Schools', Curriculum Matters documents written by Her Majesty's Inspectors, and the response thereto. The Bullock Committee Report's recommendations 'had not been implemented...and their implications have not been followed through with sufficient rigour or in detail'. Callaghan's speech drew attention to the need 'to meet the demands of contemporary society and the competitive economy nationally and internationally'. 'Curriculum Matters' had noted widespread opposition among teachers to 'grammatical analysis' and had suggested an enquiry to focus on an 'agenda and ultimately a curriculum'.

Tollefson (1991: 58-78), a committed opponent of the political Right, saw the Kingman Report and its prioritisation of Standard English (SE) as a good example of the ideology inherent in language planning:

> The identification of SE with the nation and with English citizenship assumes that the standard variety is _normal_...the Kingman Report denies that the standard is essentially the result of domination by its speakers...That this policy inevitably grants advantage to children whose home language is SE - and disadvantages immigrants and native speakers of non-standard varieties of English - is never acknowledged. The policy is a clear example of ideology, and its impact is to preserve and protect the hegemonic domination of the educational system by SE speakers.

The recommendations that emerged from the Kingman Committee were however generally regarded as 'bland'. The model of English proposed was more 'linguistic' than 'pedagogic'. In this, it responded more to the concerns of those outside education who wanted attainment to be geared to the English needed for later life than to those of the teachers and teacher-trainers who wished to concentrate on the intellectual, social, personal and aesthetic development of the child. However, the analysis of the purposes of teaching English and about English in schools, as laid out in its Chapter Two in seven paragraphs, only allocated two of these to economic purposes. In one, these were 'the humdrum passages of life where tax returns, mortgage returns, insurance claims are completed'; in the other, the passion of the politicians was dismissed in the remark 'Competence in language is essential to competence in any job'. The Committee did not recommend that dialects and other varieties should not be taught; it did not recommend that 'grammar' should be taught without understanding of communication and comprehension, it took the view that access to the standard language was a right but should not be an imposition. It went so far as to accept the view of professional linguists, and state (page 43) 'All languages are rule-governed systems of communication, and none is linguistically superior'.

The Kingman Report was indeed welcomed by the Labour Opposition as a victory over the Government for its liberal pluralist tone. The Labour Party felt that the Conservatives' political ideology was based on the issue of national identity and hence on the teaching of the standard language, on a Right-Wing belief in reinforcing the centrality of the traditional monolingual middle-class, opposing a Left-Wing view supporting multiculturalism and regional and social variety.

The Kingman Report had not appeared at the time of writing of another opponent, Fairclough (1989), where a final section on 'Language and Power' was devoted to comments on its terms of reference - regarding them as excessively instrumental. Fairclough proposed the inclusion of 'Critical Language Awareness' as a subject in schools, based on a model of language for educational purposes. Instrumental education ('training') focuses on the

> transmission of knowledge and skills, whose content is assumed to be unproblematic and whose social origins are ignored. One finds an analogous concept of literary education, often advocated by the same people, as the transmission of dominant cultural values, teaching children what conventional wisdom regards as 'great literature'. (p. 238)

The aims of education, by contrast, are for Fairclough to 'develop the child's critical consciousness of her environment and her critical self-consciousness, and her capacity to contribute to the shaping and reshaping of her social world'. Critical Language Awareness in schools would therefore be part of a general project to emancipate and empower children, enabling them to 'contribute to the transformation of existing orders of discourse' (p. 243). Fairclough declared himself to be 'a socialist with a generally low opinion of the social relationships in my society and a commitment to the emancipation of the people who are oppressed by them' (p. 5).

Most British linguists who were concerned with education in the schools tried to adopt a less overtly political stance, as can be seen in papers and discussions by umbrella organisations like the Committee for Linguistics in Education or the National Congress on Languages in Education. Points expressed included the view that a school curriculum is a selection from a culture, and that it should contribute to pupils' understanding of social norms and practices. Some contributors tried to maintain that their aims were to encourage children to think for themselves, and that this necessarily meant that they must question the status quo. They felt aggrieved that teachers who raised such ideological issues among their pupils should be accused of political bias or indoctrination.   Others felt that what they were doing was simply to give children the methods to understand better the culture in which they lived, including the analytic tools to analyse purportedly 'neutral' reporting, forms of language and thus to analyse the ways in which reality is socially constructed. Many professionals seemed naively unaware that such liberating intentions could be easily misunderstood and would inevitably lead to conflict with authority. Other organisations, such as the National Association of Teachers of English, in effect declared outright opposition to the changes proposed.

The LINC Reader

The Kingman Report did not go far enough for the Conservative government. The Secretary of State accepted only its recommendation 17, that 'a nationally devised, administered and funded scheme should ...provide training for selected staff in institutions ... and in schools'. The training materials and process were allocated £15.2 million over three years. When these, prepared by a group of linguists and educationalists, were presented to the new Secretary of State in 1989 however he had them withdrawn from the planned wide publication for all, and they were eventually only made available to teachers who expressly requested them, in loose-leaf 'unpublished' format, and with a 'health warning' included: 'At the request of government ministers and of DES officials, LINC has agreed to state that these materials are for teacher training purposes only' (LINC: Language in the National Curriculum. Materials for Professional Development. 1991). Despite this, some 30,000 copies were distributed and used in training, in co-operation with BBC programmes.

The following extracts, from the LINC Reader accompanying the materials, exemplify two aspects of the battle between linguists, English specialists and Government. These are the belief among the working group that they had freedom to interpret and adapt the Kingman model, and their belief that they could openly state, in a Government policy document, their disagreement with the Secretary of State and the Conservative party on such matters as the necessity for class teaching ('classroom analysis' and 'transmissive methods'). One might almost read the preface as a declaration of political opposition:

> The LINC team is committed to the following main principles for KAL (Knowledge About Language) in primary and secondary schools:
> 1. There can be no return to formalist, decontextualised classroom analysis of language, nor to the deficiency pedagogies on which such teaching is founded.
> 2. Language study should start from what children can do, from their positive achievements with language and from the remarkable resources of implicit knowledge about language

which all children possess.

3. A rich experience of using language should generally precede *conscious* reflection on or analysis of language. Language study can influence use but development of the relationship between learning about language and learning how to use it is not a linear one but rather a recursive, cyclical and mutually informing relationship.

4. Being more explicitly informed about the sources of attitudes to language, about its uses and misuses, about how language is used to manipulate and incapacitate, can *empower* pupils to see through language to the ways in which messages are mediated and ideologies encoded.

5. Metalanguage should be introduced where appropriate to facilitate talking and thinking about language but children should be allowed to come to specialist terms as needed and in context.

6. Teaching methodologies for KAL should promote experiential, exploratory and reflective encounters with language; transmissive methods are usually inappropriate for the study of language in schools.

A Secretary of State who had robustly condemned the 'trendy theories' of the progressive teacher trainers, and who was not sufficiently upset by this, could then continue to learn that

> ...the LINC group has realigned the Kingman model of language in order to give special emphasis to the third and fourth 'parts' of Kingman - the development of language and language variation - with greater emphasis than in Kingman given (*sic*) to the variation in language in different social and cultural contexts. In fact, a principal and underlying motivation for the LINC project is a concern with *language variation*.
>
> A concern with social, cultural and textual variation does not preclude a concern with the forms of language (contained in Part 1 of the Kingman model of language). However, such forms should be examined not in and for themselves but in relation to functional variation...
>
> The LINC approach to language is much influenced by functional theories of language. The main proponent of such theories - over a period of almost 30 years - has been Professor Michael Halliday, and the LINC model owes much to Halliday's work...
>
> A functional theory of language is a natural complement to

influential theories of language development constructed in the 1970s by Professor James Britton and others working to similar principles...Such theories culminated in the Bullock report.

The reference to experts whose work had been carried out during the 'trendy sixties' and whose opinions and research were anathema to the pressure groups and individuals working to revise British education, particularly to Drs Lawlor and Marenbon, together with the refusal to concentrate attention on the forms of (the standard) language, dealt an inevitable blow to the acceptance of these materials by the relevant Secretary of State.

National Curriculum Orders

The Kingman Report was followed by National Curriculum orders, devised a year later than those for mathematics and science in order to give time for a Committee chaired by Professor Brian Cox of Manchester University, one of the authors of the 1969 and 1970 Black Papers and a member of the most influential Conservative Educational policy groups during the 1980s, to produce its report (Cox, 1989). The reception of the Cox Committee Report by linguists and educationalists was in general favourable. The reasons for this are many and variable: most important is perhaps the fact that the curriculum was presented as providing suggestions which teachers could interpret, rather than instructions which gave them no room for manoeuvre. That this was not what was intended by the politicians may be gauged from later comments by Cox, who is said to have felt that Mr Baker very much disliked the report. He had wanted a short report, with strong emphasis on grammar, spelling and punctuation, which would have been easy for parents to read. Cox and his group were more anxious to persuade the teaching profession to implement the recommendations with good will. Other ministers were equally condemnatory. One found   'repugnant' the Committee's insistence that a child's dialect should be respected. Mrs Thatcher herself, apparently, asked for only one alteration. In the Attainment targets for Writing Cox had put: "Use standard English, where appropriate". The Prime Minister asked for "where appropriate" to be deleted.

The Cox Committee Report's recommendations were incorporated into the official National Curriculum for English. In 1992, changes were suggested and the Secretary of State commissioned a review, requesting 'advice' particularly in regard to standard English:

a greater emphasis on the vocabulary...(and) the importance to effective speaking of clarity of diction...

...whether the programme of study for the reading of fiction in key stages 3 and 4 could be better designed to ensure a study of the great tradition of the novel: for example by identifying a smaller group of pre-20th century authors of central importance from whose work some selection is <u>required</u>.

Basic writing skills, grammatical knowledge and spelling were the topics upon which the New Right had expressed its views forcefully.

In April 1993, the revised version of the English Order was presented. This accepted many of the criticisms voiced by the New Right and moved the curriculum in the direction desired by the more radical thrust of Conservative thinking over the 1980s. The following formal consultation, however, took place against the background of the appointment of a new Chairman to the National Curriculum Council (Sir Ron Dearing), brought in to mollify the teaching profession and to revise all the National Curriculum orders. In effect, therefore, the 1993 order was not implemented and was superseded by the 1994 version.

Both the 1990 and 1993 versions were more 'political' than had previously been the case, changing the literary works to be used to make greater emphasis on traditional works of the 'canon', insisting to a greater extent on traditional grammar and approaches to language learning, stressing correctness rather than imagination, and reinforcing the role of standard English, giving little support for the teaching of dialects and none to language maintenance for minority languages. The extent of the political interference leading to the 1993 changes can be assessed by the bitterness of the attack Professor Brian Cox then conducted against the National Curriculum Council and its Chairman, an 'oil company executive', the Secretary of State and the Conservative Party generally in a television programme in 1993.

Extracts from an analysis of the 1993 order by CLIE (the Committee for Linguistics in Education, a joint body of the British Association for Applied Linguistics (BAAL) and the Linguistics Association of Great Britain (LAGB)) showed the concern of linguists at the changes from Cox. They had little doubt that the 1993 order would have been difficult to implement.

1. The revision goes way beyond its terms of reference...unlike the Cox report, it lacks any explicit rationale for its structure and content.
2. In the removal or drastic reduction of material on knowledge about language, media studies, drama, and information

technology, and in the failure to acknowledge a multilingual, multicultural dimension within our society, the revised proposals offer a narrowed and impoverished curriculum.

4. The structure of the existing curriculum has been damaged by the incorporation of spelling and handwriting into Attainment Target 3 (Writing), which gives these skills undue significance in the determination of a child's achievement in writing.

5. ...teachers are required to teach children to speak in standard English from the age of five, and to assess their spoken language in terms of the conventions of standard English at the end of Key Stage 1 (age seven). This means that pupils are expected to speak standard English before they are reading or writing fluently, yet the best way for those who speak non-standard English at home to make the forms of standard English their own is by reading and writing extensively...

7. (ii) The requirement to speak standard English by the end of Key Stage 1 does not recognise the difficulty for those who come from homes and communities where standard English is neither used nor accepted of adopting a different speech style. (Perera, 1993, 25)

In 1994, the National Curriculum Council and the Schools Examinations and Assessment Authority were combined in the Schools Curriculum and Assessment Authority (SCAA) under a new chief executive (Nicholas Tate). The general review produced draft proposals for change in May 1994 and a final version in October 1994, accepted by the Secretary of State in November 1994 with the intention that there would be no further curriculum changes for five years. This 1994 version (NCO, 1994) weakened or removed many of the points which had been seen as contentious, even in the version of the 1993 order which had been published after consultation. In relation to standard English, for example, this latter order had noted at the beginning:

2. The significance of English as the language of government, business, the professions and general communication means that, in order to participate confidently in public, cultural and working life, all pupils need to be able to speak, write and read Standard English fluently and accurately.

In the following definition of standard English, mention was made of other dialects:

The richness of dialects and languages in England and Wales can contribute to pupils' knowledge and understanding of language.

The aim should be to equip young people with the ability to use Standard English when circumstances require it: in their written work and in many speaking and listening contexts. It is important to encourage pupils' ability to extend their speaking and writing repertoires: to make their language 'fit' the context.

The 1994 order modified this further to:

2. In order to participate confidently in public, cultural and working life, pupils need to be able to speak, write and read standard English fluently and accurately. All pupils are therefore entitled to the full range of opportunities necessary to enable them to develop competence in standard English. The richness of dialects and other languages can make an important contribution to pupils' knowledge and understanding of standard English. Where appropriate, pupils should be encouraged to make use of their understanding and skills in other languages when learning English.

Although the changes may seem subtle to the uninitiated, the significance of the differences is not lost on the initiated: no mention of 'business' or 'equip'; the use of words like 'entitled'; the change from 'can contribute' to 'can make an important contribution', and the general organisation of the changes mean that the 1994 orders are more likely to be accepted over time. Indeed, the teachers' boycott of testing was formally lifted in January 1995 by the unions.

Ideology as a Policy Motive

The National Curriculum and the political agenda underlying its introduction and contents originated in a political ideology, clearly expounded and openly stated as the aim of government. Insofar as language was concerned, the aim was to ensure that standard English was taught to all children, while their own social dialects or languages other than English were kept out of mainstream education. The general motive was therefore the implementation of a political agenda aimed at developing a particular type of society. Like any ideology, the view put forward ignored other points of view. Two particular points which were deliberately set aside were the question of language varieties and their domains of appropriate use, and secondly the role of language learning and teaching in education, although this latter may have been a matter of ignorance of how to present the political aims of the curriculum in a manner suitable to the education of the young.

The opposition between the views of the politicians and linguists we have examined in this chapter falls into at least three areas. There is a difference between the extent to which each knows the language facts: what standard English is, what grammar is, what a dialect is. There is a further difference in the nature of the emotion, in some cases, passion, demonstrated: generally the academic linguists try to be dispassionate while the politicians deliberately aim to stir up feelings, although many linguists and academics quickly lost their cool in the heat of discussion. There is a further difference in the extent to which each group approved of intervention: most academic linguists were content to let teachers decide, while the politicians were generally in favour of issuing direct instructions to the educational administration and in some cases became political control freaks.

Given such contrasts in attitudes it is hardly surprising that there would be a clash between the linguists and the politicians. Politicians seemed to take pride in an utter lack of knowledge of the linguistic facts about language varieties and about the nature of standard languages. Their taste for direct intervention in language matters during this period of British educational history, meant that although language policy in education was a simple consequence of a prior ideological aim, the motive seemed to be based on deliberately putting aside available knowledge about a number of relevant aspects of the question. One cannot blame just the politicians involved for this dialogue of the deaf: their opponents were equally determined to pay no attention to the views of the properly elected government, to the reasons for them, or to the facts of political life.

Better knowledge of the dialects of English, both regional and social, might have prevented the idea gaining ground that it was the English of southern England that was to be forced onto unwilling Yorkshire or Scottish children. Better knowledge of the range of social dialects of English could have avoided the feeling that the middle classes were trying to impose their way of speaking on the working class. Better knowledge of the fact that what Bernstein had called the elaborated code of the middle classes could not be taught in abstraction from the cultural concepts that went with it, might have avoided the idea that the aim was to force young children from deprived backgrounds to adopt a Right-wing agenda by expressing themselves in Received Pronunciation. Better knowledge, indeed, of the actual range of abilities, backgrounds and origins of schoolchildren might have helped avoid the impression that London policy-makers were intent on preventing many children gaining access to advancement. Indeed, it was not until the language of rights was used, and the teaching of standard English was advocated as an aid for children to gain access to the advantages of society including employment, that the government started to gain some support.

There was equal ignorance on the part of supporters and opponents alike. The lack of a coherent, argued position representing the point of view of linguists and teachers as a profession was clear. The Committee for Linguistics in Education for example had representatives from a number of associations in the field, and was concerned with 'a wide range of aspects of English and language teaching'. Nonetheless CLIE did not succeed in uniting the profession(s), and the concerns of teachers of English, of English as a Second Language, of Mother-Tongue Teachers and of Teachers of Foreign Languages were often misunderstood by one or another group. The British language and linguistics field was characterised by a plethora of associations and interest groups, which did not unite in a coherent position on language or languages and which were hence unlikely to propose a coherent British language policy. The situation in the late 1980s directly contrasted with the coherence of the Australian professions and pressure groups, whose joint action and clear understanding of the political environment, and how to present their case, led to the Australian National Languages Policy of 1987.

The development of the National Curriculum has generally gone forward in the UK without much benefit from experts, including linguists in this case, instead following in many areas the agenda of pressure groups, consultants, and strong-minded individuals, and being opposed by the brute force of an outraged teaching force in the context of an industrial dispute. Constructive argument and debate was notable for its absence, and was replaced by sometimes wilful ignorance. This was particularly evident in the English proposals, within which sections on the bilingual child had been included (e.g. Cox, 1989), only to be attacked by some educationalists for not providing policy proposals on the maintenance of 'immigrant' languages, which was neither the purpose of the Cox committee nor their remit. Similarly, the advice for teachers in the LINC materials contains nothing about learning foreign languages, and its insistence that 'transmissive methods are inappropriate' is evidently at variance with the needs of foreign language learning. Even in the one section on multilingualism there is no understanding of any relationship between language maintenance, essentially building on (some) knowledge of a language already spoken, and foreign language learning where everything has to be acquired. The National Curriculum orders on Foreign Languages similarly ignore the

English curriculum orders, in questions such as understanding the existence of dialect or in any attempt systematically to understand the foreign society.

Ideology as a motive in language planning has not therefore been the prerogative of politicians blindly pursuing an educational dogma. There is little doubt that the ideology, the beliefs and values, of the Conservative educational thinkers of the early 1980s, blinded them to accepting any full and accurate picture of the nature of language, of the range of language varieties and of their social role. But similar ideological preconceptions meant that many educationalists and linguists were unprepared to accept any view on the social role of language different from their own. Ignorance of the issue of social cohesion and the importance of a single language to this, and a preconception that acceptance of diversity was the only way to ensure adequate recognition of the dignity of social and ethnic groups, ensured that minds were closed in the academic community to any point of view other than the fostering of individual creativity in children in an atmosphere of multiculturalism. Ideological preconceptions here also predisposed activists with one issue in mind to ignore and condemn learning methods which might be more appropriate to different tasks.

Chapter 3

Image

The attempts by the British Council and by the US government to support the greater use of English as an international means of communication have been widely documented (Phillipson 1992; Ager 1996b). A network of schools and language classes, established in conjunction with local interests, linked with the Paris branch of the Alliance Française, and heavily funded by the French government, forms part of the overseas cultural policy of France (Ager, 1999). Such actions may be regarded as positive, simply part of cultural aid and cultural diplomacy (Ministry of Foreign Affairs of Japan, 1999), or as negative manifestations of colonialism and worse (Phillipson, 1992).   The aim of cultural diplomacy, of which this type of language policy is often a part, is that of image projection and management: trying to ensure that a favourable view is taken by other countries of one's own history, traditions, cultural productions, religion and manner of being.   This motive is by no means   reprehensible in itself: indeed the European Convention on Cultural Cooperation commits states to support their own language and culture in other member states, and to facilitate such action by other states in their own territory. Nonetheless, the motive for such types of governmental action seems to be a search for advantage, whether economic, commercial, diplomatic or cultural.

There is a difference between promoting English abroad and promoting other languages. The power and presence of English in international communications in all fields, but particularly in sport and finance, is such that Britain and the United States tend to make money out of teaching the language abroad while other countries have to spend resources in order to encourage speakers of other languages to learn theirs. Laitin (1997: 288) rather cruelly says 'People are willing to pay high personal costs to learn English, they have to be bribed to learn French or German. The microeconomic handwriting is on the wall'. It is unfortunate that journalistic jingoism on this topic occasionally tends to pity Johnny Foreigner and to pour scorn on the attempts of governments to protect or to support their language on the international scene, while congratulating itself on the inevitable superiority of English. Such xenophobic attitudes are however not far from the thoughts of policy-makers with other language backgrounds, who condemn the superior attitudes of supporters of English while attempting to make the case for their own language on the grounds of its undeniable intrinsic superiority over English, its unassailable case to be the language of international communication as a vehicle of economic or cultural superiority, or its outstanding richness and subtlety in contrast to the paucity of expression of English when used as a lingua franca.

The two cases we shall examine first are those of German and Japanese, particularly over the last decade or so. The 1939-45 war is now a long time ago, and the motive which might have been important for both countries, of improving their image after the 1945 defeat, has long been superseded. What is current practice and how is cultural diplomacy and language policy now seen? As the third case study in this chapter we shall investigate some aspects of language policy in the creation of the new European Union. Here, since a new political entity is being created, policy should on the face of it be agreed, and be a matter of ensuring that non-European views of the Union are favourable. But what is that cultural policy, and how 'European' is it?

Language Spread: the Case for German

German is not the language of one state alone. It is the official language of Germany, Austria, and Liechtenstein, one of the official languages of Switzerland and Luxembourg, a regional language in Belgium and Italy, and is widely spoken by recognised minorities in parts of France, in eastern Europe particularly Hungary and Romania, and in immigrant countries such as Brazil, Argentina or the USA. As a pluricentric language it has no one cultural centre, and its history, symbolic importance and practical utility vary widely between countries (Ammon, 1995). During the Nazi period in Germany itself language policy was a central part of the Reich's identity formation, was closely associated with xenophobic National Socialism, and was heavily promoted abroad as the Reich expanded. The most obvious manifestation of this was in language reform aimed at removing foreign lexical borrowings and ensuring the use of the 'native' language, including print styles and handwriting. For long after 1945 the use of German was resented outside Germany, particularly in eastern and central Europe where previously it had been widespread, as symbolising

Nazi policies for dominating Europe. This resentment was somewhat moderated for political reasons since the DDR was politically within the Iron Curtain, and German could not be rejected as a manifestation of Western imperialism. Russian, heavily promoted to fill the gap and to be used as a replacement 'official' and school language, soon suffered the same rejection for very similar reasons. German was not one of the official languages of the United Nations. Language policy was for long a low priority for the Bundesrepublik, although less so for the East German Democratic Republic. Since the late 1950s, and particularly since reunification in 1990, the fear of German political (but not of economic) domination has subsided, and Germany has been spending a considerable amount on officially promoting its language abroad. Some idea of the nature of this expenditure can be gained from comparing investments for different languages: 6 million US dollars by the British Council over 18 months in Eastern Europe, 70 million per annum by the Spanish Government world-wide, 22 million by the German government for Central, Eastern and South-Eastern Europe alone in 1992 (Clyne, 1995: 11).

The Goethe Institut is one of the Bundesrepublik's main vehicles for promoting German abroad: 'to promote the German language and to foster international cultural co-operation'. Like the British Council, it undertakes language teaching directly in addition to its role as cultural diplomat, employing numbers of teachers, course administrators and course developers. Formally, it is an independent, non-profit making organisation, with 135 branches in 76 countries. The Institute's offices are well-funded and act as repository for book, videos, audio sources and computer software, while all the activities are generally free of charge.

The German Academic Exchange Service (DAAD: Deutscher Akademischer Austauschdienst) is equally well-known in academic circles for its fostering of personnel exchange in the pursuit of language work and for German studies more widely. It organises the selection of some 500 language assistants (Lektoren) for Universities and schools and in some countries provides them with salary supplements in order to maintain their income at the levels of the German academic system. Both organisations respond to governmental priorities, for example in shifting resources to Central and Eastern Europe after 1990. In addition to official organisations, the Volkswagen Foundation and other private organisations have long provided grants and other support for German-related cultural activities abroad. A large German Institute was thus created in Birmingham (UK) in the 1990s to foster German studies in the region.

State policy for German abroad is not simply a matter of cultural diplomacy and good works. German is protected and supported politically by many parts of government. This support takes the form of specific activities in the cultural domain as we have seen, but it also includes symbolic actions designed to ensure that German's official status in the European organisations is borne in mind. As a reaction to the French attempt to restrict working languages in the European institutions in 1994, the Bundesrat called on Ministers to ensure a continuing prestigious role for German, going so far as suggesting simply three working languages as the Union was enlarged: English, French and German (for references to the Bundesrat's continuing role in such supportive measures see Quell, 1997: 74). Such Parliamentary pressure continues to be important to governments: the first meeting held as Finland took the European Union Presidency in July 1999, an informal summit of Ministers of Industry held in Oulu to discuss high-tech Europe, was boycotted by both German and Austrian Ministers since German was not included as a working language. This attitude, perhaps provoked by French insistence on the use of their language throughout the European institutions and certainly strengthened as new members have joined and as the Brussels bureaucracy has grown, is nowhere near so strident as that of the French government. It is nonetheless insistent.

German attitudes towards creating and maintaining a favourable image of Germany abroad are positive, quite vigorously pursued and widely shared by the population at large. Although official concerns since 1990 have concentrated on the two priorities of integrating the former DDR and overseas people of German extraction (Aussiedler) to the new Bundesrepublik and the creation of the European Union, German policy for supporting cultural exchange and for fostering the understanding of German language and ideas throughout the world remains important. But despite informal contacts and various attempts to strengthen joint action by the German-speaking countries, most notable recently in the proposed reform of German spelling (Clyne, 1995: 180-5), there is no central language organisation with sufficient authority to make language policy for German, nor to provide international support for the dissemination of German in non-German-speaking countries. It may be this pluricentric aspect of German that makes it less easy for the Federal Republic to project abroad the image of German it would like to see.

What then is the case for German? It has three potential roles for the world: as a symbol of German-speaking countries; as a language of international communication; and as a language of culture. This latter aspect is of importance to any language, and although German-language literature is of undoubted value, it is no part of our intention to attempt a comparative evaluation of its intrinsic worth to humanity. German is the first language of by far the largest number of European Union citizens, outranking the 60 million or so speakers of English or French. But there can be little doubt that the former dominant role of German as the first foreign language taught in schools throughout Eastern Europe from the Balkans to the Baltic has declined since 1945 and since the collapse of the Communist satellites in 1990, to be replaced by English. As a language of international communication, German has a strong vehicular role for a number of speakers of other languages. This is particularly true for Dutch , little known outside Holland and Belgium, and for central Europe, where Hungarian speakers are obliged to learn other languages for communicative needs. German is hence, potentially at least, of fundamental importance as a lingua franca, of even greater importance since Germany itself is now the main economic and financial motor of the European Union. But again it may be too late: English and American have become the principal language of international communication.

Japanese Abroad

Japanese attitudes towards their own language sometimes seem to be a mixture of pride and amazement. The language was and is felt to be far superior to any other means of human communication and at the same time so impossible to learn that nobody other than someone of pure Japanese extraction could possibly acquire other than a smattering of its beauty, complexity, subtlety and charm. The first reaction by Europeans to the Japanese written language in the sixteenth century was to agree on the complexity, but not the charm; it was an invention of the devil aimed at preventing the spread of Christianity. The country was closed to foreigners from 1639 until 1853, in a move which was paralleled by the order that Japanese people should not travel abroad. Isolation in an island state became the Japanese reaction to others. After 1853, Japan not merely caught up with the West but, in the view of many, became just as 'advanced'. Japan became a colonial nation, conquering Korea; it rapidly transformed itself into an industrial nation, laying the basis for what would become the world's second largest economy. Politically, it became a nation demanding its place among others; at first intent on reversing the unequal treaties it had been forced to sign with them, and later dominating much of the Pacific Rim in military occupation. In today's world of increasing tourism by Japanese citizens individually as well as in organised groups, an economy based on exports and dependent on manufacturing increasingly based abroad, tours of duty by Japanese nationals abroad, and better knowledge of others by the Japanese themselves, the twin inheritances of isolation and internationalisation remain of central importance. Although Japanese products are well-known everywhere, the country is not part of the international tourist circuit, its language is not extensively taught or understood, its diplomats are not major international figures and both country and people remain remote.

Japanese language policy for the written language in Japan has struggled with nationalist, conservative views which try to preserve the complexities of two separate syllabaries (kana), an ever-increasing range of Chinese ideographs (kanji), many of which can relate to more than one spoken representation in Japanese, an alphabetic script (romaji) and the increasing number of Western, usually English, loan-words often written solely in romaji. The opposing drive for efficiency would simply replace such difficulties for education and industry with romaji, and although this nearly happened immediately after the second World War, it is now impossible. The complexities and politics of the debates opposing imperialism and democracy, modernisation and conservatism which have raged since 1868 over possible policies, over the role of the government and the bureaucracy and over the Japanese calligraphic tradition are not our concern here (but see Gottlieb, 1995). It was the 1945 defeat and the subsequent occupation, followed by economic growth and the need to internationalise, which sharpened the debate about the consequences of language attitudes for Japan's international role. By 1970, Japan was the third richest economy in the world by Gross Domestic Product, and 'Expo 70' at Osaka aimed to demonstrate the fact to the world. But internationally, Japan was inexperienced, still shielded by the USA from the harshness of the Cold War and hence shocked by the USA's recognition of China and its imposition of import tariffs, actions carried out without informing Japan. Japan felt it needed both to widen its international contacts and to tell the world that it had other things to offer than cash, cars and computers.

The oil crisis of 1973 meant that Japan did not regain 1972 output levels for ten years, by which time her exposure to the unstable Middle East and to heavy industry had both reduced. By the 1990s, Japanese official attitudes have become more aware that the world is not made up simply of markets to be exploited but that Japan itself could benefit from increased understanding of Japanese civilisation and language by others. 'Japanese have been compulsively concerned with how they are perceived in other parts of the world. With the maturation of Japan's economy and society 'internationalization' became an obsession with many' (Reischauer and Jansen, 1995: 37). The foreword to a 1999 volume produced by the Japanese Ministry of Foreign Affairs is instructive in locating this feeling within a generalised policy of greater internationalisation:

> The reason why 'international contribution' was chosen as the book's theme is that, as a result of Japan's growing importance in the international community, Japan's contribution to it is of growing interest in Japan and in other countries. We often hear criticism like 'Japan provides money but not people' or 'Japan's international contributions lack a comprehensive principle'. Nimi Jun, Director of the Overseas Public Relations Division, Ministry of Foreign Affairs. (Ministry of Foreign Affairs of Japan, 1999: 6)

This volume is an attempt both to set the record straight, in terms of the assistance Japan now provides to other countries, and an attempt to explain to Japanese citizens themselves as much as to foreigners the necessity and the nature of this contribution. Like many other countries, this could nonetheless fairly be described as still self-centred:

> it is impossible for Japan, with its great economic potential, to ignore international society or to hope for its own prosperity alone. What is being required of Japan is active leadership and responsible action in supporting and assisting an international society that is facing many difficulties. This will increase the number of friends, around the globe, who understand and support Japan's way of thinking, and it will ultimately contribute to Japan's own national interest, that is, the welfare of the Japanese people. (Ministry of Foreign Affairs of Japan, 1999: 103)

The contribution is not small, as this volume indicates: in 1996, Japan's Overseas Development Assistance was 9.439 billion dollars, the largest provided by any single country, and had been the largest contribution for six consecutive years. Admittedly, a high proportion (58.6%) was in yen loans rather than aid, although Japan's untied loans rate at 81.4% was much higher than France's (50.9%), the UK's (45.8%) or the USA's (37.4%), and it amounted only to 0.2% of GDP rather than the 0.7% which is supposed to be the international target.

Japan's present Constitution has remained unchanged since it was imposed by the American occupying forces in 1946. It was intended to ensure Japan could never again attempt to develop a 'Greater East-Asia Co-Prosperity Sphere' through aggressive militarism. As a result of the occupation and subsequent events,   Japanese politicians have concentrated on developing prosperity at home, and on diplomatic and commercial relations with the USA to the extent that foreign policy has practically disregarded other countries.   Japan has taken only very cautious foreign policy initiatives, particularly within Asia. Hence, perhaps, the ignorance of their own history by Japanese youth: schools do not explain the Japanese role in Nanking, Manchuria or the reasons why atomic bombs were dropped on Hiroshima and Nagasaki. Japanese-Korean relations are formal rather than friendly. Japanese tourists in Asia are sometimes shocked by their reception abroad, being unaware of the nature and impact of Japanese actions during the war in the early 1940s. Hence, too, the rather limited programmes of youth exchanges, the presence of only 40,000 Japanese students in the USA, the minute number of marriages between Japanese and non-Japanese, the small number of foreign tourists or students in Japan. Although there is a   scheme for the state-supported promotion of the learning of Japanese abroad, it is nowhere near so vigorous or well-supported as the JET programme for inviting young people to act as teachers of English in Japan.

It may be Japan's experience of defeat and the undoubted success of her policy of national economic development above all else that has led to this situation. But underlying Japanese attitudes are deeply embedded in her history (Cortazzi, 1993). Common myths abound: drugs, Aids and illegal or even legal immigrants are regarded as diseases of foreign countries. Meat- and milk-eating foreigners smell different from the rice- and fish-eating Japanese, although this opinion is much less true of young people today who eat as many hamburgers as other countries do. The widespread ignorance of other countries, and the continuing felt need to survive by hard work and export, since Japan contains limited natural resources of her own, have led to a lack of trust, even dislike, of other countries and their citizens.   Foreigners are rare in Japan; the aliens, mostly of Korean extraction, living in Japan, either came to the country against their will as forced labour during the war or are employees, often of Japanese companies.   Pride in the Japanese way of life, in Japanese culture and even in cuisine sometimes takes the form of decrying the cultural products of other countries. Nationalism, as elsewhere in the world, has its supporters, as the election of Shintaro Ishihara as governor of Tokyo in 1999 demonstrated, even if this vote was as much a protest against political corruption as an act of support for emotive ultra-nationalism. Even on an everyday level, there is a widespread feeling that Japanese can speak to Japanese about others because nobody else in the world is listening; even if they are, they cannot be expected to understand 'internal' matters. Even major contemporary politicians can reveal a depth of ignorance about other countries, and at the very least, a lack of tact in describing them, which astonishes:

> Prime Minister Nakasone appealed for every Japanese to buy at least $100-worth of foreign goods. (He undid many of his own best efforts at internationalisation by) suggesting that, after all, Americans couldn't compete successfully because the Japanese were so much better educated and more intelligent. The insult was further compounded by his attempted 'explanation' that Americans as such weren't actually less intelligent but that, having so many blacks, Hispanics and other ethnic minorities, the United States was intrinsically disadvantaged compared to homogeneous Japan. (Tames, 1993: 215)

Japan has a programme, nonetheless, aimed at disseminating her culture and language abroad. The Foreign Affairs booklet referred to above tacitly accepts the need for this, and Japan officially maintains a programme for improving international relations. The Japan Foundation is the main instrument for it, carrying out a range of activities, including sending Japanese teachers abroad, funding the learning of Japanese in many countries at all levels, and opening Japanese Language Centres at home and abroad. The Japan Language Institute was opened in 1989 in Urawa, Saitama Prefecture, to act as a training centre for language teachers in many countries, and was followed by the Japanese Language Institute Kansai near Osaka in 1997. Awards and special prizes are given annually to overseas individuals and organisations in recognition of deepening mutual understanding between Japan and other nations. The 1998 list was chosen from 167 nominations; it gave two awards, one to an American Emeritus Professor and one to a Japanese composer; and three special prizes, one to a French artistic advisor and tour organiser, one to the Pusan Korea-Japan cultural exchange association, and the other to the Suntory Foundation (Japan Foundation Newsletter, 26: 3). The Japan Foundation was created in 1972 to

> efficiently carry on activities for international cultural exchange and thereby to contribute to the enhancement of world culture

and the welfare of mankind, with a view to deepening other nations' view of Japan, promoting better mutual understanding among nations, and encouraging friendship and goodwill among the peoples of the world (Article 1 of Japan Foundation Law). (Japan Foundation)

The Foundation's original endowment of 5 billion Yen had grown by 1998 to 106.2 billion through annual grants, interest on the original endowment and donations from individuals and corporations. Its activities include Japanese studies, language education, and two-way international exchange in the arts, publication, sports, media and culture generally. The Japan Foundation is not the only agency involved in such actions. The Foreign Affairs Ministry itself undertakes occasional actions such as organising Essay Competitions for 18-32-year-olds in Europe, with the prize of a study tour of Japan, as it did in April 1999 with the title 'Japan-UK relations: What more can be done?' Private organisations, too, like the Daiwa Foundation make grants available to academic institutions to further Japanese studies.

But generally it has to be said that Japan's official policy towards encouraging the study of Japan and Japanese is cautious rather than aggressive. The image of itself Japan would like to foster abroad seems to be based on non-controversial arts such a flower-arranging and calligraphy. Cultural diplomacy as represented in the Foreign Ministry booklet of 1999 is so cautious and self-deprecating as to be practically invisible:

> Visits by people overseas to such performances and exhibitions of Japanese culture typically bring about positive sentiments and a greater sense of familiarity with Japan. As a way of promoting friendship with other countries, such modest but steady efforts to introduce Japanese culture abroad should be continued. (Ministry of Foreign Affairs of Japan, 1999: 185)

The self-deprecation, and the strange mixture of inward and outward-looking approaches have not gone unnoticed by seasoned observers of Japan. Some see the cause as a permanent concern with Japan's own identity:

> As with foreign-language instruction in the schools, there are not enough persons of influence who care. Japan is a startlingly international country on the surface but an isolated, inward-looking country beneath its cosmopolitan sheen. This is primarily a psychological problem and is probably the most significant fact

about the Japanese today. (Reischauer and Jansen, 1995: 394)

A European Language Policy: Jobs for Functionaries, GATT and the Media, and the Labelling of Foods

European integration means many things to many people. For the politicians who devised the idea of joint action on the European level after the second World War the idea of integration developed on two levels, of economics and politics. The pragmatic desire was to avoid the need for reparations payments by Germany to France, which had been the fundamental reason for the second World War, by devising a Common Agricultural Policy based on payments to agriculture from industry. This was associated with the need to promote joint action on coal and steel, and to develop atomic power. The main aim, the rather more high-level, but in fact equally pragmatic, post-war need to prevent another European war opposing France and Germany, meant associating the two countries politically. Later, the hope that a European organisation could compete with the growing industrial and economic power of the United States and the need to keep the French franc and the German mark in step led to the Single Market, the European Union and eventually a common currency. Personal friendships between de Gaulle and Adenauer, Mitterrand and Kohl, cemented the political process. The major incentives have been political rather than cultural; elitist rather than democratic; commercial rather than economic. European integration so far has been essentially a technocratic, administrative process based in the European Commission, modelled on the workings of the French state machine and basically benefiting large-scale agribusiness, some types of industry, and finance. The slow development of democratic institutions, and the restricted powers of the European Parliament, are proof enough of these priorities.

As the Community, and now the Union, have developed, one of the many difficulties slowing down closer European integration at the level of the citizen has been that of image. How can one project an image of Europe to European citizens which they will buy into, which they can understand and support? How could one enable the peoples of Europe, with their different languages, histories and traditions, to understand one another better on a continuing basis? Even at the level of the European institutions, how could one ensure that the whole enterprise did not collapse under the burden of coping with eleven official languages, which would of course mean 110 language pairs in translations? How could one then continue to help the peoples of Europe to understand one another in the future by ensuring a common approach to language learning? Has the time come to create, develop or modify the image of Europe, and how could a common policy towards language affect this? How necessary is a common language to an integrated Europe, particularly if this is to become in effect a new nation-state? How relevant are the two main models of large democratic multicultural federations, the USA and India, to this issue? The first answers seemed to require a common language for all Europeans, or at least and in the first instance, a common language for all the bureaucratic institutions. Later, the creators of the European Union have seemed to decide that the best way of improving the image of Europe is to retain language diversity. A policy for a single European language, if it were not English, would simply fail in practical terms. A language policy which deliberately proposed English would receive no diplomatic support from French speakers and command only lukewarm approval from most others. A policy which merely continued earlier French domination would not meet the needs of northern Europe, and could lead to Europe being isolated from the world at large. Other languages each had their claim, but no single language seems to be the answer. European language policy, aimed within rather than outside the European Union, is to a certain reflected in three questions: which language should the functionaries use? how can one best preserve a European cultural identity? and how can the practical, simple and direct issues of safety and commerce be addressed?

Jobs for functionaries

After the 1939-45 war, most institutions operating on the European level which would eventually be regarded as European used French as their administrative and working language. By 1997 however, the majority were facing a major dilemma: unless they dealt only with European matters, their external relationships were normally conducted in English. This was true not solely of discussions with the United States and the English-speaking world, but with Asia, the Far East and indeed with the Near East and with Russia. Even if they dealt only with matters internal to the European Union, they found effective working almost impossible in the face of the potential of 110 language pairs caused by the use of their own national language by every representative of a particular nation. If all international civil servants adopted the attitude required of the French by official circular in 1998, that is to express oneself in the native language even if no translation was provided, complete standstill would have occurred.

The actual use of languages in the bureaucratic institutions has been studied by many scholars and is nervously watched by governments. For example, an annual report on the situation of French in the world is prepared for the Haut Conseil de la Francophonie, chaired by the French President. Its 1995-6 report briefly mentioned the French proposal of 1994, when in the pursuit of efficiency in the growing community it was suggested that the number of working languages be limited to five from the eleven officially possible. The proposal

> brought about very sharp responses from many countries, particularly Greece, the Netherlands, Denmark and Portugal. A resolution was adopted by the European Parliament on 19 January 1995 stressing that 'any proposal limiting language use merely strengthens the distance between the citizen and European institutions'. (Etat, 1995-6: 99)

The proposal was rapidly dropped by the French, who proceeded to proclaim their interest in pluralism and language diversity. Similarly, when the German Ambassador was asked in 1992 in London about his government's interest in German as a working language, he was quick to make clear that 'we are in no way pressing for this' (reported in Quell, 1997: 72).

Quell (1997) studied the choice of working languages and the language preferences of 274 trainee Commission workers in 1993. The survey reported the languages actually used by this group of future European bureaucrats as percentages of their time:

Table 3.1 Percentages of language use

Type of use	Eng	Fre	Germ	Span	Ital	Dan	Greek	Dutch	Port
oral	47.1	38.3	5	3.2	2.9	1.3	0.3	1.1	0.8
written inside	49.1	45.4	2.1	1.2	0.6	0.1	0.5	0.4	0.5
written outside	54.6	35.4	4.8	1.2	1.7	0.6	0.5	0.4	0.4

Source: Quell, 1997: 63

These figures are surprising on two counts: firstly that although English is clearly in the lead for communication outside the Commission, it is much less so inside despite the fact that written communication inside the Commission is intended for widespread use among a number of offices and to/from a number of different Directorates. Secondly, the fact that the other languages are used to the extent they are in internal oral communication. This may be due partly to the fact that respondents were asked not to indicate their main language of use but all the languages they used and to give the percentage of their time for which each was used, and much informal communication was clearly carried out in the native language of the trainee. Partly, also,   in oral communication the listener was 'clearly defined and immediate' and if the trainee had the listener's language available it was preferred. Although this group of trainees could have no direct effect on a possible language policy for the Commission, they were asked their preferences for a language regime. Since the Indian language situation demonstrated so clearly the power of the state bureaucracy in influencing policy it is perhaps worth recording the preference of the group for a two-language solution, English and French. But although this was the preferred solution for 38% of the group, the next choice was a trilingual solution of English, French and German (24%), while English alone was preferred by 17%. There was a clear split between northern Europeans who preferred English and the southern Europeans who preferred French, while there was a very noticeable 18% who preferred no limit at all and would have been quite happy to continue using all languages as working languages.

The European Parliament has taken a different approach to its language problems. In working parties English and French are the norm, and little or no translation is available. In debates, each member uses his or her own language and translation is provided. The cost is high: at least 33 interpreters need to be present at three per booth for the eleven languages, and this does not cope with the full number of language pairs. But it is in the Parliament that national feelings run highest and that national pride demands that the language used be employed as much to express oneself as to make oneself understood. Other European organisations have come to similar conclusions.

Overall, the likelihood is low that a restrictive language policy will be adopted, one which will reduce the number of languages used in the work situation to a minimum or even to the bilingual solution apparently favoured by Commission trainees. There is after all no central power with sufficient democratic legitimacy to impose a solution such as that adopted in the USA or in India. The European Parliament is not a European government, nor is the European Commission a European bureaucracy with sufficient power to act as a group of autonomous state policy-makers. Unless or until the European summit meetings of Prime Ministers can persuade their countries to cede further power to the Commission, or indeed can persuade themselves to do so, it is highly unlikely that such a sensitive matter will be resolved. Meanwhile, 'the logic of the market is clear: English has become the lingua franca of the EC. For political reasons, however, this social fact has not been officially acknowledged' (Laitin, 1997, 289). In terms of jobs for the boys, although France persists in believing that nominating a Francophone Commission President will ensure the domination of French, the reality of the working environment is that without English the bureaucrat is lost.

GATT and the media

Up to the end of the Uruguay round, nominally by December 1993, the General Agreement on Tariffs and Trade regulated international commercial exchanges. After that time the agreement was transformed into the World Trade Organisation, with a wider brief and a more permanent interest in free trade as understood by the main economic power, the United States. It was during the Uruguay round that the concept of cultural exclusion was developed. The original impulse for such a policy came from industries which foresaw their own disappearance. American film production has an enormous home market, from which almost any film maker can generate a satisfactory level of profit. TV networks are voracious consumers of filmed material, and the quantity of material needed to fill the American domestic market is such that an enormous amount of material covers its costs at home and is then available for export and distribution at prices which are minimal. If European TV networks and film distribution companies needed material, it was plentiful at very low cost. But inevitably, the cost of producing similar or better quality material in European countries would remain high. The logic for the distribution networks is simple, and the inevitable destruction of the Italian, French, German and British film industries could be foreseen. The answer put forward during the 1993 negotiations relied on the French defensive approach of protectionism against American imports, permission to continue with subsidies for home productions and to export the finished products. Cultural productions were eventually excluded from the full force of free trade provisions.

Although this is not specifically an example of language policy the concept of cultural exclusion is naturally affected by, and affects, the languages of European countries together with the associated cultures. If American productions were to be bought, even with the cheaply dubbed soundtracks that many find offensive, American cultural norms would eventually replace the European. The Disneyfication of culture would follow the Macdonaldisation of food. This is particularly serious because the basic story lines of fiction are to a large degree universal: cowboy films are attractive to most cultures world-wide, as are the child-centred fantasies of Star Wars. It is because cheap American filmed material is good and popular, not because it is bad, that it represents a danger for European difference and diversity. As with other commercial products, if the variety of languages in which such material is shown can be reduced, so will the costs. The pressures to unify and simplify are great, and the language policy of the global corporations exporting cultural products is to do everything in English. Their motive is to manipulate the image of English so that it becomes acceptable: the cultural product itself already is universal enough to be so.

The motive for a European cultural and linguistic policy to retain diversity and difference is a mixture of considerable insecurity, even fear, over the future of any language apart from English, the desire to ensure a negative image for American English, and the associated desire to ensure a positive image for European languages. Problems abound, not least among which is the fact that English is a European language, too, a fact of which some commentators seem occasionally to be unaware. There is clearly also an economic motive: the desire by many countries to ensure support for a viable home industry and its ability to export its productions. Europe-wide, the desire for a European image requires that this be different from the American if Europe is ever to establish its own identity. Pressures for Europe to create and extend an image policy in the cultural domain, including language, are based on the need to develop and foster an image of Europe in all the countries of Europe as much as outside the continent. The difficulties inherent in any such project, and getting it supported, are probably insurmountable. They may lie behind such actions as President Chirac's frustration with European enlargement, and his proposal of 2000 that France and Germany set up an inner group with its own secretariat which could make decisions and would represent the 'real' Europe.

The labelling of foods

European integration has, as one of its aims, a Union-wide policy on agriculture and on the labelling and description of foods. An agreed approach to labelling is a clear requirement before cross-border trade can be undertaken, common marketing and safety policies introduced, and fraud successfully combated. It is however hardly surprising that getting agreement on common standards of production and description among food producers and processors has been very difficult. In the early days of standardisation France and Germany could more or less

impose their will. After the entry of Great Britain, Denmark and Ireland
it became clear that harmonisation was the best that could be hoped for,
and that there were some very basic labelling problems that were to
prove problematic. Three such were the decisions to be made on
sausages, on ice-cream and on chocolate. These presented problems
because the products were so very widespread, had developed in very
different ways in different countries, and also because the words were
easily translated into different languages. The need for a Europe-wide
policy was not quite the same as for products that were differentiated
within their own home markets. The making and conservation of beer in
Germany had been tightly controlled for centuries, for example, and the
German public saw threats to its purity and specificity which were
inevitable if German manufacturers were allowed to drift closer to the
European norms. The eventual compromise remains uneasy, and
sausages, chocolate and ice cream were, and still are, likely to become
even more anonymous internationalised products as pressure to adopt
the lowest common denominator increases.

In general, Germany and France had tight controls to ensure that
sausages were made from pigmeat, while Britain allowed large
proportions of cereals and other items while still permitting the use of
the name. Ice-cream may have originally been in essence frozen cream.
It had long since been prepared from vegetable and other non-milk
solids in the UK, and cream was no part of the recipe. While France and
Italy jealously protected the names of frozen cream (and crème glacée),
both had other words (gelato and glace) which could be used for less
pure products and wished to apply this distinction to all European
producers. Chocolate was a similar issue. The proportion of cocoa solids
used in Belgian manufacture ensured that the taste was generally bitter
and specific. In Britain, additives included milk solids, sweeteners and
vegetable fats, but the eventual product was popular and the taste quite
different from that of 'real' chocolate. Unsurprisingly, the battles over
the labelling of foods opposed large-scale manufacturers and small-scale
artisans, but also involved not merely traditionalists and conservatives
who wanted no change in their foodstuffs but also those who felt that
large-scale manufacturing represented an undesirable activity, and
wished to preserve a comfortable way of life which only an elite could
continue to afford in the modern world. In these battles, as elsewhere,
language policy is rarely about language alone.

The European state

Does the example of European language rationalisation, in the

Weberian sense, mean that Europe is closer to becoming a state in its own right? Certainly the development of a common currency, of similarities in the workings of bureaucracies, of Europe-wide enterprises and organisations, of a European Parliament, of European symbols such as the flag are indications that the conditions for integration and statehood are nearer to hand. Language rationalisation policies should logically follow. Indeed, Europe might have been better constructed had the politicians started from the idea of developing a common culture and a common approach to language, rather than from the bureaucratic and economic end. A European language policy aimed at creating an image of Europe with which people could identify could either be a repetition of the monolingual solutions of France, Britain and Germany, transposed to the European level through the imposition or acceptance of a common language, or move closer to the multilingual policies of post-colonial India. Laitin (1997: 286) considers that in many post-colonial societies, rather than a move towards monolingualism, 'the normal path seems to be toward some form of institutionalized multilingualism'. Basing his arguments on the strength of regional movements, he posits a Europe-wide policy of 2 plus or minus 1 where one language is English as a lingua franca, one is the state language, and the third is a regional language. Some citizens would need to learn only English (in the UK and Ireland); most would need to learn two in order to add English (in Germany, France and the Netherlands); others would require three (in Catalonia, for example). This he considers the most likely and most stable position.

The regional solution has the support of the Commission, which has tried to develop the power of the regions as an antidote to the blocking power of states. The Committee of the Regions attained a status similar to that of the Economic and Social Council in 1996, and its base in the German Länder, the two parts of Belgium, the French administrative regions, the Spanish and Italian provinces gives it much greater power than in the past. Regional expenditure is now a third of the Commission budget.

Despite Laitin's neat proposal there is little doubt that most experts who have made proposals in this field have come up with a scheme which does little more than suggest that his or her own language preference should become the European lingua franca, replacing English in this role of necessary. Proposals, not all of them serious, range from French (Truchot, 1991, who notes that French is the only language present in all educational systems) to German (Leitner, 1991, who notes that German has the greatest number of speakers in Europe). Central

Italian has at least one major supporter (Posner, 1994, who notes it is the most central Romance language, is easily learnable, and is tolerant of variation). But so has Latin (Salagnac, 1995) and Esperanto (Erasmus, 1994, who notes the advantages of a non-national language as a means of communication). The general conclusion seems to be that , if any policy is to be advocated at all, it should follow the history of nation-states and seek a one-language solution. But no expert is prepared to propose the obvious, the adoption of English as the lingua franca.

There is of course constant pressure on politicians in the Council of Ministers to advocate their own national language, and on Commissioners to do likewise even though the Commission, as supposedly a European institution with supranational loyalties as opposed to the multinational Council, should be a more likely sphere for a European solution. The bureaucracy within the Commission and its Directorates should similarly be pressing for a European solution, although as we have seen the solution here seems to be rather a matter of force majeure. At the institutional level the issue should present no more problems than those which confront the nation-states themselves. But it is well known that European countries have generated a range of responses to their national situations.

The main problem preventing the 'English' solution, for most European countries is that English is also the language of the United States of America. Had this not been the case, had France not abandoned Canada and not sold Louisiana, there is little doubt that French would by now be the dominant world language. English would then have been a contender for the European language, although it is more likely that German would have been the automatic choice. But then of course, since French itself would have been the language of the United States, the problem would merely have shifted its label. European countries would still have objected to possible domination by the language of a non-European state.

Image as a Motive for Language Policy

Image is correctly defined as the reflection of identity, and as an intended projection of that identity. The image of an individual, company or country should simply be the view taken of it by the external world. Although organisms can create their own identity, they should logically have little control over how this looks to the outside world, and we should be dealing with only one independent motive, identity. But image is not quite so simple. Individuals, companies and countries (try to) manipulate their image in order to generate for themselves the most favourable possible external opinion on what and who they are. Marketing, advertising and sales promotion depend on adapting the image while keeping the identity. The whole concept of added value depends less on actually creating worth and much more on creating an impression of worth, so that fashion decrees much higher prices for one shape of dress than for another even though both cost the same to make.

Official language policy-makers thus try to create the most favourable impression they can of their 'product', and do so firstly by attempting to spread knowledge of their own language and culture as widely as possible. Considerable effort is deployed by countries whose native language is not English. In these examples, the image motive is closely associated with feelings of insecurity, or at least with a feeling that the national identity does not quite fit the view of it that its own diplomats possess. Both Japan and Germany seem to feel that the world does not place them at the level of prestige that they deserve, whether by dint of their culture, traditions and history, or their economic might. Their language policy, like their cultural diplomacy, is devoted to correcting this impression. Those whose native language is English, however, gain considerable financial advantage for themselves from the fact that English is in effect a world language. They continue investing in the export of their language so that the net balance remains resoundingly to their advantage. Their investment is caused less by insecurity than by simple economics: exporting English is profitable. Although most English-speaking countries use a language which is generally widely understandable and indeed most play on this wide-spread comprehensibility, at the same time they stress the unique nature of their own variety. Policy here is to cash in on international intelligibility, which requires universality and a surrender of individualism, but at the same time to foster the individualism of one state or group by claiming difference and specificity. The British claim they originated the language and own Shakespeare and Milton; the culture proposed by America is that of the twentieth century; while Australia, New Zealand, India and South Africa fight to establish their own specific characteristics and their own contributions to the world language. Associated with the economic motivation is that of the desire to create and maintain a positive image.

In the case of federal or multicountry states or supranational developments like Europe, the one-language solution is simply untenable as a policy solution. European attitudes in individual countries ensure that diplomats promote their own language, and are unprepared to accept any one, even European, language as representative of all. Thinking diplomats accept the equal value of languages, their individual vitality and attractiveness. Policy for supporters of greater European integration hence consists of attracting as many people as possible to support the new political entity by seeking a new symbol, and by ignoring the language issue in all but the most minor of domains. The general European policy is to accept diversity: in effect to ignore the problem. Accepting diversity means accepting the consequences, in terms of increased interpreting and translating, practical dependence on a limited number of languages and mentioning the topic as little as possible. In these cases, the motive might be closer to the instrumentalism we shall examine in Chapter 6. For the moment though we should consider further the issue of insecurity.

Chapter 4

Insecurity

This chapter deals with language policy motivated by feelings of insecurity. Gypsies in central Europe have long been regarded as outsiders, and such nomadic, asocial or sometimes antisocial groups have often inspired fear in settled, regulated and controlled political entities. Partly this may be simply fear of the unknown, but there is also the worry that social cohesion may appear a chimera, and that the rules of society might prove inadequate for the management of the citizen. In France, new words and terms are often introduced from American English as scientific, technological and social change introduces new concepts. Some politicians and others fear that such linguistic inroads could destroy French culture, the French way of life, French science and even France itself.

Language Policy in Central Europe: Fear of the Gypsies?

The Czech and Slovak Republics came into being in 1993 in the Velvet Divorce, some four years after the Velvet Revolution of 1989 when the former Soviet satellite countries freed themselves from Russian domination. The position of Gypsies (usually there called Roma) in both countries has been greatly affected by the declarations of citizenship both new Republics have made. At least 250,000 Gypsies probably live in Slovakia and 100,000 in the Czech Republic. In Hungary, too, with about half a million or more Gypsies, Gypsies have suffered as a result of the new nationalism. In all three countries, citizenship laws have declared an official language, and arrangements for linguistic minorities including Romany-speaking groups have generally indicated a desire to exclude them from the benefits of citizenship. Insecurity in the face of such minorities is probably a causative factor.

It is not easy to determine who is or is not a Gypsy. Apart from the family and tribal divisions, many travelling groups are sometimes labelled Gypsies, sometimes not; there is an inbuilt difficulty in discovering precise numbers of people who are on the move; and many previously nomadic groups have settled, some losing their wish to identify with other Gypsies in the process. Some have assimilated while others have not; some are Muslim while others are Christian and yet others do not profess religious affiliations. Language, too, is not clear: there are many dialects of Romany, some of them heavily influenced by Rumanian while others have borrowed words and expressions from the languages surrounding them. It appears unlikely that there can now be created a standard, widely understood Romany language. To add to the difficulties, there is no political authority structure in the Romany-speaking communities, so governments often have difficulty in deciding who to talk to, while the communities themselves rarely interact with other citizens, avoid the authorities and indeed rarely participate in government at national or local level.

Why should the Gypsies pose a threat? They are after all underprivileged by definition: traditionally they have been poor, have been nomadic as much from need as from desire, they have received little from any society in the way of education, social benefits, political rights, land or finance. They have a history of exclusion from regulated and normalised societies in Europe: they have been taxed, persecuted, imprisoned and killed. They were travelling artisans, not allowed to travel too far and formally enslaved to the ruling power, but their lack of permanent settlement and their particular economic role made them occasionally useful if subservient. As they moved slowly northwards and westwards, particularly after the collapse of the Ottoman Empire in the nineteenth century, Gypsies generally fared less well than at earlier times in their slow movement from the Indian sub-continent. In the present century, long after the times of mediaeval barbarity, Gypsies have continued to be persecuted. Jews and Gypsies were the two 'racial' groups singled out by the Nazis for annihilation, and many were sent to concentration camps. After the 1939-45 war, massive population movements affected Gypsies, as others, in Hungary, Czechoslovakia and throughout central Europe. But the Communist regimes exercised policies towards Gypsies between 1950 and 1990 which were both good and bad: good, in the sense that Gypsies occasionally received recognition and the advantage of treatment as a national minority; bad, in the general desire of Communism to avoid special cases in society and any special treatment. In addition, social and welfare policy was by no means consistent:

> The Czech policy was variously typified by a blend of condescension and impatience, of paternalism and despotism, of

benevolent inactivity and strenuous attempts at radical solutions
...in 1958...the authorities concluded that the Gypsies' group
identity had to be demolished if they were to advance at all.
(Fraser, 1995: 277)

The 'dispersal and transfer' policy aimed at moving Gypsies from
concentrations in Slovakia to the west. This provoked 'the emergence of
ugly racial bias on a serious   scale'. The authorities reverted to
assimilation as the only solution and generally dropped schemes for
teaching in Romany. In Hungary teaching in Romany was more widely
encouraged and towards the end of the Communist period a number of
schemes were in operation. The collapse of the Soviet regime has since
generally resulted in freer movement; nomadism has to a certain extent
returned but at the same time so has ethnic hatred. One result of the
varied policies over the centuries is that, apart from the obvious
divisions (tribes, families, Romany-speaking or not) Gypsies fall into
three categories from the point of view of whether they live in towns and
are in the main reasonably assimilated, in villages where they frequently
live alongside the majority population but have not assimilated, or in
special Gypsy settlements where problems of poverty, unemployment
and lack of education are greatest (Vasecka, 1999).

In terms of language-related policy, the motive of fear of minorities
underlies much legislation in all three countries. In Slovakia, where 22%
of the population is formed by recognised minorities, legislation applies
to Gypsies but also to Hungarians; in the Czech Republic, to Gypsies
but also to German speakers; in Hungary, to Romany speakers but also
to a number of other linguistic minorities. The laws on nationality in the
Czech and Slovak Republics as they divided decreed that after 1994 each
citizen would have separate nationality. Many Gypsies in the Czech
Republic have found themselves classified as Slovaks because they
moved, or were moved, west in recent times or have found it impossible
to document their position adequately (Siklova and Miklusakova, 1998).
Catch-22 traps also occur: to obtain Czech citizenship one must obtain a
document of release from Slovak nationality. But the effect of
surrendering nationality is that one becomes stateless, and hence cannot
obtain proof of Czech nationality! The result of the confusion is that
many Gypsies in the Republic are denied benefits, cannot work legally
and are liable to expulsion. In late 1997, a flood of Gypsies, desperate at
the situation, tried to emigrate to Britain or Canada, and the position for
minorities is undergoing review in both the Czech Republic and in
Slovakia since the Canadian authorities introduced a visa requirement.
A 1998 report now proposes a number of measures to improve the

position of the Gypsies, including special educational plans and provision to avoid Romany-speaking children being sent to special schools because they do not speak Czech.

Gypsy children constitute just over 5% of the school population overall, but nearly 96% of that of special schools (Guardian, 17.6.99). Formally, the test for entry to special schools is a psychological and IQ test taken on starting school. Although the government insists that the final criterion for special school entry is the parents' wish and no child can be directed there without the parents' consent, the 75% of Gypsy children who do not 'pass' this test do not, it is contended by Gypsy representatives, for cultural and linguistic rather than intellectual reasons. In 1999, various human rights organisations collaborated to set up a test case submitted to the Czech Constitutional Court alleging racial discrimination in the case of twelve 9-13-year-olds. The case was followed by observers from Bulgaria, Hungary, Romania and Slovakia and its outcome was 'expected' to cause these countries to reconsider their own legislation if it were successful.

The 1995 Slovak State Language Law required that Slovak alone be used in dealings with the state administration and in education. It was not until 1997 that the Constitutional Court decided that this provision was unconstitutional, but the purpose of the Law had been clear from its preamble: Slovak is

> the most important characteristic of the Slovak nation, the most valuable piece of the cultural heritage and expression of sovereignty of the Slovak Republic and the general means of communication of its citizens. (Times Higher Education Supplement, 19.1.1996)

It was the Hungarian minority in Slovakia that opposed this law, even though one of its aims was to improve the status of Slovak as against Czech (although the languages differ little) on the basis that Slovak itself had long been treated in Czechoslovakia as a minority language. The Slovak view was that the concerns of minorities were adequately catered for in separate legislation, although

> One of the reasons for such anti-minority legislation would appear to be fear of the Slovaks to increasing Hungarian influence in these areas, areas which for centuries came under Hungarian rule. According to Culture Minister, Hudec, the Slovak language must be protected in these regions and brought forward out of the hinterland. (Contact Bulletin, 13: 1, 5)

In Hungary, the law on minorities requires that only groups demonstrating at least one hundred years of presence in Hungarian territory, and whose members are Hungarian citizens, are recognised. Elected councils have been in place since 1995, and in 1997 it was proposed that the minorities be granted additional parliamentary representation, although it is unlikely that this will be in place until early in the new millennium.

Neologisms in French

French, like all other languages, has a constant need to invent new words, terms and expressions to cope with changes in the social, political, economic, scientific, cultural and particularly technological environments. In recent years the influence of the USA in technological innovation has been such that new inventions and processes, particularly those to do with communication technologies, have come about so quickly that often the item has been adopted in many languages complete with its original American designation. For politicians, particularly those in countries like France with a long tradition of independence, with a well-developed industrial base of their own and with pretensions to global importance, simply keeping the original term has been unthinkable, and there has been a constant fear that if the term is retained then the result can only be industrial, financial, technological and possibly cultural domination by the Americans. In considering this question of neologisms in French, and particularly the Anglicisms of recent years, a distinction must be made between the normal linguistic processes including borrowing, semantic change, calques, translations and others and the terminology developed and, in France, legally imposed, by the political authorities.

Responses to this sense of insecurity in the face of the invasion of foreign terms and components first became important for the official world soon after 1970, with the creation of the first Ministerial Terminology Commissions. These Commissions were set up to develop French terminology acceptable to French-speaking users, not just in France but also in Francophone countries. The initiative in fact came from Quebec and from the visits to Canada made by Michel Bruguière, the newly appointed Secretary to the Haut Comité pour la Défense et l'Expansion de la Langue Française, set up by de Gaulle in 1966. After the political victories of the Parti Québecois and a growing sense of the need to reject American domination, the Quebec provincial authorities had decided on a course of action aimed at strengthening the commercial, financial and employment roles of French speakers in the

Province. As a fundamental part of this reform, the Quebec approach prioritised language policy, and particularly sought to remove Anglicisms from technical language. In France, ministerial commissions were set up in most parts of the French administration, and their work was eventually brought under the overall control and direction, or at least approval, of the French Academy (see Ager, 1999).

Braselmann (1998) examined a number of the replacements for Anglicisms decided on by the Terminology Commissions over the twenty years to 1994. The study principally concerned neologisms listed in the 1994 _Dictionnaire des termes officiels de la langue française,_ but ranged widely over the various official decisions and Circulars which proposed words, terms and expressions relevant to particular domains. Braselmann was concerned to discover that the terms proposed often lacked systematic linguistic understanding; occasionally offended against the norms the French language had long adopted for word-creation; sometimes invented new terms which simply reminded users of the original English; were often illogical; were tainted with anti-Americanism and sometimes, indeed, had the result that French idiosyncracy in effect cut the country off from international progress and buried the proverbial head in the sand:

- Replacement forms are too often led by the foreign term: the creation of acronyms, words formed from initial letters, paraphrases often do no more than model themselves on the original English and thus in effect perpetuate it.
- They destroy the clarity of French - there can be up to 12 substitutions for one English term (eg. ground)
- They introduce changes to French word-formation, word order or other characteristics of French (_couper sec_ for cut - which uses an adverbial construction which is not standard French). Such a formation is itself condemned elsewhere precisely because it is not 'proper' French.
- Words like _vtt, facob_ and _publipostage_ contradict the norms of French and give credence to new methods of creating neologisms. Such procedures, despite being also condemned elsewhere, then become not merely accepted but develop into an officially approved method for creating new words, a _norme nationale._
- English forms like prepaid are so widely used that the replacement is forced to adopt the non-French word order and becomes _prépayé,_ not using the standard French _payé d'avance,_ which already exists and would have been much the more normal

method of creating the term.

- A form like *payer-prendre* for cash and carry allows the original English still to be clearly seen.
- A form like *jardinerie* for garden-centre does not give the same meaning; why not use *pépinière* instead?
- Why condemn the 'natural' development *tour-opérateur* from tour-operator and invent *voyagiste*, when the former term had already entered the language and been widely adopted? Such a pernickety rejection of an English-seeming form seems unnecessarily purist.
- Given the confusion over word order, a form like *carburéacteur* is misleading: is it *carburant pour réacteur* or *réacteur pour carburant*?
- French work on the witchhunt against Anglicisms, particularly internationally accepted words like computer, cuts France off from other countries and actively opposes the idea of building a consensual Europe.

To be fair to the Terminology Commissions it must be said that the work has been conducted under the overall guidance of the Délégation Générale à la Langue Française, the successor of the various committees and councils set up since 1966. Professional help is therefore at hand. But essentially the replacement terms proposed are the result of committee work and discussions conducted by the prime users, in Ministries and among suppliers and clients, and established as far as possible in conjunction with the terminology groups of other Francophone countries. These include not only the well-resourced Canadians but also Belgians, Swiss, occasionally Tunisians and others. The replacements are the work of non-linguist specialists in specific subject areas. Individual terms are discussed at length, while compromises are often necessary among the terms preferred by different firms, countries or individuals. It is perhaps hardly surprising that their work does not always meet with the approval of the general language user, nor that they are on increasingly dangerous ground as they leave their specialist areas and approach everyday language usage. The controversy over 'politically correct' forms officially proposed for women at work (*auteure, Madame la Ministre*) or over spelling reform is sufficient indication of the strong public sense of ownership of French.

Insecurity as a Motive for Language Policy

The Gypsies of central Europe have been at the bottom of the social heap for centuries. Consistently rejected by most ruling authorities, they have nonetheless retained their identity. Partly for this reason and partly because their rejection of 'normal' society holds considerable dangers both for concepts of normal social behaviour and for all the norms of regulated, ordered, democratic social management, they are feared and in many cases hated. Policy authorities refuse them citizenship from a sense of frustration at their unwillingness to request or accept citizenship as other citizens do. Their way of life, their culture, their language and their beliefs single them out as opposed to any other individual or group, and it is this desire to be different that is very difficult for social authorities to accept, when their job it is to manage and run things in a fair, equal and ordered manner. Gypsies represent a danger to settled, regulated society. They are a danger particularly for the sense of identity the settled state itself has.

There are many other examples of language policy based on fear of the outsider and the fear that an attack from outside might be so effective as to change or destroy the identity that has been constructed. The Toubon Law, passed in France in 1994, although expressed in terms of a Rights agenda and apparently aimed at ensuring that French citizens have the right to use their own language in their own country, in fact marks a reaction against external dominance and is inspired by a fear of international American and all it conveys, or was thought to convey by the Law's supporters. The nature of this law has been well covered elsewhere (Ager, 1996b: 156-68 and Ager, 1999: 134-44). While France has consistently developed her language policy over centuries as a significant element in identity creation and in protection of this from others, protecting the nation through corpus policy is more recent and has reaffirmed the importance of language. Language has played a major role in affirming identity but also in marking the boundaries of society and community. Language has acted as a major component in the cement of symbolism, which has helped create unity and bind people together, and in excluding others from membership of the charmed circle. The fear of others has been of a possibly successful attack and hence of political, cultural, religious and social domination, to a certain extent of territorial loss, but mainly of a dilution of the specific nature of the society that France, Hungary, Slovakia and the Czech Republic have sought to create. In the case of France, the feared domination was more economic than political, although the rhetoric surrounding the alleged American invasion has drawn little distinction between the political, economic or cultural domains.

The Slovakian case is fascinating in that it, like many other areas of the world, represents an example of the double minority issue. A group which comes to exercise majority control after a history of oppression and lack of power may feel itself to be still potentially powerless, in danger, and acts as though it did not possess the authority it has. It hence acts with more force and violence, and sometimes becomes more intolerant, than the previous controlling authorities. Slovakians regard themselves as a minority in need of protection, while Gypsies within Slovakia are a minority within a minority and thus doubly rejected. A similar case exists in Northern Ireland, where the Protestants fear the situation which might occur should the North lose its separate existence and be merged in what would then be a mainly Catholic Ireland. In the meantime the northern Catholics fear the Protestants, since they regard themselves as in the minority and look at links with the mainly Protestant British mainland as ensuring the continuation of an anti-Catholic majority. Both communities regard themselves as doubly rejected. Both act both as if they were an oppressed minority and at the same time as if they are in the majority.

It hardly needs saying that the sensitivity with which such matters are discussed by outsiders is often misunderstood. Insecurity is an emotion, not a rational construct. If outsiders misunderstand, fail to see the point, regard the emotion as misguided, insecurity is if anything increased. A case in point is our own use of the term 'Gypsy' in the present chapter. Current usage by the relevant community in the UK prefers 'Roma' as the descriptive label, and for some the term 'Gypsy' is so reminiscent of past discrimination that its use is felt to be an insult, even though none is intended and indeed the opposite is the case. But connotations change, and change rapidly, as every dictionary lexicographer knows to his or her cost, and apologies can themselves be misconstrued. At the time of writing this chapter the term Gypsy, as a descriptive label, had been in use in all the references cited.

Fear and insecurity as a motive for language policy, even where this is in effect micro policy not carried out by official authority, is hence determined by two factors: an external threat significant enough to provoke action, and sufficient awareness by the threatened community of its situation and of the effect on its own identity. The threat must be identifiable, and may be political (potential domination of the community), economic (potential loss of income for members of the community), or communicative (lack of an effective affective link between members of the community, coupled with lack of adequate mean of expression for some domains and particularly for public ones). The ability to meet the threat requires the existence of both a way of identifying the threat and a potential answer, as well as a mechanism for implementing this. There has to be an identifiable political, ethnic or linguistic minority community which can plan for different language use, and which is coherent enough for all its members to acquiesce in it. There also has to be a linguistic solution: an available language (which might be adapted), a mechanism for insisting on language use in all domains, a set of rules for membership, particularly for citizenship, which include language as an identifying marker.

Attitudinally, the superiority and attractiveness of the policy-makers' first language, his or her L1, is matched by fear that this attitude is unjustified. Vitality, the use of language in the many domains of active life, is the key and hence activists try to ensure the use of the language particularly in public domains, by force if necessary. Domination would squeeze out the L1, so the language of others is excluded as far as possible. Here, as elsewhere, language policy is not just about language. The Gypsy threat has been diffuse. It has rarely been conceived as a linguistic threat to established languages, but more as a social menace and a threat to ordered and regulated society. The economic threat to France was met by well organised and systematic opposition. Interestingly, the French political Left has often been as vociferously anti-American as the political Right; both have combined in a common anti-Americanism and xenophobia.

Chapter 5

Inequality

This chapter will consider three attempts to change or influence language behaviour in relation to three areas of social exclusion: gender, powerlessness and ethnicity. In each case a group of people have been shown to suffer discrimination because of a particular trait or characteristic they share. Their language use, or the language use of society in relation to them, has demonstrated that they are regarded in different ways from other members of society, to their disadvantage, and that they are thus in some way not regarded as equal to other members of society. Clearly, although there may be universal features which enable us to identify similarities and draw general conclusions about such phenomena, the specifics of individual types of discrimination due to inequality depend on the nature of the individual societies and countries in question. Language and gender differences and attitudes are in fact quite different as between France and the USA, and are closely associated with other characteristics of the social roles of women and men in each society. Power, and particularly political power, is associated with different personal, tribal, ethnic, linguistic and religious characteristics as between different European countries, so the powerful in Italy do not necessarily share the same origins, characteristics or even views as their counterparts in Norway. Social justice can be quite differently manifested in rich and in poor countries, and the rights citizens can expect to enjoy might be quite different as between countries with established Islamic or Christian churches.

Action on language, aimed at the correction of inequalities in society, is sometimes carried out by governments and those in authority as part of their own deliberate policy. Much more frequently action is a response to injustice or unfairness brought forcefully to the attention of the political authorities, not always by the suffering groups themselves. Action on language can also be undertaken by a linguistic, ethnic or any minority community, many of whom are more likely to suffer the effects of social inequality than the holders of power in a political sense. Action provoked by a sense of injustice can thus be a matter of policy or of planned behaviour; can affect the language use of the state or be directed at the language(s) of groups within it. Motives for the correction of inequality manifest themselves   in a number of ways. Almost by definition, they represent the views and feelings of people whose social situation is disadvantaged, and who wish to change a situation which they feel is unfair to themselves and often cruel. As people and groups who are disadvantaged, they have little access to power, and their main motive is to change this exclusion to enable themselves to at least enter mainstream society. To this extent, the motives of those who are themselves excluded are selfish. But one must then ask what the motives of the policy-makers, who are by definition the powerful in society, could be, if they intend to correct injustice. These reasons can be extremely varied: it may simply be a matter of pressure, of force and violence, which have obliged the powerful to accede to at least some of the requests and demands of the powerless. The disadvantaged often join with other groups and create a force which it is difficult to counteract. But even without this, the powerless are helped by some of the power brokers in society whose own motives may be a mixture of humanitarianism, pity, altruism, an attack of conscience or a number of other equally complex feelings. In some cases, the power brokers have themselves been members of the disadvantaged group(s): they have been poor, they share the same colour of skin or ethnic membership, they are of the same gender, they share a religion. In some societies these characteristics do not prevent access to power, and when such people have it they implement (at least some of) the policies which aim to help such groups. In other cases the powerful are driven by political ideology: support for the disadvantaged in society has long been a main tenet of the Left, and in most democracies the Left does gain power in due course and is able to put its beliefs into practice. In most societies altruism is not a feature of the policies of the powerful, however, and there are more examples of Left-wing movements moving towards Right-wing policies when in government than the opposite. The final motive on which policies are made may be mixed, correcting inequality but also furthering aims which are closer to the wishes of the elite. Typically a utopian motive may thus be allied to a selfish one: policies in support of Australian community languages may be associated with policies supporting a greater export drive; anti-sexist policies in publishing may reflect not just a demand to correct inequality but also the demands of readers who would otherwise not buy.

The result of the successful implementation of policies based on these motives is the support of social equality and social cohesion. The three cases we deal with seem to reflect issues firstly of the equitable distribution of resources, secondly of the language or indeed human rights of the marginalised group or groups, and thirdly of what might be called the resolution of social problems associated with manifest injustice. To distinguish the three levels of severity of the general situation, we shall use the terms inequality for unequal resource distribution, inequity for unequal rights, and injustice for more severe manifestations of exclusion. We shall return to these distinctions after reviewing the cases themselves.

Language and Gender

In the USA, women academics brought the existence of inequality to public attention during the 1960s. The case for non-sexist language began to be made seriously during the early 1970s and 1980s. Robin Lakoff, in _Language and Woman's Place_, pointed out in 1975 that if language demonstrated inequality this was not because women were genetically inferior but because their place in society was unequal: males dominated females and this domination was reflected in language. The general point was made that women were widely denigrated in US society and notably in academic life, and their life chances, in career, economic and other resource-based terms, were badly affected by society's sexist habits in language. One particular point, the case for avoiding the 'he/man approach' and the use of such gender-marked pronouns to refer generically to human beings because such use of pronouns in English is offensive to women and 'maintains societal sexism' (quoted in Martyna, 1983: 26), shows how the general point can have specific application in particular language use. The womens' movement and many writers of the time and later have made clear the degree and nature of the inequality that is here objected to, its social, political and economic consequences, and it is no part of our purpose to repeat these, nor to rehearse the many arguments, debates and discussions which have followed. Suffice it to repeat the comment by Sontag (1973: 186): 'language is the most intense and stubborn fortress of sexist assumptions', one 'which crudely enshrines the ancient bias against women'.

Attempts to change this bias and to correct the inequality in the allocation of resources include the many governmental actions taken by Western governments in recent years in fields such as employment practices and advertising. There are specific examples, too, of deliberate language policy adopted by governments and by international organisations, in UNESCO in 1987, in the Council of Ministers in 1990, in France in 1986, in Belgium in 1988 and more formally in 1993, in Canada in 1975. Generally, however, in English-speaking countries where government statements on recommended language use are rare, antisexism in language has been instituted as a code of acceptable and unacceptable terms and usages put into effect by publishers, publishers' readers, proof-readers and printers rather than by state authorities. The style manual for the New York Times, for example, makes the general point that

> In referring to women, we should avoid words or phrases that seem to imply that _The Times_ speaks with a purely masculine voice, viewing men as the norm and women as the exception. The principle is similar to that involving certain racial and religious designations, and some of the same questions must be asked: Is the term being used essential to the story? Is it denigrating? Would it be appropriate if applied to someone of another race, religion or sex? (quoted in Fasold et al., 1990: 525)

In addition, many such manuals make quite precise recommendations about referring to people by name, using last name only in the second reference; using such terms as spokesperson, chairperson instead of spokesman or chairman, or indeed using the singular 'they' instead of 'he/man'. Micro policy of this type has been widespread in policy manuals, style sheets or guidance handbooks for newspapers, publishers, proof readers and others: 'Newspaper style manuals are really language policy documents for the news organization that commissions them' (Fasold et al., 1990: 522). The effectiveness of these style manuals in the domain of 'androcentric generics' (i.e. the 'equitable use of language where gender is concerned') was studied by Fasold et al. in reference to The Washington Post, and it was found that indeed the manual was extremely effective to the extent of being felt to be a constraint in some reporting.

A finding such as this does not mean that language practice as a whole in North America now avoids linguistic sexism as a consequence of the points made after 1968. Indeed, the politics of the 1980s ensured that the debate would continue, and there remain many examples where non-sexist language recommendations have been twisted or have other results than those intended. Ms, for example, originally intended to enable women to be referred to by a title without reference to a male-female relationship, is often now used to refer to an unmarried or divorced woman; chairperson or chair often designates females whereas chairman is retained for males. Discourse strategies weaken the impact of terms like sexual abuse, date rape or sexual harassment by extending their meaning beyond that originally intended by the feminist movement. It is simple to imply that they are the creations of fevered imaginations, for example by writing of 'the thing called date rape' or of 'so-called sexual harassment'.

Sexism in language, as in society, is a feature of particular languages and particular societies as well as a general issue. In English, most of the style guides and recommendations suggest three principles of linguistic correction: neutralisation, stereotyping and symmetry (Hellinger, 1995). Neutralisation is the priority, so both 'false generics' like man (to man a project, chairman) and sex-specific terms like stewardess or usherette should be avoided. This prioritisation is language-specific, however: in German grammatical gender plays a different role than in English, and while the use of masculine and feminine pronouns may, for some, demonstrate the inbuilt sexism of English it simply indicates obedience to grammatical requirements in German. Sexism in German is shown in other linguistic ways. Pronoun splitting, or the use of the plural for the singular are appropriate devices for English (the trainee must stand up; he or she may then speak; they may then speak). German could use der/die Auszubildende or repeat the noun in the plural (die Auszubildenden).

Such linguistic differences affect and are affected by the social differences. Sexism in French and in France is quite different from that in the USA. Antisexism, too, has unsurprisingly run a different course. The most obvious example of this for language policy is the unsuccessful attempt in 1986 to propose an Arrêté which would define the linguistic changes deemed to be necessary to avoid discrimination. One of the main differences with American experience is that this was an official initiative, undertaken by the Minister for Women's Rights and organised as part of an attempt to reduce discrimination in employment (see Ager, 1996b: 176-82). Linguistically, the stress was on designations of occupations. The proposals were initially for a declaration of principles, a sort of manifesto of Women's Rights, to be followed by a list of forms to be proscribed in public documents and in advertisements for employment, and those replacements to be recommended. Public reaction was immediate and violent. The Terminology Commission, the formal vehicle for the discussion, was condemned in Parliament as containing cranks and frivolous individuals who had no better way of wasting time; the prestigious French Academy weighed in with a formal letter of warning which it published in the Press, claiming that the Commission intended to attack the very nature of the French language; the Press had a field day. In the end, the very mild final recommendations were published on the day the Socialist government of 1981 to 1986 was voted out of office. They were lost from sight and apart from the occasional woman politician who is prepared to be called Madame la Ministre have never since resurfaced openly, although the recommendations are slowly entering official usage. Correction of inequality in terms of gender differs as between France and the USA. This is partly due to differences such as those between a private and a public initiative or between the domains of publishing and those of the much wider work-place, but also perhaps to the quite different nature of the two societies and their view both of woman's place and of the nature of their own language. The American proposals were generally well-received and faced little serious opposition. The French ones were rejected out of hand by public opinion, led by bastions of the Establishment.

For some US commentators also, the correction of this discrimination has in certain circumstances gone so far that the pendulum may have swung in the opposite direction.

> While there were a few women officers, Council members, and committee members before the 1970s, women are now over-represented in ASA governance relative to their share of the membership. (Rosenfeld et al, 1997: 747)

Elections to the American Sociological Association's leadership involve three offices (President, Vice-President and Secretary) together with twelve committee members. There are two routes to nomination for the governing Council: either through the Committee on Nominations, itself elected from a slate of candidates nominated by the Council and which presents a ranked lists of candidates, or through a petition to add a candidate to the ballot, signed by one hundred members for the offices of President or Vice-President or by fifty members for other posts. Potentially, three factors might have ensured a greater proportion of women candidates and successes: the womens' movement and subsequent changes in gender attitudes; the specific influence of the group Sociologists for Women in Society, political activism and block voting; and/or a general process of elite dilution. The study by Rosenfeld and others came to the conclusion that 'women and men candidates differed little from each other or over time in productivity, honours or experience', so that the elite dilution theories did not seem applicable, except insofar as 'women were elected earlier in their careers than men and were less often employed in the most prestigious graduate departments'. When all three factors were analysed together, 'gender affected election success, with marginal effects for productivity; effects of SWS membership and professional location were not statistically significant'. The authors conclude that

> most of the rise in womens' election success occurred in the 1970s and early 1980s, with women generally remaining over-represented as candidates and winners since then...Gender is one distinctive characteristic, and apparently is indeed used as a criterion by voters...General changes in attitudes and opportunities seem to be the exogenous factors behind womens' election success.

There is little doubt that changes in gender attitudes in the USA and elsewhere since the 1970s have affected not merely professional associations in the social sciences but society generally, nor that the existence of pressure groups such as Sociologists for Women in Society have 'had an impact' on attitudes and behaviour including the desire for leadership, voting behaviour and many other aspects of modern life. It is widely felt that such changes have been symbolised by such movements as that for 'political correctness' in language, and particularly by attempts to correct the inequality represented or thought to be represented by a sexist use of language.

The European Charter for Regional and Minority Languages

> After several years of prevarication and a decision not to sign the Charter on the part of the last Conservative government, it was indeed good news to hear the announcement that the new UK government would be signing the Council of Europe's Charter for Regional or Minority languages. Derek Fatchett, Minister of State at the Foreign Office declared that the government readily subscribed to the 'general principles of recognition and support for indigenous minority languages and removal of discrimination against them'. (Contact Bulletin, November 1998, 15: 1)

The European Charter for Regional or Minority Languages was developed as the result of a conference of local and regional authorities held in Paris in 1984. It has gradually emerged since as a legal Convention binding those member countries of the Council of Europe which ratify it to recognise and support the rights of minority languages.

By 1999 eight countries had done so while a further ten had signed to agree its principles, which are four:

- to recognise languages as an expression of cultural wealth;
- to eliminate discrimination;
- to promote respect, understanding and tolerance;
- and to take into consideration the needs and wishes of the relevant linguistic communities.

Measures should be undertaken to promote regional languages in education, the media, the law, public services, cultural activities and economic and social life while progress in each country is periodically reported to the Council of Europe. The Charter represents a particular legalistic and policy approach to the rights of minority languages, one which many of the European language associations have adopted and which, in our terms, is a matter of correcting social inequality. In this respect it follows traditions of formal textual declarations important to many countries, but particularly to those such as France. From this point of view its main import may be symbolic. Nonetheless, governments take it seriously: the French government had to be persuaded by the Poignant Report of 1998 to adopt it, while the UK government was only prepared to countenance it once the Northern Irish peace process had seriously started; the Greek government has had considerable difficulties with the future of its own province of Macedonia, once the former Yugoslav province of the same name became an independent state in 1991. The European Union, as well as the Council of Europe, has been active in this area. The European Parliament has passed at least three resolutions in support of minorities: in October 1981 (Arfé Report I), 1983 (Arfé Report II); and February 1994 (Killilea Report), and an Intergroup for Minority Languages meets every six months. There had been a budget line in the Commission since 1983 funding projects in minority languages, until the 1998 'discovery' of the absence of legal authorisation for many lines of EC expenditure led to a formal proposal for the expenditure of about 2.5 million Euros to cover EBLUL and Mercator (information) centres. EBLUL (the European Bureau for Lesser Used Languages) was legally established in Dublin and Brussels in 1983.

The motive for persuading member countries of the Council of Europe to ratify the Charter as a Convention is the feelings of persecution, marginalisation and lack of recognition many European minority language associations have expressed over the years. 'It remains incomprehensible that the (German) Federal Government demands rights for German minorities abroad but chooses to neglect the minorities with German citizenship in its own Basic law (Frisians, Danes, Sorbs, Sinti and Roma)' as Karl-Rudolf Fischer, in charge of minority issues in Schleswig-Holstein, was reported as saying (Contact Bulletin, 1994, 11, 3: 2). Ladin activists complained about the differential effects of the Italian Law of 1993 protecting Ladin in the province of Trentino, pointing out that it is better protected in Bolzano. The unfairness activists in France feel is suffered by Occitan, as opposed to Catalan, is clear from the following extract:

> Catalan has less speakers than Occitan in France but is in a stronger position ... though spoken by an estimated 48% of the population in 31 'Départements' ... (Occitan) has less resources at its disposal and its status is therefore weaker... the curriculum and course outline (for Occitan) is very much based on the middle ages. Catalan, on the other hand, ... has a curriculum much more orientated towards the modern word of today. (Contact Bulletin, 1993, 10, 3: 9)

In the case of Wales, the demands of activists, the statements surrounding the 1993 legislation and the language of the Act stress 'equality' between Welsh and English as the guiding principle. Although in each case there are resource implications to the recognition of minority languages, the main purpose is a declaration of rights and entitlements.

The European Charter is of course a political and diplomatic document. It has the great advantage that it is in fact not one document but many. The full version has a number of sections, articles and paragraphs, but governments can pick and choose those which they wish to implement. The French government thus chose 39 articles for its version, signed by the government at a ceremony in Budapest on 7th May 1999. The Charter was nonetheless rejected by the Constitutional Council as being contrary to the Constitution which clearly states that the language of the French Republic is French, so the Jospin government had to request the President to submit a constitutional amendment before ratification could be proposed to Parliament.

The Australian National Policy on Languages

The successful implementation of the Australian National Languages Policy in 1987 (Lo Bianco, 1987; Lo Bianco, 1990) was the result of a long period of preparation and at least as long a period during which pressure on policy-makers was relentless (Clyne, 1991; Ozolins, 1993).

Although we shall here concentrate on the late 1980s, it is worth noting that the policy itself did not last long in its original form as outlined in the Lo Bianco Report of April 1987 and the government Press release of 26 April 1987. Even by December 1987, after the re-election of the government, the policy had undergone some subtle changes, mainly in stressing the implications for overseas trade of the new policy for teaching foreign languages and in foregrounding Asian languages. It was changed again in 1991 to a subtly different approach outlined in _Australia's Language: the Australian Language and Literacy Policy_ (Dawkins 1991) which itself suffered a number of modifications, and, particularly, became in effect a number of policies implemented at State, rather than Federal, level, during the later 1990s (Clyne, 1997).

As in most societies, policies on language had been implemented in Australia for a considerable time before 1987. Some were openly stated: it was necessary for citizens to be able to understand and express themselves in English. But in practical terms foreign-language speakers were present from the beginning of settlement in 1788, and welcomed at all levels of society, and their presence made multilingual language policy an essential part of everyday life as well a political fact. The first governor of the colony, Arthur Phillips, had a German background; the household of the first governor of Victoria, Charles la Trobe, was bilingual in English and French; 'As from 1848 there was a thriving "community language" press' (Clyne, 1991: 8); English-speaking candidates for the early state parliaments issued statements in German appealing to communities whose first language remained German. In education, too, many languages were taught and bilingual education was a commonplace, with more than a hundred bilingual schools, mainly in the south of Australia, by 1900. Although linguists were interested in the languages of Aborigines, and philanthropic societies discussed their situation in the early 1800s, very little official concern was devoted to them while early policies and practice aimed at extinguishing the first Australians, destroying their culture or at least excluding them from any significant position. Practical language policy at governmental level in the new colony consisted however of ignoring any language other than English.

It was nonetheless not until the first World War that English only became the formal rule, tolerance of 'community languages' disappeared, and language policy could be considered unjust. German was banned, place-names were changed and English became the sole language of education. Attitudes and official policy became thereafter even more monolingual and indeed xenophobic. Australia tried to get even closer to Britain, the mother country. Even in policy for the teaching of foreign languages, where French, quite logically the first modern foreign language for Britain, France's near neighbour, became in effect almost the only language taught in Australian education. Immigrants were sought only from Britain or Europe, although despite the economic crises of the 1920s and 1930s numbers remained small. It took the second World War before the fear of population decline, added to fear of Japan and compounded by the pressing need for manpower to reconstruct the country and enable industrial growth, led to a deliberate search for immigrants. A mass immigration policy was inevitable. It was strongly opposed by many Australian workers and trade unionists who saw it simply as a way of keeping labour costs down. Equally inevitably immigration could not come solely from Britain. Immigrants would be 'displaced persons', refugees at first from northern Europe but thereafter from eastern and southern Europe. Immigration from Asia or the Pacific was not so much discouraged as actively prevented. The White Australia policy, supported by all the political parties and by public opinion, lasted until 1966.

The Labor government of 1972 to 1975, led by Gough Whitlam, marked a change of policy and the development of multiculturalism, partly following Canadian thinking (Grassby, 1973). Clyne (1991: 19) sees this as reflecting two motives: part of the world-wide recognition of the rights, cultures and languages of ethnic groups following the upheavals of the 1968 'revolutions', together with a realisation that Australia now contained within itself a number of groups and traditions which no longer reflected a British monoculture. In effect, Australia was now becoming conscious of its own identity and of its differences from Britain. Ties were being loosened, political parties and particularly the Labor party now had members who did not themselves come from the British tradition or from British origins. It was less socially impossible to reveal one's origins as a convict's descendant. Irishness was no longer held to be somehow a mark of inferior status. Despite deliberate efforts in the post-war period to disperse 'aliens' and prevent their concentration in 'national groups', communities had formed and assimilation and 'absorption' had taken place very unevenly. As a result, ethnic communities retained their languages, their religions and customs, and parts of Melbourne and Sydney and elsewhere had a recognisable Greek, Italian or Serbian flavour.

Attacks on such multiculturalism and multilingualism came from a number of sources. These were not confined to those who believed in assimilation and integration at home. As much danger was seen in immigration from Asian countries and in any recognition that Australia should be more and more aware of its Pacific situation and of the nearness of populous countries who could provide large numbers of migrants, on the one hand, or whose growing wealth might pose a threat to the ownership of Australian businesses and tourist opportunities on the other. Associated with these economic fears was also a more subtle worry. As a former colony founded in large part by rejects from British society, and by many of Irish working-class origin, an attitude characterised as the 'cultural cringe' was never far from the surface of Australian life. In the debates over Australian identity, a 'profound sense of inferiority and diffidence' (Ozolins, 1993: 14) lay in the back of the Australian mind.

Such an attitude may be partly responsible for the political acceptance of policies aimed at correcting inequalities, unfairness and discrimination. The immediate cause of the changes lay in the election of the Labor government of 1972. In 1978, the responsible minister Frank Galbally systematised services and programmes which should be developed for migrants, including multicultural broadcasting and television, and his report, advocating 'the right to maintain cultural and racial identity...provided (it is) interwoven into the fabric of our nationhood by the process of multicultural interaction', remained official policy from the early 1980s until 1993.

The National Languages Policy of 1987, an eventual outcome of this movement, adopted four principles:

- English for all
- support for Aboriginal and Torres Strait Island languages
- a language other than English for all
- equitable and widespread language services.

As announced in December 1987, the Commonwealth of Australia committed $28.65 million to the National Languages Policy. Eight programmes were funded at the following levels for 1988-89 (Lo Bianco, 1990). In addition to these sums, considerable additional amounts became available, either through educational programmes in individual states or through such actions as special support for languages in higher education:

- Adult literacy action campaign ($1.96 million)
- Asian studies programme ($1.95 million in 1989-90)
- Australian second language learning programme ($7.7 million)

- English .as a second language program (new arrivals element) ($35.4 million within an overall total of $82.1 million for the Commonwealth English as a second language program)
- Languages Institute of Australia (initial allocations totalling $1,090,000)
- Multicultural and cross-cultural supplementation program ($2.5 million over four years)
- National Aboriginal languages program (one million dollars)
- the Australian Advisory Council on Languages and Multicultural Education ($190,000).

After the Senate enquiry and report in 1984, the policy was eventually adopted by the Hawke Labor government in 1987, formed part of its re-election platform in 1987, and was endorsed in December of that year when fairly large-scale funding was allocated to a number of programmes as the list above shows. The motives of those proposing the policy have been analysed in Ozolins (1993: 206-49): the main thing about them is the level of collaboration and co-ordination that they represent among very different groups. Ozolins lists these as the language professionals; the government bureaucracy itself in the form of the Federal Department of Education; and the councils of the ethnic communities. While the first two may be regarded (by critics) as somewhat self-seeking, the language professionals at least combined both those teaching languages other than English (LOTE) and those teaching English: in many English-speaking countries the two groups have been noted more for their attacks on each other than on co-operation between them in pursuit of a common policy. The role of the bureaucracy in policy formulation, characterised by some commentators as the 'autonomous state' (Skocpol, 1985), had a clarifying role in the Australian situation, systematising and simplifying many of the language issues that the Department of Education and the state governments had had to deal with, through the use of a three-fold classification of language issues under the headings of needs, rights and resources. The bureaucracy wanted co-ordination and a set of principles for setting priorities, and its work, although it made the job easier for civil servants, also cleared the road for language professionals and for the political 'pushers', the ethnic councils.

These latter formed the 'ethnic lobby' (Ozolins, 1993: 214). Multiculturalism, formally adopted as the guiding government ideology in the 1970s, represented what might be termed the humanitarian approach to a diverse society, mixing aims of social cohesion, the maintenance of cultural identity, equality of opportunity and access, and commitment to society. It was based more on correcting injustice than on correcting inequity or social inequality. The formation of the Federation of Ethnic Communities Councils of Australia (FECCA) in 1980 demonstrates both the awareness of social divisions and discrimination and the need to create a new Australian identity based on diversity. But this ethnic lobby, like many Australians, was not altogether sure that multiculturalism was the right answer: for many individual ethnic groups what was important was the maintenance of their own language and traditions. While many were worried about the associations the political Left made between class and race, seeing both as simply examples of the class struggle and multiculturalism as an attempt at social engineering, other ethnic activists were worried about the political Right and its belief that integration and assimilation was the best course of action to avoid cultural pluralism and the disruption of the state. Whatever the perception, the power of the ethnic groups after the mid-1970s must be acknowledged:

> (The Senate Committee enquiry of 1983) was the result of a great deal of ground work by the ethnic communities...the National Languages Policy came into being because John Menaduc was willing to take an ethnic community perspective. (Croft and Macpherson, 1991: 105)

Even by 1986 multiculturalism had become the target for budget reductions, and the reaction from ethnic groups to these reductions sparked a number of protests and forced the Labor government to try to 'reestablish its credentials with its ethnic constituency' (Ozolins, 1993: 193). The July election of that year enabled the government to put forward the National Policy on Languages as part of its response to the pressure from the ethnic groups.

The motives of those actually making language policy, the government politicians, were more mixed as became clear when the policy itself was funded: the December 1987 version was different from the April one. It is fairly clear that motives for supporting languages other than English were not limited to community support: the politicians were also concerned about learning languages (for example classical languages) for purely educational reasons and, more particularly, about learning languages of commercial importance for Australia's export industries.

Here, however, those who might have been thought to be the main supporters for language learning and use in Asian languages, Japanese in particular, the Confederation of Australian Industry, reflected the views of many industrialists in other countries by rejecting any demand for specific languages. The viewpoint of many industrialists is that export personnel have to cope with a variety of countries and markets, and hence that although an awareness of cultural difference is required and personnel should have some knowledge of a foreign language, the details of negotiation and particularly of legal matters need a specialist - although few industrialists are prepared to share the costs of training a Japanese-speaking lawyer versed in international contracting.

What then were the motives for the implementation of the National Languages Policy in 1987? They are (at least) three: concern to accept immigrant communities by giving greater recognition to their diversity and acknowledging it as such; concern to unite society by ensuring access to power, but through the use of one 'unifying' language, English; and an economic motivation aimed at ensuring that Australia's situation as part of Asia and the Pacific rim was recognised through the development of linguistic capability in the languages of near neighbours. Whether the correction of inequality and injustice was foremost in the minds of politicians is somewhat doubtful, although the Labor policy-makers of the time might have been more inclined to adopt it than their Liberal opponents. Many commentators on the Australian situation throughout the 1990s have nonetheless cast doubt on whether anything other than the economic motive was positively accepted by the politicians. Lobbying by the ethnic communities certainly ensured that the language question got on the political agenda, and their motive was certainly to do with getting rid of what they saw as discrimination. Nonetheless, the significant factor in the fact that the policy was implemented was the coming together of a range of interest groups, added to the political awareness of the promoters of the policy in ensuring that the policy did not become a political football and was pursued single-mindedly and coherently over a long period. That the policy could easily have remained a dead letter is clear from the fact that New Zealand never adopted any form of open language policy despite the existence of many of the same factors.

By the 1990s the original L1s of immigrant communities have in many cases disappeared from use, particularly among second generation immigrants. In examining the Polish, Welsh and Chinese communities in Australia, Smolicz (1992) came to the conclusion that language loss of this sort entailed a close examination of core cultural values, and how these related to communities' assessments of themselves as such. For some communities, language is regarded as 'the' core cultural value:

without it, members of the community simply disappear into the host community and retain no special distinctiveness. For others, language is one among many core cultural values, and members of the community can retain some distinctiveness even when their L1 has become that of the host community. Other people have in effect rejected any language other than that of the host and majority community, and feel neither the need to be distinctive nor any wish to be. The Polish respondents (18, mainly post-1980 residents in Australia) led Smolicz to conclude that the Polish language was a fundamental core value: there were few other ethno-specific core values, even Catholicism, and without the language individuals drifted away from the Polish community. But drift they did:

> Polish was regarded as intellectually debilitating, socially downgrading and politically divisive...The comments in the memoirs suggested... that it was a passive submission to the status quo in society. They found it easier to use English...and they were not prepared to make the greater effort needed to use Polish in contexts where it was not specifically required. (Smolicz, 1992, 284)
>
> I was not accepted in the Polish community because I could not speak Polish. (Smolicz, 1992: 287)

Both the Welsh and Chinese communities contrast with the Polish. Of 27,209 people born in Wales there remained 1708 Welsh speakers in the 1986 Australian census. Typical of the memoir comments elicited by Smolicz (1992: 288-97) were the following:

> The children are Australians and this is where they belong so I don't see any point in them learning Welsh.
>
> When deprived of the language as the core marker of identity, the Welsh resort enthusiastically to 'residual' or 'non-authentic' expressions of ethnicity...flags, leeks, Welsh cakes and daffodils...The evidence presented in these memoirs confirm the view that the Welsh language is the core value of Welsh culture and that when it vanishes, the culture is reduced to fragments .
>
> I suppose it's a bit silly to be Chinese and not to be able to speak a word of Chinese...I don't think I'm interested enough.
>
> There is no motivation really...you cannot see the relevance
>
> In Australia I don't think it's important to be literate in Chinese.

The success of the Australian Languages Policy in regard to the situation of immigrant languages is clear. The motive here has been basically similar to that of those promoting the European Charter: to clarify language rights. In addition to the ethnic councils fighting for migrant languages, those supporting the use of Aboriginal languages in the Australian Languages Policy formed another set of groups with strong political interests and motives, but concerned with what they felt to be injustice rather than inequality or inequity. Some of this concern with the Aboriginal question became obvious outside Australia at about the time of the creation of the Languages Policy, through interference with the bicentenary celebrations and the arrival of the replica of the First Fleet in Sydney Harbour, but it was the Mabo judgment that openly represented the major shift of opinion in society and at least a start to the recognition of past injustices in the treatment of Aboriginal peoples. The Mabo judgment of 1992 showed a new assessment of the situation of Aborigines in Australia. The case, between the Murray islander Eddie Mabo representing the Meriam people, and the Queensland Government, concerned title to land. Queensland maintained that when the Murray Islands were annexed in 1879 both sovereignty and ownership passed to the colony. The judgment in the Australian High Court, while accepting that sovereignty over all parts of Australia had passed to the British Crown from 1788 as an act of state which courts could not dispute, decreed in a majority decision (six to one) that it would be 'an unjust and discriminatory doctrine' to hold that the indigenous inhabitants of the colony had no proprietary interest in the land. The principle applied to all Aboriginal people in Australia, and in effect meant that where a particular group could show continuing contact with land, they possessed prior title to it. The major practical outcome of the judgment affected mining and pastoral (farming) companies in the interior.

The judgment went part way towards formal public recognition of the injustice of the current situation of Aboriginal peoples. There remain difficulties, particularly in the contrast with the situation of First Nations in America and Canada, and in the issue of sovereignty (cf. Reynolds, 1996). If Aboriginal peoples possessed sovereignty before the establishment of the colony in 1788, and if they possessed social organisation and a system of laws and punishments, it could be appropriate that they should continue to apply these today even where they conflict with Australian law. Problems have arisen where the laws and punishments differ markedly from those of 'civilised society': marriage conventions, the treatment of children and the death penalty are areas where such conflicts have occurred and continue to occur.

Discussions on the nature of the Australian Constitution, on the November 1999 referendum on a possible Republic, have meant that the issue of reconciliation with the original inhabitants of Australia is of great concern at this time. There seems to be a desire to express in some formal way both regret and apologies for the past treatment of Aboriginal people by the settlers. Indeed in 1991, a Council for Aboriginal Reconciliation was set up. Various proposals have been made for formal reconciliation, ranging from a treaty accepting Aboriginal self-government and autonomy to practical acceptance of Aboriginal laws and customs. It seems to be generally accepted that a new Preamble to any revised Constitution is the most likely document. But the constitutional convention preparing this suggested in 1999 that the preamble should refer not simply to Aboriginal rights but also to

> Almighty God, the Federal system of representative democracy and responsible government, affirmation of the rule of law, recognition of cultural diversity and respect for the land, while acknowledging the original occupancy and custodianship of Australia by Aboriginal peoples and Torres Strait Islanders... matters to be considered should include gender equality (Sydney Morning Herald, 15.2.1999).

Japan, by contrast with Australia, is a country long noted for its isolation, voluntary and otherwise (Miyawaki, 1992). It is as monolingual as Australia was traditionally considered to be, yet despite the pressures towards cultural homogeneity, inevitably contains some linguistic minorities. Two of these, the Ainu of Hokkaido numbering possibly some 25,000 (no accurate figures are known) and those of Korean extraction (possibly 690,000), have a history of discrimination if not persecution. Hokkaido was not extensively settled by the Japanese until after 1868. The 1899 'Protective Act for the former Aborigines of Hokkaido', still in force, has in effect destroyed the Ainu community's economic, social and cultural traditions, including the language. The Ainu are generally regarded by contemporary Japanese as almost subhuman: 'Ainu tourist circuses are often combined with caged bears in zoos, a sight equally depressing, symbolic of the freedom lost by the Ainu' as the 1997 Lonely Planet guide to Japan puts it. Nonetheless there remain isolated attempts to raise the prestige of the culture, particularly in Shiraoi, and keep the language alive even though remaining native speakers number less than ten.   People of Korean origin have long lived in the Japanese islands. Japanese culture itself traces its origins to Korean and Chinese influences from the fifth century, while Korea, invaded by Japan in 200 AD and regularly since, was annexed by Japan between 1910 and 1946. During the 1938 to 1945 war more than two million

Koreans were transported to Japan and forcibly integrated into the Japanese labour and fighting forces. Since 1910 at least Japanese policy has been to deny rights, particularly language rights, to Koreans. As a result, 80% of children are now monolingual Japanese speakers; 95% use Japanese names. Although Korean schools use both Korean and Japanese, they are classified as 'miscellaneous' along with cooking and driving schools; their graduates cannot enter Japanese Universities and employment opportunities in Japanese firms are non-existent.

The forced linguistic and cultural assimilation of both Ainu and Koreans in Japan represent another example of the more severe level of social inequality. Social injustice at this level exists elsewhere, of course, and the example of discrimination against Roma speakers in central Europe comes to mind. The practical outcome of changed and changing views, both by mainstream society and by the relevant minority group, has in the Japanese case led to practical language shift. In Australia, too, Aboriginal languages have not survived as means of communication for a modern democratic society, and although they retain vitality in relevant groups, the great majority of Aborigines in contact with mainstream society are at least bilingual and in most cases have lost their original language.

The Correction of Inequality as a Motive for Language Policy

The examples above lead us to draw a number of conclusions about this motive. It would be hoping for too much from human nature to expect that policy-makers, themselves holders of power by definition and hence members of an elite, will voluntarily and selflessly cede power to those without it. On the face of it therefore, the correction of inequality is an unlikely motive for policy of any sort, and indeed such analysts as Tollefson (1991), Fairclough (1989) and many others see language planning generally as being a form of imposition or domination rather than the opposite. Inequality can only be corrected, particularly in the Marxian interpretation of history, by brute force: it needs a pressure group, a powerful lobby, threats or violence to bring about change. This interpretation sees language difference as reflecting power differences: domination, by males or by ethnic groups holding power in society, ensures that the language use of the dominated group or groups lacks prestige and the motive to correct this is in effect a motive to change society. Such analyses see little difference among our three levels of inequality, inequity and injustice; all are expressions of severe injustice.

On the other hand the policies in Australia and the USA came about through social change; through greater awareness by a wider group that inequality existed and should be corrected. These more democratic attitudes led to the adoption of less unequal policies by the relevant authorities. Pluralism works. An alternative explanation is that the linguistic differences represent cultural differences rather than domination: it just happens that the cultural group (white males or Europeans) who hold power in society do not understand the language of the other group. On this analysis, if each group could understand the other better the inequality might be reduced by this simple fact.

It remains true, that in order to bring about such changes, in a pluralist democratic society a pressure group is needed whose purpose is to ensure awareness of the relevant inequality and of the need for it to be corrected, and to show how this might be done. The women's' movement and particular organisations such as Sociologists for Women in Society deliberately set out to ensure that gender inequalities were corrected. The same is true for the Australian Ethnic Council and for the variety of interests that came together in FECCA. Whether the relevant linguistic policy was adopted and implemented by governmental organisations or by less official authorities such as editors and in style manuals is immaterial. Responding to pressure groups and being made aware of inequality has led in the cases referred to here to change, to a large degree successful, in language use.

The case of the European Charter for Regional and Minority Languages is a little different from those of gender inequality or the ANLP. Language planning proposed by groups of people affected by a sense of injustice has rarely taken this form, where the relevant communities using the dominated languages have not themselves taken joint action to implement language behaviour which aim to correct the situation. Here, the representatives of those communities are attempting to construct policy rather than planning. Attempting to persuade political authorities to take political action when the relevant communities themselves are by no means clear about their own actions is rather strange, and the ambivalent reactions of some governments to the proposals shows this. The Greek, French and British governments, those most intransigent to 1998, all have linguistic minorities within their borders and all have expressed considerable caution about the implications of their adhering to the policy. The pressure for Corsican autonomy is matched by the problem of Macedonia, while the northern Irish question has led to long delay by the British government. It is when such issues lose their problematic nature for the relevant governments that the Charter may pass into law in all European states.

Behind all these considerations is the distinction to be made between the language policies of states or those with political power, and the language planning of communities and groups which may possess some power in domains like education. The distinctions Ruiz (1984) made between problems, rights and resources in language policy is fundamental to our distinction between inequality, inequity and injustice. These discriminatory practices may be solved by making a 'claim to something' as opposed to a 'claim against someone' in certain cases; overall, social inequality remains a motive whose manifestations differ as between individual countries and societies but which retains universal characteristics recognisable in all human societies (Hornberger, 1998).

Chapter 6
Integration and Instrumentality

We have so far been dealing mainly with states, governments and communities concerned with making or influencing policy, principally affecting language-as-object. At this point we turn attention to the economic motive and its relation to the political and social ones, to the role of individuals and to issues of planning as well as policy, affecting not just language-as-object but also language-as-instrument. Independent states make policy for the language behaviour of those for whom they are politically responsible. They make every attempt to implement this policy and to see it through, sometimes, but not always, to a measurable conclusion. Governments, political leaders and other identifiable figures design and implement top-down policy, whether this takes the shape of macro policy in the form of laws, directives and instructions or micro policy in the form of influence on action by state representatives such as teachers, bureaucrats or law enforcers. Motives in either case are political, aimed at influencing the way society behaves, and language policy decisions are usually taken deliberately. Minority, ethnic and language communities also change language behaviour however, whether this is their own or whether they hope to influence that of others. Such communities and human groups, defined in the first place by characteristics other than the political, differ from governments and states not only because, by definition, they do not construct policy in the formal sense, but also because their ideas about language behaviour may be less clearly identifiable. They may possess few institutions to influence language behaviour, and any influence they may have is rarely measurable. Pressure groups in the community frequently make conscious and deliberate plans about language, but these are about language-as-object and usually try to influence the prestige allocated to a particular language or variety. Individual community leaders and pressure groups cannot usually point to successful outcomes in phenomena such as language shift, although there have been notable exceptions. Eventual changes in language behaviour by the community may seem to be almost instinctive, responsive simply to environmental change. Community 'bottom-up' influence on language is similar to the actions of the independent individual coping with his or her own immediate situation. Again, the actual changes which take place in behaviour can take the form of conscious strategies for action or a seemingly unconscious, responsive reaction to the changing environment. Gardner and Lambert (1959), as we have noted, designated the extreme points of individuals' motivation for acquiring foreign languages as instrumentality and integration. The first assumes that individuals are interested solely in acquiring sufficient communicative ability to satisfy their own specific goals, usually economic targets, while the second is based on the desire of individuals to associate themselves ever more closely with a target community to the point, eventually, of assimilating to it. Gardner and Lambert's work was based in Canada, where the target community consisted of either French or English speakers but where both were part of the same country, and the sample investigated was of adult learners. Other situations, and other types of language behaviour, may shed more light on this social-to-economic motivational spectrum for language planning, and enable us to see how far it applies to communities as well as to individuals. But the ideas of self-advancement for the individual on the one hand, and solidarity with a human group on the other, give a starting point for consideration of the non-political motivational spectrum applicable to communities and individuals. They also provoke some doubt whether the language behaviour of individuals and communities is indeed simply responsive. Our concern in this chapter is to explore the language behaviour of individuals and communities, and through this to question whether such behaviour is planned and what the motivation might be for such planning. Our inbuilt assumption is that individuals act in much the same way as communities.

Immigrants to the USA have for decades included people moving for negative as well as for positive reasons. 'Negative' here means refugees fleeing from persecution, whether religious, political, economic, social or racial, while 'positive' reasons are mainly economic, although migrants do move to marry or to join a society they like. The push factor, moving for negative reasons, should imply that many migrants simply want to recreate their former society in a new place, often continuing to use its language and only using that of the host community when necessary. Economic migrants, motivated more by the pull factor of a rich and well-resourced country, seem more likely to adopt the host language, but to do so as simply a tool to a better life. For all types of refugees and migrants, motivation to change language behaviour may be essentially instrumental, aimed firstly at improving life chances, career development and personal financial success. Does this mean that all migrants are essentially reluctant to assimilate? Motives for learning and using a lingua franca, a language intended solely as a communication instrument, seem similarly unlikely to reflect an integrative aim. African multilingualism in the marketplace offers, on the face of it, a clear example of the need to acquire languages in order to cope with daily requirements, to purchase food and other necessities. International English for trading is frequently quoted as an example of a sophisticated trade pidgin whose sole raison d'être is to permit basic communicative exchanges for purposes of commercial exchange. Finally, the instrumental-integrative spectrum is further examined here through five case histories, including one English-speaking person learning Japanese for instrumental reasons, another person who uses English for specifically academic purposes, and three immigrants, to the UK or other English-speaking countries, whose motives are less clear.

Immigration

'The assumption in 1803 was the same as today: the language of America (if not of all Americans) is English' (Ricento, 1996: 131). The American approach to language since the creation of the United States has been consistent with this myth of homogeneity: the use of one language, English, will guarantee democracy through preventing any group (including those speaking any other language) from having special privileges and rights. The Constitutional system of checks and balances safeguarding against the tyranny of any one group or individual did not envisage any counterbalancing system of language rights: the aim was to facilitate the melting pot, and while the American Constitution did not go so far as the French in eliminating the privileges of groups, it did envisage some sacrifice of group privilege in the cause of democracy for the individual. The main thrust of de-facto American language policy through the nineteenth and twentieth centuries has been to absorb linguistic minorities, 'civilise' native Americans and adopt gradualist assimilation policies only where more direct ones could not work. Specific groups like the Pennsylvania Dutch and French speakers in Louisiana have slowly assimilated to the general model, and although groups of Italian immigrants have often retained their use of specific dialects of Italian, this is rarely their only or even main language. The 'great wave of immigration' after 1890 sharpened the English language requirement: the first law requiring English as a precondition for citizenship was passed in 1906, while the national origin quota restrictions preventing immigration from any one country by more than 2% of the 1890 census numbers already in the USA were not abandoned until 1967. Not until 1992 did Congress permit bilingual ballots in districts with at least 10,000 members of a single language minority group. How far were these policies accepted by immigrants, and were their motives for acquiring English therefore simply instrumental, aimed at gaining economic, political or social advantage for themselves and their families, or does it appear that there was any desire to integrate linguistically, as opposed to the natural desire of any immigrant to associate closely with the host community?

Over the period since 1950, and despite large international movements from Vietnam, Korea, Haiti and elsewhere, immigrants to the USA have been mainly Spanish-speaking and have originated from dependent territories (Puerto Rico) or from neighbouring countries (Mexico, Cuba). The result has been that Spanish is now spoken by a high proportion of the population in large areas of the United States, particularly in the southern states and in such centres as New York. The extent of Spanish speaking is such that most states (48 of the 50) have been inspired to consider legislation affirming that the official language of the state is English, although in many it is impossible to conduct daily business (shopping, contact with local authorities) without some knowledge of Spanish. At least one southern town has now declared Spanish its official language, and declared its support for 'illegal' immigration across the southern border. The future role of Spanish is thus possibly the main issue for language policy and planning in the United States, despite the presence of large numbers of immigrants speaking other languages.

The instrumental motivation for language acquisition should logically apply to two separate groups: to immigrants who need English in order to manage a large part of their daily activities, and to the host community who, because of employment patterns, find it necessary to acquire sufficient Spanish to shop, contact local authorities and utilities. It is common experience that the integrative motivation is the prerogative of the first group. The host community is generally so opposed to any desire to integrate with Spanish speakers that considerable efforts are undertaken to ensure that Spanish is and remains a marginalised language. Who speaks for the 'immigrant' and the 'host' community? Two groups of organisations seem to concern themselves with language matters. On the 'English language' side, determined to protect the privileged position of English, the two main organisations are US English and the Federation for American Immigration Reform (FAIR). Their public pronouncements are often motivated by an 'unreasonable and unfounded fear that linguistic pluralism will weaken national unity' (Ricento, 1996: 154) and have 'hit upon a pulsating raw nerve of linguistic and cultural fear in the American psyche' (Zentella, 1997: 72).

Countering the efforts of the anti-immigration groups are a number of coalitions and professional associations, including many language associations. These include the National Association for Bilingual Education (NABE), Teachers of English to Speakers of Other Languages (TESOL), the Modern Language Association (MLA), among many others. Other, more ethnically oriented, groups include the League of United Latin American Citizens (LULAC), the Puerto Rican Defense and Education Fund, the Mexican American Legal Defense and Education Fund (MALDEF) and the National Council of La Raza. (Ricento, 1996: 151)

Most academic analysis of the question has concentrated on the question of language rights, whether those of the majority or of the minorities. There has been little examination of the motives of the migrants, and this unfortunate situation has been exacerbated by the concentration in the research literature on legal cases, on legislation and on attitudinal study, mainly of groups opposed to immigration. Official policy at the Federal level has switched between traditional monolingualism and support for assimilation, on the one hand, and multiculturalism and affirmative action supporting minorities on the other. The debate, reflecting widespread conflicting attitudes such as 'immigrants steal our jobs' opposed to 'free movement should be welcomed and encouraged', has often degenerated into the exchange of slogans and accusations of racism and Fascism, countered by those alleging dumbing down and a desire to destroy social cohesiveness. In this debate, the stress on a Rights agenda by both sides has led to a general feeling that the language issue in the United States is a problem which can only be solved by drastic action, and the motives of individuals and the relevant communities tend to be lost while the politicians adopt positions, reflecting the strength of feeling of the pressure groups.

The behaviour of migrants themselves is varied when it comes to the issue of assimilation or of retaining a separate identity in the host country. It is widely agreed that assimilation and integration come about anyway during the second or third generation. Employment in the host community, outside 'ethnic business', is an intermediate test (but only one) of a desire to obtain economic advancement within the norms of the host community itself, and could therefore be a measure of (immigrant) community motivation towards integration. Employment, too, is closely associated with language. While unofficial or illegal employment can get by and ignore the host language, as soon as migrants enter more organised employment they must cope with regulations ranging from tax declarations to safety instructions, communicate with fellow workers, management and organisations such as Trade Unions or Social Security.

It is all too easy to oversimplify the situation of migrants and the assimilation/integration issue. The situation is not static. To take an example, urban, skilled and semi-skilled Puerto Ricans were deliberately recruited between 1900 and 1945 as cheap labour for the North-East US industries since they were American citizens and could not be excluded by the 1924 Immigration Act that restricted European migration (Grosfoguel, 1999). After the 1950s, Puerto Rican migrants, 79% of migration from the Caribbean area, were mainly rural and unskilled, but fed the same industrial need. After the 1970s, Puerto Ricans immigrated less, falling to 7% of Caribbean migration, and their place was taken by new immigrants from other Caribbean countries and elsewhere. Because of their origins (particularly their social class), mode of recruitment and the public perception (by the destination community) of them as a group, Puerto Ricans have generally become labourers in US manufacturing, and when the manufacturing boom ended have remained marginalised. In the 1990s, more than 50% were unemployed or out of the labour force. '"Public opinion" seems generally to have racialised Puerto Ricans as "spics" and marked them as "lazy, violent, stupid and dirty"' (Grosfoguel, 1999: 245). As a consequence, Puerto Ricans for their part have resisted assimilation, even to the extent of refusing hyphenated labels such as those adopted by Italian-Americans, Mexican-Americans or Korean-Americans. Apart from questions of social class, employment patterns and public opinion, yet another further complicating factor is the difference between traditional migration where the group moved to a new location and cut off all contact with their former home, and the current situation in which migrant groups not merely retain contact by post, e-mail and telephone but move back and forth, return or send family members 'home', sharing their time between the locations. The 'commuter nation' label was applied to Puerto Ricans because air travel is now relatively cheap and many Puerto Ricans could travel frequently between the island and the mainland. Yet another complicating factor is economic and social progress outside the US mainland. Like Hawaii, the island of Puerto Rico itself seems largely to have adopted the US national identity, with middle-class suburban cultural practices, among Spanish speakers, which are often very different from those of returning working-class urban ghetto dwellers in the US.

Despite the complications of the situation, its dynamic nature and the variation between migrants from different countries, employment prospects and thus instrumentalism has often been the main motivating factor for migration. Integration into the host community's employment practices has seemed an ideal but merely a secondary motive, and assimilation into the host community's cultural and linguistic norms simply the necessary consequence of the move. But here again it is difficult to generalise, and migrants' employment patterns reveal very different situations. Individuals migrate to take up jobs in the host economy. Migrants' networks are soon established, facilitating further immigration which is not merely family reunification, but is semi-independent of actual employment prospects. Such self-motivating migration, together with resource flows as migrants send money 'home' or as older generations return to live out their retirement, and as ethnic enterprises and enclaves are created in the destination economy, can then restructure both the sending and receiving economies, creating new employment possibilities and reshaping the whole question of integration (cf. Light et al., 1999). Indeed, the extent to which immigration creates new employment prospects in the host community can be measured by assessing how far cross-ethnic employment take place: that is, how frequently immigrants of one ethnic origin establish employment opportunities for members of other ethnic groups, including members of the host or destination community itself. The example Light et al. studied in the 1990s was that of the Los Angeles garment industry, where 'Hispanics were 87% of the employees of Korean-owned garment factories' (Light et al., 1999: 13). Overall, in a situation in which three quarters of the industry was owned by and employed first generation immigrants and employed 3.5 percent of the labour force of Los Angeles County,

> about 30.3 percent of garment industry personnel were in simple ethnic economies (i.e. employing one ethnic group), 47.2 percent in the immigrant economy (i.e. coethnic), and the remaining 22.5 percent in the mainstream economy. (Light et al., 1999: 20)

Examples of such processes abound, in addition to that of the Los

Angeles garment industry. Italian peasants migrated to Cairns, Australia, to work sugar-cane plantations in the 1920s, encouraging whole villages to follow them. Employment patterns diversified; enterprises, particularly in food production and treatment, were created and internal migration within Australia followed. Similar patterns are being followed with migration from India and Pakistan to parts of Bradford, Birmingham and Leicester in the UK. It is common experience in the UK that Asian entrepreneurship is widespread and that resulting enterprises employ labour of many ethnic groups.

Such cross-ethnic mixing inevitably has effects on language behaviour and on the language motivation of communities, generally leading to more rapid adoption of the host country's language and to language shift. But the dynamic nature of migration, and the constant travel of the 'commuting nation', works against this and is more likely to lead to bilingualism in the destination community and, to a certain extent, in the source community.

Immigration in the USA is by no means always typical of immigration elsewhere, however. Immigration by Spanish speakers to the US has three very specific characteristics which mark it as quite different from recent European immigration. Migration has not been the result of an imperial past: many Spanish speakers entered the States through Mexico, firstly as temporary or seasonal workers. In the USA, Spanish is not in the same category of languages as German or Italian: Spanish was spoken in many States well before English and has some right to be regarded in the USA as an indigenous rather than as an immigrant language. The Civil Rights movement of the 1960s and 70s has had a major affect on public policies and attitudes, and Spanish in particular has benefited from changes in attitudes towards blacks and towards the underclass generally. Motivation to acquire the main host language is hence not merely economic and instrumental nor merely integrationist. Nonetheless, despite the special situation of Spanish speakers, they show no signs of wishing to live in a monolingual Spanish-speaking environment within the USA. There seems therefore to be good reason to believe that the bilingualisation of the United States is becoming an institutional reality. Whether this bilingualism will itself turn out to be a stage on the way to a new monolingualism, and whether this will be Spanish monolingualism, lies as yet too far in the future. As far as the motivation of immigrants is concerned, the US situation show fairly clearly that instrumentalism and integration are necessarily intertwined, and that early instrumentalism may soon lead to a desire to integrate. More importantly, the extent of immigration and its changing nature affect both source and destination communities, and hence constantly modify the nature of motivation. More importantly still for our purposes, much immigrant behaviour and the consequent language behaviour seems planned, rather than the fortuitous result of economic or political chaos.

The Lingua Franca

The multilingualism that is normal in many African countries can be viewed from a top-down or bottom-up perspective (Fardon and Furniss, 1994: 4). For language planners and experts concerned with issues of administration and policy, and considering the situation from a top-down 'managerial' point of view, African societies are linguistically complex. Most African states contain a large number of different languages, spoken by groups whose size varies from many millions to a mere handful. Languages typically cross frontiers; European languages, Arabic, Swahili, pidgins of various sorts are used in specific domains or functions, while indigenous languages are spoken among ethnic groups, although the ethnic boundaries do not necessarily coincide with linguistic ones, and neither coincide with political frontiers. The problems facing language planners are typically those of educational and acquisition planning, deciding which languages should be made available in schools and elsewhere. The second concern is to ensure corpus planning: standardisation, the elaboration of dictionaries, grammars and writing systems. Sometimes, too, issues of status arise directly as well as indirectly, since most corpus and acquisition programmes depend on the political will to support one group of speakers or another. If politicians intend to strengthen or weaken the relationships between ethnicity, language and nationhood language policy may be pressed into service.

From the 'bottom-up' anthropological perspective of what actually happens, the most striking feature of the African situation is the multilingualism of individuals.

> Multilingualism is the African lingua franca...a multilayered and partially connected language chain...a set that is always liable to be reconnected more densely to a new environment by rapid secondary language learning, or by the development of new languages. (Fardon and Furniss, 1994: 4)

While motives of nation-building, identity formation and the correction of inequality may be important to language planners at the official level, the motives of individuals seem fairly clearly to be principally instrumental: it is essential to survival to be able to manipulate the languages and language varieties needed for particular purposes.

> Because of the utility of such languages as Akan in Ghana, Wolof in Senegal, Hausa in Northern Nigeria, Lingala in Zaire, not to speak of the more widely-spoken Swahili in Eastern Africa, speakers of different languages are embracing them as second languages. (Bamgbose, 1994: 34)

Practical multilingualism and the use of linguae francae is evident in the most basic of activities. In specific studies of African market-places, Calvet (1992) noted that in one market in Cotonou of 396 people interviewed, 381 agreed that Fon (French spelling) was in effect the market's most spoken language, even though not all of them spoke it. Only 118 had this as native language while 232 were at least bilingual including Fon. Similar multilingual situations were typical of market-places in Brazzaville, Abidjan and elsewhere. In one of the markets in Abidjan in the Ivory Coast, different sorts of products were offered for sale by different ethnolinguistic groups: smoked fish by one group, vegetables by another. But exchanges between sellers and purchasers, themselves of many different linguistic groups, were conducted in Dioula (French spelling), in French or in English. Both sellers and purchasers clearly had to acquire at least enough of these languages to be able to use them for commercial and interactional purposes.

The contrast between the top-down and bottom-up perspectives on language use is important for the linguistic reality of many situations in different countries. Typically, formal language policy and planning will support the native languages of different ethnic groups. This may affect educational policies, political affiliations, ethnic conflicts and many other aspects of life. But in some cases the lingua franca of the market place has few native speakers. In Sierra Leone for example, 'ethnic groups began to acquire the Krio language through migrants moving into Freetown to seek job opportunities' but there were few moves to include Krio in educational policy or even in early standardisation programmes. Yet 'The persistence of (Krio's) major function as a lingua franca throughout the region means it cannot be replaced by English, the official language' (Fyle, 1994: 53). Although Krio, a pidgin based on English, has few native speakers it has acquired a certain degree of prestige through its associations with English, so it is more and more useful in careers. Its acquisition is a matter of planned behaviour by individuals and to a certain extent by communities, not of policy by authorities.

The instrumentality motive is rarely pure: that is, the use of a lingua franca has associations which may also be of cultural importance. While it is true that individuals in many situations need to use a variety of languages for instrumental purposes including simple sustenance, career progression, giving or receiving instructions, getting a job done or simply asking for information, languages retain all their other associations and symbolic value. The use of Wolof by the American Ambassador on local television in 1986 'did much to enhance the reputation of Americans' (Swigart, 1995: 223). Poor use of Wolof by a Presidential candidate in 1988 offended some sections of Senegal society, but pleased others who appreciated his 'levelling of status' in using Wolof rather than French. Language choice among multilingual groups is of course affected by group membership and by such factors as religion and gender. Among French-Wolof bilinguals in Dakar, women

> consistently speak Wolof more than French in comparison with their male age-mates of comparable educational level...the common correlation between formal education and competence in French...French language is associated with Christianity in Senegal while Wolof and other indigenous languages are associated with Islam...the Diola and the Peul actively resent the dominant role played by Wolof in Senegal. (Swigart, 1992: 158-90)

If it is essential to acquire a language in order to negotiate in the market, make purchases and survive in Africa on a day-to-day level, it is for some people equally important, and probably important in the same way, to have available a means of communication to enable them to buy and sell on the international level. In order to facilitate globalisation and the development of international commerce, a sort of lingua franca has developed which enables communication to be established in specific commercial fields. Nowhere is this more obvious than in international banking and finance.

International English is different from other Englishes. As the language is used more and more, regional varieties of English become more numerous and recognisably different from each other. The Encarta World English Dictionary, released in 1999, shows the following: American, Canadian, Caribbean, African, South Asian, East Asian, Australian, New Zealand, British, Irish, and, as sub-varieties, Maori, Jamaican, Patwa, Trinidadian, Bajan, Inuit, Sri Lankan, Hawaiian, Scots, Ebonics. One must therefore ask whether there is one International English or whether this variety is itself divided according to where it is used. There may also be sub-varieties according to field of use: banking

English is different from that used in air transport. Nonetheless the common view is that International Standard English does exist, that all varieties are mutually intelligible and that speakers of the language, by common accord, deliberately ensure this degree of intelligibility by, in effect, avoiding terms and expressions they recognise as local or marked when communicating with other groups or on the international level.

In neither the African case nor in that of international English has there been any form of conscious or open political planning, although clearly individuals and communities have planned their behaviour in response to specific motives. Although some African countries have tried to develop specific educational plans for language use, the desperate poverty of many countries and the pressure from international agencies for reduced public spending have effectively stopped much central planning. International organisations often have a language policy and global corporations frequently standardise on one form of communication, and in many cases these plans require the use of English. But the enormous growth of international English is in no sense the result of an international conspiracy to impose the language, despite the attempts of some commentators to see devious British or American plots at work (cf. Ager, 1999: 98-115). It is rather the result of a whole range of factors: historical in the world-wide presence of the British Empire, commercial in the successive economic dominance of Britain and then the USA, political and military in the wars of the twentieth century and their effect on the losers. Currently, the motivation that individuals and communities demonstrate is economic and pragmatic. It is also not all integrative: no international users seem to wish to become more like the British, the Americans or the Australians. If anything, increasing use of the language is accompanied by a rejection of the cultural norms of the main English-speaking nations.

Individuals and Language Acquisition

Five in-depth interviews were conducted in early 1999 in order to clarify the nature of instrumental motivation for foreign language acquisition. The five were A, a British male aged 32 learning Japanese in the Japanese electronics industry; B, an Indian male now retired from employment in a public utility in the UK; C, a female University lecturer aged 60 who had fled Nazi Germany during the 1939-45 war and now lived in the UK; D, an Italian male aged 58 who had migrated to Australia in 1987; and E, an Algerian female aged 35 who, while remaining employed in Algeria, was following doctoral studies in English.

Individual A

Aged 32 at the time of interview, A had achieved rapid success during three years since being appointed in a managerial capacity in a Japanese electronics firm located in the UK. As part of his management training period he was required to spend two years in Japan working in different placements within the organisation, ending with one year in domestic sales where Japanese would be the only language used. He was anticipating both financial advantage as a result of the two-year placement and career advancement thereafter. Motivation for learning Japanese seemed clearly instrumental: it would have direct career consequences. Command of Japanese in the UK offices of the company, while helpful, was not essential despite constant contact by phone, fax and email between the UK and Japan to fill orders and file reports on UK client contacts. At more senior levels the job requirement would be to consult with Japanese manufacturers in order to vary specific products, negotiate adaptations to future products made in Japan and discuss policy matters with Japan. These remained instrumental motives.

In terms of integration, however, A had become 'fascinated by the Japanese', had sought placement in Japan with wife and child and was actively seeking occasions to get first-hand contact with various aspects of the culture and life-style. A had soon learned to accept non-Western Japanese cuisine and eating habits ('dancing sushi') and to do so less as an adventure and more as a normal way of life. The surface habits of a 'salaryman's' life in Japan became less and less foreign: Japanese drinking habits, liking for spa bathing, acceptance of the norms of Japanese social interaction (bowing, the exchange of business cards), living under pressure for space, had become second nature. A was looking forward particularly to working for his second year in Japanese exclusively.

Many aspects of Japanese culture remained unacceptable, however: condemnatory attitudes towards foreigners, self-centred beliefs in the supremacy of Japanese language and culture, acceptance of a high level of corruption in business and political life. There were particular causes of concern: the lack of individualism, the need to consult widely before taking any action, the difficulty of being accepted, the lack of comprehension on the part of others in the office of any expression of concern for wife and child. Overall, A's attitude remained instrumental, albeit with a degree of surface integration. 'If I win the sweepstake, I'm on the first plane out of here'. 'I spend my day being laughed at by work colleagues because I don't understand the finer points of etiquette; this is neither pleasant nor is it likely to change'.

Individual B

An Indian male, B had retired from employment in a public utility in the UK in 1994. He had worked in a research laboratory where the normal language was English. He had retained close contact with both his home environment and also numerous relatives living in different countries (USA, South Africa), and, since retirement, had spent lengthy periods in India. He had just returned from a three-month visit to his home environment when interviewed. His motivation on migrating to the UK had been economic: it had proved impossible to pursue a career with adequate rewards and at an appropriate level in India. The integrative motive was nonetheless strong, and B had good relations with English-speaking neighbours and the immediate environment, including fairly frequent attendance at neighbourhood events (parties, meals, clubs). His interests extended to non-Indian activities like local politics and sport. His main UK contacts however with the local Bangladeshi and Indian community were strong; he often acted as leader or representative at events important to the community and which brought it into direct contact, sometimes conflict, with the UK authorities. His son had attended an English school, married a non-Indian wife, had two children and the three generations intended to remain in the UK. Indeed, the son had on several occasions refused to take his small children to India on the grounds that Indian family conditions, food and shelter were not suitable for children. In this case, the original instrumental motivation had considerably changed. B was in the now common situation of many twentieth century migrants: by virtue of ease of travel, he was able to operate in two communities at once, to use two languages and to feel at home in both of them.

Individual C

C is a female University lecturer aged 60 who had fled Nazi Germany during the 1939-45 war with her parents in trying circumstances. Her mother and siblings had returned to Germany after 1945. She had married a Canadian national, had two sons and intended to continue living in the UK. Motivation for entering the UK at first had been simple survival, while the motive for remaining was a mixture of instrumental forces in that career opportunities became available in the UK and were then pursued, and integrative in that both the working and living environment were found agreeable. Career development had led to a senior position in education which required considerable negotiating and management skills. Her language behaviour was such that it was often difficult for interlocutors to detect any accent or linguistic habits which would indicate someone not of UK birth. C now felt it difficult if not impossible to contemplate returning to Germany despite having family connections there. Her personal assimilation reflected her desire to be regarded as a normal member of the host society.

Individual D

D is an Italian male aged 58 who had migrated to Australia in 1987, following earlier moves to the UK and to the Irish Republic. The motive for originally entering the UK was integrative, and D expressed strong views on the attractiveness of the English-speaking environment at that time. He had moved to Ireland with wife and family for different integrative reasons, however. He wished particularly to ensure that children were brought up in a Catholic environment. He also retained a very small number of specifically Italian habits, notably a liking for Campari, ice cream and pasta. The move to Australia was as a result of instrumental motivation: there were inadequate career opportunities in Ireland and a suitable opening occurred in Australia. Wife and family followed after a considerable period (two years) and wife's career openings had not followed a path as successful as that which she had hoped. Nonetheless, D's integrative motive towards Australia remained strong: the pair had taken Australian citizenship, and D had written reports and reviews strongly opposing policies aimed at maintaining ethnic and language identities separate from those of the majority community. The resultant language behaviour meant that only slight phonetic traces of non-English origin remained, while D's skill in language manipulation meant that such interests as solving cryptic crosswords were comparatively child's play.

Individual E

E is an Algerian female aged 35 who, while remaining employed in Algeria, was following doctoral studies in English at a UK University. E was a teacher of English in the Algerian system who had retained her post despite considerable difficulties. She was determined to complete research work which required understanding of the foreign language. E was specifically studying the concept of the 'discourse community', in her case an international group of medical scientists. In identifying methods of accessing such communities she had identified the acquisition of specific linguistic skills as fundamental. She saw no need for any other integrative aim in her sample of scientific workers, and clearly adopted the same view herself. The motive for language acquisition was for her, and for the group she was studying, specifically instrumental, although possession of this instrument would lead to inclusion in a specific community using English. She needed English only because current language policy in Algeria was now stressing the use of international English as a lingua franca for the scientific community. Indeed this motive influenced the mode of acquisition she adopted, the particular variety of English she aimed at and the channel in that the majority of the language samples involved were of written scientific discourse. The motive here is instrumental, but associated with this is the integrative desire to become part of a very specific discourse community using a particular form of the foreign language.

The varied experiences and motives of these five adults can be expected to differ from the motives which ensure success in foreign language learning during the period of formal education. Young (1995) examined the language-related motives which 14-year-old schoolchildren expressed in Britain and France. She undertook a massive comparative survey of over 500 school students and came to a number of conclusions about the differences and similarities between the two countries. The main factors affecting motivation for this age-group unsurprisingly included a number of external influences, including in particular the peer group, parents and teachers. Internal and psychological factors included those of instrumentality and integration, but she found that for many fourteen-year-olds it was difficult to make a clear distinction between these. The aim of achieving good examination results was often closely associated with liking for manifestations of the target culture, particularly so in the case of English for French children where an interest in pop music and American life-style was very evident. More important factors included the individual's own demonstrated success in language learning and prior achievement. Family background, including parental career patterns and experience or knowledge of career possibilities, was a major factor. French schoolchildren were in general more motivated for language learning than British ones, although this may have had much to do with the geographical situation of the two main centres studied: Birmingham and Mulhouse. The most successful children, she found, were in both countries those with parents aware of the external world. From this, one might deduce that instrumental motivation was of much higher importance than integrative, although there were many individual cases of successful learners with strongly integrative motivation.

Integration and Instrumentality as Motives for Language Planning and Policy

We have looked in this chapter at the differences and similarities between the language-related behaviour of communities defined in various non-political ways, and at that of some individuals. Although Gardner and Lambert came to the conclusion that integration with a target community was a different motive from instrumentality, later research questioned this separation and we have noted that in most of the cases we have examined there is no sharp difference to be found between them. Where instrumentality is a clear first motive for such actions as migration or language learning it is often accompanied, particularly as language behaviour develops, by a desire to gain closer acquaintance with a destination community. Similarly, the integrative motive automatically inspires individuals to improve the linguistic tools they use. Overall, the motive is perhaps to be found at a deeper level than the impulses of integration or instrumentality. There is a desire on the part of the individual or community to assess how far their own behaviour is appropriate to the circumstances they find themselves in, and what consequential action they should take. In some cases, the organism (individual or community) discovers a bad fit between the skills it possesses and the environment in which it operates or wishes to operate. Depending on the disparity, and on the effect of this disparity on the organism, the organism is motivated to improve existing skills, add a new communicative mechanism for use in some domains like commerce, or, in the case of the worst fit, to shift from one language to another. The motive seems in all these cases to be a search for a better match between organism and environment. One thing is clear: language behaviour is not random nor unplanned.

Chapter 7

Measuring Motivation in Language Planning and Language Policy

This chapter reviews the three components of motivation outlined in the Introduction and looks at ways of measuring these so that meaningful relationships between them might be made.

Language Attitudes

An attitude can simply be a state of mind, a 'disposition to react favourably or unfavourably to a class of objects' (Edwards, 1994: 97). The concept of attitude and of attitude change is of importance to some schools of social psychology (cf. Stahlberg and Frey, 1996), which also hold that the attitudes of individuals derive from their beliefs and, at a deeper level, from the sets of values that they hold. In the terms we used in the Introduction, attitudes hence depend on identity. Attitudes, lying near the 'socio-psychological surface' of individuals, are generally easier to discover than the sets of beliefs, in their turn supported by a scale of values, which underlie them. Values, the most fundamental level, are often indeed difficult to uncover, since they are unspoken assumptions, myths and taboos of which the holder is often unaware, and are shared to a greater or lesser extent within a society or community. For the most part they depend on the history and context of the relevant society, and are developed and adopted in the process of socialisation from parents, peers and social institutions such as the school. Beliefs, too, the second 'layer', are often not openly stated. It goes without saying that beliefs and values, together often called an ideology or world-view, are socially conditioned, subjective and in essence emotive: there is no such thing as an 'objective' value and even apparently fundamental ones such as the sanctity of human life or the importance of the family are clearly not accepted by all societies at all times. It is rarely easy for social scientists to measure directly which values and beliefs an individual holds. The process is usually indirect. Values and beliefs are indeed usually guessed at through measuring attitudes, either through simple observation of actual behaviour, of the actions undertaken by an individual, or through collecting and systematising statements of opinion, for example by administering a questionnaire and summarising it through such presentational methods as a five-point Likert scale (e.g. strongly disagree, disagree, no opinion, agree, agree strongly). The interpretation of Likert scores, and indeed of any evidence such as this, is by no means obvious and is rarely unbiased. Nonetheless, major studies of the values held by the population of European countries, based on surveys conducted in 1981 and 1990, have been published (Harding and Phillips, 1986; Ashford and Timms, 1992), and opinion measurement is a standard technique in sociological analysis and in market research.

Clearly, values are closely associated with identity. What makes an individual's or a community's personality or identity different from that of others often only becomes clear when different sets of values and the consequential attitudes are confronted. When two religious beliefs come into conflict the battle often rages around attitudes, while the real problem lies more in the identity conflict. Muslim believers trying to retain their identity and values in Western societies often find that when conflict arises over, for example, Pakistani cultural attitudes towards marriage or criminal punishment, the conflict very quickly escalates to one of Islamic and Western identity. But attitudes can change, as they do between migrant generations, whereas attempts to change the deeper values and particularly identity are much more difficult.

At the level of an attitude, three types of component are distinguished in the social psychological literature as knowledge, emotion and (potential) action, otherwise called the cognitive, affective and conative (or behavioural) components (Fasold, 1984: 147-79; Harding et al., 1986: 1-5; Baker, 1992; Edwards 1994: 97-102; Stahlberg and Frey, 1996: 206-9). The cognitive aspect is formed by the individual's thoughts and knowledge about a 'class of objects': in our case language behaviour and language use. The affective component is made up of the attraction or rejection an individual feels towards what he or she knows about. The conative element, the 'reaction' of Edward's definition, is the extent to which an individual is disposed to take some form of action in relation to the object.

The cognitive aspect: Knowledge about language

Where language is the object of knowledge, one knows both the language code and the use of the code. Knowledge can either be of language structure, divorced from its users, or of language in use, including all environmental considerations involved in language-as-instrument, the interactive and social aspects of using a language. The sort of knowledge most people have in relation to the structure of a language concerns its grammar or lexis, and awareness of such knowledge seems to come about mainly when comparison is made: with another language, or with an earlier state of the same language. As people compare the characteristics of today's grammatical forms with those of the past or with those of other languages, they become conscious of their advantages or disadvantages. Often, too, such knowledge tends to be comparative in an emotional sense - people like this or that feature of the code, consider this grammatical feature to be better or worse than another. Knowledge is of the structure, history and comparative advantages of a language.

Knowledge of language in use concerns the relationship between language and the social culture of its users, implying awareness of the differences between language varieties and the range of settings in which each would be appropriate. Knowledge of the range of language varieties and their relationship with particular settings or domains; and knowledge of the relationship between language and society seem to recur in the literature on sociolinguistics or the sociology of language as significant elements in the social awareness of language, and hence in the attitude language users adopt towards their own or other languages (Chambers, 1995). Such knowledge posits either a strong connection between language and society or a weak one.

In the strong version of the deterministic belief that a particular language in some way uniquely represents a particular society, it is held that a language like French represents France and is a component in French identity, in ways which are similar to those markers of French identity like the flag, the Republican concept or the basic Republican values. An attack on the language would thus be an attack on France, and preservation of the language from external invasion is seen as preservation of French culture and way of life. Knowledge of the variety-domain relationship requires a more sophisticated understanding and experience of a particular society and of what is meant by appropriate behaviour. The deterministic belief here is that a specific language variety is restricted in use to a specific domain, so that for example only aristocrats can use aristocratic language, that there is a specific religious variety which must be used in religious texts, or that serious topics like the meaning of life can only be discussed in 'academic' or 'philosophical' terminology.

A major set of attitudes which seem to be based primarily on knowledge about language is that normally called purism. Thomas (1991: 76-81) identified five types of purism, which he called archaising ('reverence for the language of the past'), ethnographic ('the notion that rural dialects are somehow purer than city speech'), elitist ('a negative, proscriptive attitude to substandard and regional usage'), reformist ('adapting the language for its role as a medium of communication in a modern society'), and xenophobic ('the eradication or replacement of foreign elements'). Purism as such is not necessarily always simply a manifestation of knowledge or lack of it. Indeed, it is axiomatic that purists prefer one type of language to another, prefer a word like 'handbook' to 'manual', or 'give' to 'donate'. But the degree of knowledge affects the strength of the attitude: the more people know about language and languages and particularly about the relationship between language and language users, the less likely it is that their language attitudes will reflect the simpler, deterministic forms of purism, and the more likely that they will realise that purist attitudes reflect (socially conditioned and emotional) knowledge about language in use rather than (scientifically neutral) knowledge about a language system. Nonetheless, cognitive knowledge of and about language and languages or language varieties seems to be closely associated with a categorisation into superior and inferior ones.

The two dimensions of cognitive knowledge suggested by Ryan and Giles (1982) were limited to the second type of cognitive knowledge about language, the question of language varieties and their use. They asked whether people know about the existence of a standard variety and of non-standard ones, together with the dynamism or vitality of the variety, in terms of the range of functions it fulfils in society. The more domains in which a language or language variety can be used, the more dynamic it is and the more vitality it possesses. As with knowledge of the code and knowledge of language-as-instrument, knowledge of the vitality of a variety or language is associated with evaluation of that knowledge.

It is impossible to measure accurately what people 'know' about language code and about language in use. Two measurement scales which could help us evaluate the cognitive component of some of the attitudes we have met in Chapters 1 to 6 are a scale of 'excellence', essentially reflecting attitudes towards knowledge about the characteristics of language code; and a vitality scale, measuring (attitudes towards) knowledge about how language is used and the domains in which (a particular type of) language is used. These do not measure exactly what is known, but do enable us to measure what people think they know: in effect, the subjective feelings that people express about what they know.

The scale of excellence

Scientific knowledge about language systems is value-free by definition. Attitudes are by definition not value-free, and there is little or no scientific basis for the knowledge people express about the characteristics of language codes. Although conferences have been held to compare French with other languages in the hope that specific characteristics such as grammatical systems, word-formation or word order would provide scientific evidence to show how excellent French was as a means of communication, very little can be concluded apart from the undeniable existence of such differences. The fact that beauty is in the eye of the beholder has been shown time and again, yet as we have seen politicians and even linguists continue to repeat mantras about the supposed special and unique qualities of German, Hindi or English. The excellence of a language, its superiority or inferiority as a means of communication, simply cannot be objectively measured; what can be measured is the extent to which subjects think particular aspects of a language are good or bad, or are better or worse than those of competing means of communication. Survey respondents can be asked whether the grammatical system of a language seems to them to be good or bad, efficient or inefficient, for example. The excellence of a whole range of the supposed attributes of a particular language can be and have been proposed for such 'measurement': its aesthetics, literary worth, efficiency, richness, precision, clarity. Such measurements can then be displayed on an excellence scale, using semantic opposites as the measurement technique. The lack of objectivity of these scales is obvious, although there are recorded instances of many, such as those supposedly showing where the language is situated on such scales as beautiful/ ugly, pleasant/ unpleasant, agreeable/ disagreeable, musical/ guttural, mellifluous/ raucous. Its literary value is supposedly given by whether there exists a canon of written works; its efficiency by whether it conveys meaning clearly. The richness or precision of a language recurs in such scales, although the meaning of the terms is dubious: for some, a rich language is one with a large number of near synonyms, enabling expression of a full range of meanings; for others, a rich language conveys precise meanings without ambiguity and hence contains few synonyms. Even though richness and precision thus apparently conflict, 'knowledge' about language can happily maintain that it is both rich and precise at the same time. The clarity of a language is supposedly shown by its logical structure and by characteristics of its grammar. The 'clearest' languages are thus supposedly those that follow the 'logical' SVO order of Subject, Verb, Object (or complement). Other characteristics are supposed to render one language the most apt for the expression of the finest shades of the deepest human emotions. There are probably many other such scales on which languages have been evaluated as better or worse, despite the fact that few professional linguists would agree that they do other than represent the subjective views of users. It is practically impossible to agree that any such scales have an objective, scientific basis: the excellence scale is closely associated with the emotive one of liking or disliking.

The vitality scale

The concept of ethno-linguistic vitality was developed to account for 'that which makes a group likely to behave as a distinctive and collective entity in intergroup situations' (quoted in Allard and Landry, 1992: 172). Group members' perception of the standing of the group on a number of factors such as its demographic, economic, social and cultural capital including the use of its language is a measure of its subjective ethno-linguistic vitality (SEV). The SEV scale thus measures, in effect, the beliefs group members hold about the relationship between language and the social domains in which it is or should be used, and hence contributes to understanding their motives and attitude for reinforcing or changing these. The SEV scale seems not to be a simple matter of measuring whether subjects know about the number of domains in which a language or language variety is used, and whether such domains are prestigious. The nature of the domains - public, private or intermediate - is important. There is a clear distinction of prestige between the private domain of language use and the public or social ones. Using a language in the home, among family, kinship groups or even within the neighbourhood is quite different from using the same variety in government, administration or education, the public domains which are clearly the most prestigious. Using a language variety in religion, in commerce, at work or even in direct contacts between state and citizen such as welfare or the Post Office seems however to imply a middle set of domains, both more prestigious than the private family settings but less so than the official settings of the top level administration. Interestingly, legal settings generally seem to fall into the middle level. Interestingly also, the exact location of a particular domain on the prestige scale varies from society to society. In some countries all bureaucrats, whatever their formal branch of the administration, attempt to communicate with citizens by using only formal language of the highest rigidity. In others, such direct contact does not seem to imply formality, and civil servants are content to be less condescending.

The SEV sale can be broadened to a more generally applicable attitudinal vitality scale, which we shall use here. This scale is not limited to measuring the likelihood that an ethnic group may maintain or lose a language, but becomes a measure simply of the 'knowledge' users have about whether a language or language variety is used in few or many domains of use. A language variety used in domains situated at all three levels is more dynamic than one used in only one or even in two. Its vitality score is greater. The generally accepted wisdom is that varieties used in public domains are more vital, and are hence more likely to persist than those used in the home. But there are counter examples of varieties which have maintained their vitality even though they are little used in public domains, are spoken and have no written form, and are used mainly by lower social categories. Had this not been the case, non-official languages like Catalan and Welsh, all working-class dialects and all regional geographically determined dialects like Geordie or Brum in the UK would have disappeared long ago.

Politicians and language activists alike believe that a prestigious language variety used only in official domains seems to have more and better chances of survival than one used in private ones. The fate of official languages in Africa, particularly French, could depend on this. The history of Welsh language activism is the struggle to ensure the official use of Welsh. But there are other factors involved than use in this one level of domains: French acts as a scientific and technical window on the world and as a lingua franca with other countries for the elite and for specialised uses such as diplomacy. Such factors may be of more value to the future of French than official use in administration.

The affective aspect: Feelings about language

Feelings in matters of language are often extreme: one either likes the language or language variety or one does not. Such positive and negative attitudes may however be expressed on a number of evaluative scales of which the simple oppositional scale of attraction, liking or disliking, is the principal. All too easily, the emotive component of language attitudes is transferred towards those who speak the language, so people are often prepared to regard all speakers of a particular variety as attractive, or all communities using a despised or disliked dialect as themselves worthy of scorn or dislike. The prize examples in the UK are Cockney and the Birmingham dialect, regarded as unattractive by most of the rest of the UK, while the West Country accent is quaintly attractive. It is often difficult to tell whether those who condemn language varieties are condemning 'bad' language or 'bad' people, or whether they see any difference. It is here that one of the main language motivations lies: the desire to mark the frontiers between those to whom one belongs, and those who are the other. Chapters 1 to 6 are full of examples of attitudes based on such feelings of kinship and belonging The desire for integration seems to be much the same whether it is labelled kinship at family level, community feeling at neighbourhood or group level, or nationalism at the level of larger units.

Attractiveness scale

A scale representing a direct form of approval or rejection, related to a particular linguistic form, can be used to summarise the attractiveness of that language or variety to the group or individual concerned. Such a scale is different from those of superiority/inferiority and ethno-linguistic vitality, which are based on knowledge. The attractiveness scale summarises feelings without inquiring into the basis for them. For many social psychologists and sociolinguists the attractiveness scale is central to defining an individual's or community's attitude towards a particular language, and the cognitive and conative scales have considerably less importance.

The conative aspect: What should be done

Whatever the degree of knowledge or feelings, the attitude of an individual or group also reflects some readiness to take action. Readiness to act can be measured on a scale ranging from the extremes of prescriptivism at one end to laxism at the other. People vary in their support for action on their own use of language and on the extent to which they will support action by a credible authority. Prescriptivism leads to attempts to oblige other people to use or learn the preferred language or language variety, and has both positive and negative connotations: it is a standard and indeed necessary aspect of education, but is often regarded as obtrusive when it applies to the language behaviour of adults or is imposed by legal means. Support for intervention affects all three types of language planning or policy generally recognised: corpus, status and acquisition planning.

Readiness to act is not the same thing as a motive for action. This component of attitude simply measures the general feeling that something should be done, as part of the attitude individuals or groups have towards a language or towards language behaviour as we have defined it. Motives such as the defence of an identity or correcting social inequality might relate to the totality of the attitudinal structure of an individual or community, including readiness to act, but a motive implies not merely readiness to act but action itself: a goal, a strategy for achieving this and an anticipated outcome. We shall consider this point further below.

Action scale

Preparedness to act oneself is not the same thing as support for action by others, either. This truism is as relevant in matters of language as in most others. While many individual French people are apparently prepared to support intervention by governmental authorities it is clear by simple inspection of street signs, shop fronts or advertisements in any French town that individuals themselves are simply not taking the sort of action against borrowings from English that is specified in the Toubon Law or in the many exhortations that have followed it. The language activist who inspires others to act on language matters is a recognisable individual who often makes his or her views on language known at the same time as views on a variety of related matters. It is no coincidence that an active language policy is often accompanied by an active foreign policy or by an intensification of domestic welfare policies. From this point of view, a pure language activist, dissociating him or herself from the social, political or economic situation of the relevant community to make pronouncements on language alone, is rare indeed. Language policy, as has been noted several times, is not divorced from other types of social policy. Language attitudes may hence be closely connected to those that people show towards a number of social phenomena, and language activists are often active in other fields as well. For our purposes, a conative or action scale simply allocates a score to the expressed desire to take action in any of the areas of language planning we have mentioned: status, corpus or acquisition. In summary, Figure 7.1 gives our attitudinal scales.

COGNITIVE	EXCELLENCE SCALE
Knowledge of the history, structure and comparative advantages of a language, and value judgments of e.g. aesthetic, literary or communicative value, of richness, precision or clarity.	Inferior Superior
Knowledge of relationship between language and society. Associated with archaising, ethnographic, reformist and xenophobic purism.	Weak Strong

VITALITY SCALE

	low prestige.	high prestige.
Number and level of domains in which language or variety is used. Judgments depend on awareness of varieties dependent on time, geography, social structure, function, domain, channel. Associated with elitist purism.	Variety used in few domains of low prestige	Variety used in many domains of high prestige

AFFECTIVE	ATTRACTIVENESS SCALE
Feelings towards language or language variety.	Dislike Like

CONATIVE	ACTION SCALE
Desire for oneself to act, or support for intervention on status, corpus, acquisition or a mixture of these.	Lax Prescriptive

Figure 7.1 Attitudinal Scales

Attitudinal structure

The scales proposed by Edwards (1994) for measuring language attitudes were based on three of these scales: superiority-inferiority; attractive-unattractive; and dynamic-static (our vitality). These delimit what Hudson called an individual's   'multi-dimensional socio-linguistic space' (Hudson, 1980: 195). In conformity with the accepted definition of attitude we propose to add our conative/action scale to these to form a multidimensional space within which we could locate the attitudinal structure of an individual, or that of a group, or even that of a nation-state, towards a particular language or language variety. In order to simplify the presentation of this space and of language attitudes, which in our case are derived from the case studies of Chapters 1 to 6, we propose to reduce the complex scoring systems resulting from the many opinion surveys that have been undertaken, the speeches and statements of politicians, the claims and demands of activists, to a simple set of three values: 1 for a weak response, 2 for an intermediate or indeterminate response and 3 for the higher level. We can then list the scores of the participants in a particular situation in relation to the scales, to give us a measure of attitude and a presentation of the relevant attitudinal space or structure. Figure 7.2 gives the proposed arrangement. Any overall score - the sum of the measures in all the scales - is likely to be meaningless when we come to discuss motives, as it can be made up of very differing scores under each component. Listing the set of scores and their individual values might enable us to clarify and compare the attitudes involved.

	Excellence	Vitality	Attractiveness	Action
High scores:	3	3	3	3

A score of 3 under each scale means that the subject's attitude implies that they value a language highly and are prepared to act in relation to it.

Low scores:	1	1	1	1

A score of 1 under each scale could indicate an attitude of indifference to the fate of the language and possibly to its eventual disappearance.

Figure 7.2 Attitudinal structure

Motives and the Identity Sequence

We have already noted that the type of motives with which we are dealing are closely associated with the values and beliefs underlying attitudes. In the Introduction we proposed a set of motives to include Identity, Ideology, Image, Insecurity, Inequality, Integration and Instrumentality. Are such motives related to attitudinal structure at the surface level? We have suspected that specific attitudes and attitudinal structures are not necessarily predetermined by values or by identity. How far can the motives and attitudes of individuals, communities and states in relation to language behaviour be represented in the same overall picture? At this point we must make one major assumption: that, in relation to the policies they implement, states and communities can be treated as if they were one, unified, organism. Such an authoritarian view is true insofar as the policy or planning itself is unified; clearly within any one state or community there will be other, often opposing views and, with changes of government, other policies. For our purposes, and for measuring attitudes and motives, we must assume an organic unity within the entities with which we are concerned. The seven motives we have explored in this book do seem to be much the same, whether that organism be an individual, a community or a state. Is there a relationship between the motives?

Let us assume that an organism has been newly created. Its first task is the construction of its self, its own identity and personality. Around this it will construct its values and beliefs. As it progresses through its existence it will come into contact with others, and interaction with people, communities, ideas and circumstances will cause such values and beliefs to give birth to other motives. We theorise that, in what might be called an identity sequence, the organism constructs its own identity, modifies it against the reality of its social environment, and then defends the structure it has created. It is the different stages of this process that we have so far called motives. The organism <u>constructs an identity</u> for itself (a self, a personality), which in language terms is then realised through its own language behaviour in a choice of language or language variety. The self-identity and social identity is constructed in response to the organism's own values and beliefs. These have been developed through the organism's past experience, its socialisation, education, geographical position, tradition and history. The identity is an ideal, constructed to fit the organism's initial perception of itself and then of its environment. There need be nothing intrinsically different between the identity constructed by the individual for himself or herself, that constructed by a human community, or indeed that developed over time by a politically independent state. The key seems to be that the organism's identity is both personal, in the sense that the psyche or inner characteristics are important, and social, in the sense that the socialisation process has necessarily had major consequences in adapting and forming this initial identity. It is important that identity reflects that which marks the individual or group as different from others. The resultant language behaviour is based on a sense of status and difference, and most planning and policy motives seem to be directed to gaining social prestige for the language or language variety, and hence for the organism using it. It is this totality of the world view held by the organism of itself and its situation that is reflected in the ideology which informs it. Although this term is often restricted to mean simply a party political ideology, our meaning here is more fundamental, implying a world view applying to any political situation the organism finds itself in.

The organism then aims to foster or construct an image of this identity in other organisms and in the outside environment. This image, also intended to be an ideal, is designed to represent the identity as seen by others; inevitably, it will be favourable to the identity. One might object that the organism has no control over the image of itself others might develop, but this, although strictly true, would be naive. In the contemporary world of spin doctors, advertising and PR, considerable effort is expended on image creation and there is considerable proof that manipulation of the views that others have pays off. Again, the processes involved are no different as between the individual, the community or the state. The resultant language policy and planning can be located in a number of fields: status policy and confirmation of self and social identity, but also acquisition policy in encouraging the use of state languages abroad.

The organism's self and social identity and its own language behaviour are then again evaluated against the environment in which it exists, with possible action in mind. For states and countries, this key stage is a matter of assessing the nature of language use in society and seeing what might need changing. For individuals, it might mean seeing whether the life-time goals could be achieved with the linguistic tools available to the individual. For some communities, it is possibly a matter of despair as they acknowledge the discriminatory environment in which they live, and the low likelihood of them being able to maintain their own language or style of discourse. Insecurity can be deadly. It can also have the directly opposite result, of inspiring the organism to a major defence of identity. The image, too, is measured against the reality of international acceptance of what the state stands for, or against what others think the individual might achieve. This conscious or unconscious comparative evaluation of own and other languages, of positive and negative aspects of the environment, leads in some cases to a motive for maintaining and defending both identity and image. The key point is that the construction of an identity seems to be quite different from the decision to maintain or defend it. It may be that differences arise at this stage as between individuals, communities and states, even though these relate to the speed of action rather than to its nature. While individuals can and do take rapid action on language, communities and states necessarily take more time to lose a language, to adopt another for certain purposes, or to win the battle for domination. Corpus policy seems to be a popular method for implementing such defensive policy motives, as we have seen in the case of French official neologisms.

The stage of evaluation with possible action can provoke other motives, too. The examples seem to point to the existence of four, which for sake of simplicity we shall refer to as inequality, integration, adjustment and despair. If the organism's assessment of its own identity and of the relationship between this and its environment is satisfactory it will maintain and defend both identity and image, as we have seen. But two motives for action can be detected once inequality is discovered as between the languages of the organism and others. One is to   correct any unequal situation discovered for the organism's language, and sometimes for languages which are not the organism's own. In all too many cases the motive is not one of correcting inequality but the opposite: to ensure that the situation of the organism's own language gains from inequality. The motive is to maintain or even foster inequality. In both cases of inequality, the policy actions at state level are often formal in the sense of being legal instruments: a Constitution, an international Charter, a new regional organisation and set of responsibilities.

Next, the motive of a wish to get closer to a community perceived as desirable lies behind many attempts by individuals to learn a new, additional language, and sometimes, of whole communities or group to be absorbed into another group. The integrative motive affects both individuals and communities. It is particularly strong for individuals and for communities in a weak situation, and while personal language use can sometimes change to show how close a particular individual wishes to be to groups like other women, other social categories, club members or the young, whole groups of immigrants sometimes see considerable advantage for themselves in adopting a new language .

The intent of adjusting the organism's own linguistic capacity or ability is particularly strong for individuals wishing to acquire a new language or to add to their repertoire for commercial or cultural reasons or for social advancement.   There is another sense in which such instrumentality affects communities and states. As they assess their own situation vis-à-vis their environment, they sometimes need to make changes in order to improve their own adaptation: they reform their own language, add communicative procedures, develop new ways of increasing their word-stock. Corpus policy may be important here for communities, while for individuals the result of the instrumental motive is mainly a matter of acquisition policy.

The final motive, or stage in the identity sequence, of despair, results in language shift or language loss. Some communities discover that their situation is forlorn, or, more frequently, that their life-chances will be greatly improved if they adopt a new language. While in some cases they may retain their previous form of communication, in others it simply disappears. To a certain extent, this motive is instrumental in nature, but it should perhaps receive a different name. Despair is not a pleasant word for any form of action, but at its most extreme seems to be a fair description of what lies behind language loss.

Stage 1
The organism creates personal and social identity through values and beliefs deriving from heredity, environment and socialisation, developing its ideology. At this stage social psychology clarifies understanding of social identity construction.
Stage 2
The organism creates and fosters an image of this identity.
Stage 3
The organism evaluates identity and image against the environment. At this stage, motivational theories of goal-setting, measuring self-worth, self-efficacy and processing past success are significant to explanation. Notions of insecurity are important.
Stage 4
The selection of   motives for action depends on the outcome of stage 3. Significant motives are: the maintenance of identity; defence of this identity against attack; the maintenance of favourable social and other inequality; correction of inequality; integrative moves to associate with a desired community; instrumental moves to improve, adjust or reform linguistic instruments. If the evaluation is so negative that no other outcome seems possible, the despair might lead to language loss or shift.
Figure 7.3. The identity sequence

If this picture of a motivation being dependent on an identity sequence is accepted, we still need to account for the development of identity in the first place, and the relationship of attitudes and attitudinal structure to the sequence we have outlined. Four motivational functions of attitude are generally recognised in social psychology (Stahlberg and Frey, 1996: 215-7): ego-defensive, value-expressive, instrumental and organisational. We have already noted in the Introduction that these are in effect four different theories of motivation which can be grouped into intrinsic (ego-defensive, instrumental) and extrinsic theories. The case studies seem to show that they do not altogether account for the motives people and communities have. Some theories are more useful for understanding particular situations than others. In this respect, the division of language issues into questions of rights, resources and problems is also relevant. The ego-defensive function, for example, is a useful way of protecting oneself from doubts about the value of one's own group, by projecting negative feelings towards other groups. Managing doubts about the reality of the identity motive can be done by condemning the identity of other groups. Language problems of various types may thus be associated with this function. Similarly, expressing one's own values in relation to human rights, for example, reflects well the motive for correcting inequity. This second motivational function, the expression of deeply held values and beliefs, associates well with the rights agenda. The third function is instrumental, aimed at reaching desired goals or at satisfying needs. Instrumental behaviour such as the acquisition of a new language or improvement to one's existing skills, or the language shift of despised communities, seems to reflect such a motivational function , and is particularly relevant to the notion that language is a resource. The final motivational function is associated with the ways in which human beings systematise the information they receive from their environment. Organising the chaos of life and processing the flood of information every human being is faced with by ensuring it follows one's underlying attitude is more and more necessary in an increasingly complex world. This function is often associated with systematising information in the sense of rejecting inconvenient facts, seeking, retaining and processing information which supports one's attitudes and therefore makes the world comprehensible, rather than with changing these attitudes in relation to an increased or better flow of information.

We can measure the strength of attitudes reasonably well in numerical terms. In the case of the identity sequence, measurement is categorisation: we measure the nature, rather than the strength, of the motive. We can then see if, and how, attitudes correlate to steps in the identity sequence, look at attitudes to both L1 and L2, and develop a chart like Figure 7.4.

Identity sequence	Attitudinal structure							
	Exc'ence		Vitality		Attract		Action	
	L1	L2	L1	L2	L1	L2	L1	L2
Identity (personal)								
Identity (social)								
Ideology								
Image								
Insecurity								
Maintain identity								
Defend identity								
Maintain inequality								
Correct inequality								
Integrate								
Improve instrument								
Despair								

Figure 7.4 Motives and attitudinal structures

It might be thought that identity structures would necessarily predict attitudes, and that the intention to achieve specified goals of planning would then follow logically, too, so that we could plot particular policies or plans and link them to specific lines of our chart. But 'social psychological research has consistently found that attitudes do not have a strong impact on people's behaviour' (Terry et al, 1999: 225). The theory of reasoned action, or planned behaviour, described by Terry accounts for actual behaviour by prioritising the conative, intentional component of attitude rather than the cognitive or even that preferred by most analysts, the affective. According to this social psychological theory, motivation for action originates with the creation of social identity. Actual behaviour in any particular situation can then best be predicted from a person's intention or willingness to actually perform it. The knowledge and affectivity elements of attitude (our excellence and vitality scales) may not relate to particular points in the identity sequence, nor to the conative element (our action scale) which is affected by the subject's subjective norm created by the environment in which they find themselves. Although an individual, community or state may find a particular policy or behaviour appropriate to their identity construct, and their attitude towards it is positive (they have high scores on our three excellence, vitality and affectivity scales), they will be likely to carry it out if, and only if, the others who are important to them think they should perform that behaviour. Even for the individual, then, there is a close relationship between identity and action, but the individual's set of attitudes do not necessarily predict action. The motives and stages we have identified show the social nature, and the crucial importance, of the evaluative stage of identity creation, and the extent to which intended behaviour relies on constant checking by the organism of its relationship with its environment. 'Dynamic identity testing' might be one way of describing what seems to be the key element of motivation in language planning and language policy-making. But the goals language planners and policy-makers will pursue, and the strategies they may adopt to achieve them, can also not be simply predicted from a motive and a set of attitudes.

The Goals of Planned Language Behaviour

In the Introduction, looking at a goal-theory approach to explore motivation, we pointed out that what are often called the ends or goals of language planning can be thought of in three ways: as a long-term ideal, as a more immediate and realisable objective, or as an even more precise short-term target. Kaplan and Baldauf (1997) listed these and made it clear that the goals of individuals are often not the same as those of communities or of states. We shall further examine the differences and the range of goals in the following two chapters. At this point it is important to clarify any links between goals, attitudes and motives, and to look again at the differences that might exist between the three levels of goal.

To take the case of French regional languages, consider the following extract from French Prime Minister Lionel Jospin's inaugural speech as his new government took office in June 1997 (author's translation). The apparent motive is to maintain national identity:

> In Corsica, as everywhere else on the national territory, the Government will ensure the respect for the laws of the Republic which the population wishes and without which nothing is possible. In parallel, it will make sure that national solidarity

operates in order to catch up the delay in development which status as an island has led to. The Government will encourage the affirmation of Corsican cultural identity and the teaching of its language.

The specific policy the government proposed was to encourage the teaching of the Corsican language. This policy has a specific, measurable target: a greater knowledge of Corsican. Jospin has a more long-term aim, which we might regard as the objective: to encourage the affirmation of the cultural identity of the Corsican community. But this conflicts directly with what we might have thought Jospin's long-term ideals to be: the integrated, tightly centralised national identity of France. Jospin thus helpfully provides, in this short paragraph, a neat exemplification of our distinctions between levels of goal as well as a clarification of his purpose, as well as a revelation of the difficulties 'national solidarity' and 'respect for the laws of the Republic' face when the policy aim is to modify national solidarity and change policy in view of pressure, as we shall see below. On the face of it, goal theory explains policy motivation and its difficulties.

Why is there a conflict between the levels of goal? What is the relationship between policy, goal and the attitudes of the proposer? Jospin's attitude here reflects his knowledge of the Corsican situation, his emotive support for Corsican cultural identity and language, and his intention to act in encouragement of these. From his other speeches, his declared philosophy and his practice as a politician we can glean a rather different set of attitudes, developed through his upbringing, his education and his political experiences.Views on the nature of the French Republic and the meaning of the French Revolution have developed a set of ideas about national identity and the importance to France of maintaining it. But Jospin, who on the face of it should have followed these attitudes and insisted on maintaining the identity of France, refusing to allow regionalism any influence, took action in support of regionalism at a particular time and in a particular set of circumstances. The Socialist Party had just won an unexpected victory in the legislative elections and it was essential for Jospin to underline the differences between his policy and that of the preceding government. Secondly the official representative of France's government on the island, Prefect Claude Evin had been murdered shortly before, presumably by those fighting for the independence of the island. Jospin's policy depended on events, not on attitudes, and reflects a process of dynamic identity construction. Indeed, the strength and continuing force of the battle between traditional views on the sanctity of the Republic and its territory, and the necessity to understand the reality of regionalism on the other, lay behind the resignation of the Interior Minister in Jospin's government in August 2000.   Chevènement, the minister in question and head of the traditionalist Mouvement des Citoyens, resigned precisely because he could not accept Jospin's plan to give way to regionalism. Figure 7.6 traces the relationship between policy, goal, attitude and motive.

We propose therefore that to understand motivation we must look at motives based on dynamic identity construction, at attitudes which relate to but are not predetermined by these, but also at goals which again do not necessarily derive from either of these and may indeed conflict with them.   The next two chapters will pursue this idea, and we shall need to look not merely at the relationship between attitudes and the creation of identity, but include in our picture of motivation the goals involved. Figure 7.5 relates the three in a chart we shall use from this point.

Representing motivation									
Identity sequence	Attitudinal structure								Goals: Ideal, Objective, Target
	Exc'ence		Vitality		Attract		Action		
	L1	L2	L1	L2	L1	L2	L1	L2	
Identity (personal)									
Identity (social)									
Ideology									
Image									
Insecurity									
Maintain identity									
Defend identity									
Maintain inequality									
Correct inequality									
Integrate									
Improve instrument									
Despair									

Figure 7.5 Identities, attitudinal structures and goals

Motivation

	Policy
	teach Corsican
	Goals
the immediate target	knowledge of Corsican
longer-term objective	affirm Corsican cultural identity
long-term ideal	implement Jospin's political philosophy (nb possible conflicts with target and objective)
	Attitude
knowledge	Government knows that economic and cultural development has been 'delayed', and hence that Corsican may be excellent but has low vitality. Its traditional knowledge includes high excellence and vitality scores for French, representing French Republican values and history of the integrated Republic.
emotion	It feels a) that it should support French unity, but also b) that it should support regional aspirations; hence that Corsican is attractive.
action	It is ready to act, but in relation to circumstances rather than to knowledge or emotion, or to what it says is its underlying motive.
	Motive
	Apparently, maintain the identity of France. Actually, correct inequality?

Table 7.6 Motivation consists of goals/strategies, attitudes, and the identity sequence.

Chapter 8

The Language Behaviour of Individuals and Communities

Individuals

Language planning: Goals

As we have seen, much of the language planning behaviour of individuals is concerned with their approach to their own use of language, to language-as-instrument. The planning individuals adopt when considering language-as-object, whether their own or that of others, will be considered later in this Chapter together with the planning communities carry out, and at a point when we consider more formal planning arrangements. As we have seen also, goals at all three levels go a long way towards explaining the behaviour of individuals. We now need to put together the motives, attitudes and goals individuals demonstrate, in the light of the planning decisions they employ to achieve desired outcomes. There are only some goals, some specific targets or objectives, that individuals can follow in relation to their motives and attitudes.

One choice is to take no specific action on language, not from ignorance but in full awareness that this is as much a choice as any specific action.

At one extreme, individuals can insist on retaining their own language or language variety. They may be aware that they need to ensure that their command of L1 is as good as it can be, so the strategy is to improve the linguistic instrument or instruments available, gaining a full and complete knowledge of a language, usually one's L1. This is a matter of gaining a better knowledge of the code; improving the four skills of listening, reading, writing, speaking; or improving instrumental skills such as spelling and hence one's communicative ability; or improving one's use of the language in pursuance of a goal such as advancing one's career or gaining acceptance by a particular group. The strategy may include that of changing one's own level of ability in the use of a particular language or language variety with which one was already familiar. On the other hand, the strategy can be a matter of insisting on using a language or variety in circumstances where it would not normally be used in that society. The coherence of the individual's own identity structure may require that a Yorkshire accent be retained in London, or that formal English be used in the pub. Language choice of this type is not simple, however: while an individual may believe that they are retaining their original language variety, their accent, choice of vocabulary and many other aspects of their language variety may change through force of circumstances or even without them realising. It would be pointless for a British English speaker to continue talking of pavements in New York, and neither ginnels nor tea-mashing make much sense outside Yorkshire.

At the other extreme, individuals can adopt a new language or language variety in all circumstances. In effect, they have decided that a different language community has higher status and hence prestige than that they themselves possess, and that it is to their advantage that they abandon L1 in order to adopt L2. Such a process typically occurs where an individual enters an environment as part of social or professional mobility, as in cases where marriage brings about a requirement to communicate with in-laws of a new social group or where career advancement requires a worker to adopt new social skills. Otherwise the main reason is likely to be a sentiment of solidarity with the target group. Individuals may in this way retain or even acquire languages and varieties, even non-prestigious ones, in pursuit of solidarity with specific groups. So for example, young males in Norwich 'are more concerned with acquiring prestige of the covert sort and with signalling group solidarity than with acquiring social status' (Trudgill, 1983: 177).

Between these two extremes individuals adopt a variety of plans or strategies. Most frequently, as common sense tells us, they adopt a linguistic repertoire which enables them to move between languages or language varieties according to the circumstances in which they find themselves. They learn new varieties: the new variety can be a language one needs for instrumental purposes, such as a lingua franca or a language of international communication, and the target is simply one of obtaining the minimum ability in the language necessary to satisfy the need. When such instrumental needs are not paramount, the new language or language variety often characterises a new community or group with which one wishes to make contact.

Individuals' motives

How do these goals and strategies relate to the four scales representing attitudinal space, and to the motivational process of identity creation we have outlined? Hall's interpretation (1974: 174) of the motivational range open to individuals connected a number of motives. In narrative form he felt that ignorance or naivete about basic linguistic facts, fed by uncertainty about one's native language or one's own use of it, led to a feeling of insecurity as a major motive for action with the likely outcome either of strengthening consciousness of identity and thus of language; or of the opposite, of leading to abandonment of the language. He applied the same thinking to individuals in communities, where insecurity could well provoke (particularly purist) intervention and prescriptivism in order to strengthen the identity concept. In terms of our four scales, his motive of insecurity would correlate in such a way that the individual's own language would be regarded as less superior, less vital; it could be regarded as lying anywhere in the attractiveness range, but action would certainly be called for. Interpreting Hall's motivational structure in terms of our identity/motivational sequence, attitudinal structure and goals, and applying his argument to L1 alone, would imply the importance of the evaluative stage of identity construction, with motives following this concerned with the modification of the linguistic instrument or defence of the identity.

The origins of the two motives identified by Ryan and Giles (1982: 1-19), solidarity and status, which they saw as potentially opposites, lay in effect in the recognition and maintenance of one's own social identity in relation to that of others. A strategy for the individual of maintaining one's own language implies that one prizes one's identity and seeks to at least maintain its status and the prestige associated with it. This 'internal' view prizing the coherence of personal identity and making pride in it fundamental, is matched with an 'external' one prizing cooperation, when the individual seeks friends, companionship, association and the affective motive takes over. Paradoxically, this second solidarity motive can then have one of two diametrically opposed consequences: the individual seeks companionship in order to maintain his or her own identity (or forces others to adopt it, for example by insisting on various forms of purism); or the individual is so desirous of kinship that they voluntarily integrate with another group, abandoning their own identity altogether and submerging it in that of the external community. In terms of our four scales, the differences between Ryan and Giles' two motives would be one of the excellence and vitality of the language community against which one assesses one's own situation.

Hall (1974)

Motivation of individuals (Hall)									
Identity sequence	Attitudinal structure								Goals: Ideals, objectives, targets
	Exc'ence		Vitality		Attract		Action		
	L1	L2	L1	L2	L1	L2	L1	L2	
Identity (personal)									
Identity (social)									
Ideology									
Image									
Insecurity	1		1		1-3			3	a)coherence/strengthen identity b) shift/reject L1
Maintain identity									
Defend identity									
Maintain inequality									
Correct inequality									
Integrate									
Improve instrument									
Despair									

Ryan and Giles presuppose a different order of importance for the stage in the identity process to that preferred by Hall. Their stress on the outcomes related to solidarity and status means that they see motives for action as occurring later in our identity sequence, at the point at which concern starts to turn towards language-as-object, and the role of the language links uniting communities becomes fundamental even for individuals.

Ryan and Giles (1982)

Motivation of individuals (Ryan and Giles)									
Identity sequence	Attitudinal structure								Ideals/objectives
	Exc'ence		Vitality		Attract		Action		
	L1	L2	L1	L2	L1	L2	L1	L2	
Identity (personal)									
Identity (social)									
Ideology									
Image									
Insecurity									
Maintain identity	2		2		3		3		coherence/improve status of L1 coherence/attract others
Defend identity									
Maintain inequality									
Correct inequality									
Integrate									
Improve instrument									
Despair									

Our investigation of cases in Chapter 6 leads us to add somewhat to this range. For these five individuals, we have identified the strategies and motives each has adopted by direct questioning of them, and have classified their attitudes from similar interrogation.

Individuals in the present volume

A's eventual strategy was to add a new language to his existing repertoire, without changing his existing language. There was not much question of his doing this for integrative reasons, and his motives remained instrumental as we have seen. He did not consider Japanese as a superior or excellent language in any respect; its vitality, for him, lay in the domains of business language and also in two others and was hence fairly restricted. To a certain extent he knew that Japanese had to be used in friendly interchange with colleagues, while in everyday life, the minimal exchanges required in shops, using transport and paying household bills, Japanese was essential to him. He found the language reasonably attractive, however, and his motivation to do well in his language learning was frequently commented on by his Japanese colleagues, against which one must note his lack of interest in the advanced language skills of newspaper or book reading. In terms of the motivational process, A's instrumentalism towards Japanese is little concerned with identity questions. It is at the point of evaluating the environment that he has realised the need to add the new language, and this addition seems to have some connection with the image of himself he wishes to have his colleagues hold.

B, by contrast, is not so starkly instrumental in his approach. He acknowledges that English has superior characteristics, knows its vitality in every domain of the life he leads except that of domestic intimacy, evaluates it positively but again is not keen to learn its more difficult aspects, and is content to learn the minimum necessary to survive at what is nonetheless a complex level. His motives for action on language are mixed. In relation to English he has rather more integrative than instrumental motivation, but retains both pride in his existing language and finds it still both necessary and useful. In the motivational process, B has evaluated the self-identity he has created and discovered the need to add a new language. It is particularly in relation to his social identity that this realisation has been made. He has integrated to a certain extent with the new community, particularly with his son's family, but not at the price of rejecting the old, to which he frequently returns.

C's positioning on the motivational process seems quite different. She has reevaluated her own identity, demonstrated a desire for a much greater degree of integration than B and clearly wishes to create a favourable image of herself in the new community. Her scores on the four scales are towards the highest in each case, and the resultant strategy she has adopted is closer to language shift, for positive reasons, than towards the mere addition of English. She retains her L1, of course, but certainly not with any idea of maintaining her original identity structure.

D had also to a certain extent rejected his original identity in the Italian community or at least considerably modified it in his integrative motivation. Again, his self-identity had changed as he had evaluated it against his new environment, and he was strongly oriented towards creating a favourable image, to the extent of adopting Australian citizenship when this was not required of him. Like B but unlike C he had not gone so far as to harbour negative feelings towards his original language and was not altogether convinced of the superiority of English in every case. His strategy, like most of the individuals whose cases we have examined, is that of adding a new language.

E, like A, is positioned towards the instrumental end of the motivational spectrum. She did not see English as affecting her own identity, the image of this she wished to create, nor did she demonstrate any desire to integrate with the English-speaking environment. Despite the difficulties which have faced some Algerian females in the educational system, she remained strongly Algerian and her desire for action in relation to language extended to the acquisition of an instrument needed for her occupation and only for this.

Lingua franca

When we consider the other cases of the implementation of language strategies by individuals as outlined in Chapter 6, it is clear that the theories outlined in Chapter 7 help to organise and systematise some of the motives for action in the light of consequential strategies. In the case of the lingua franca, where motivation is instrumental and the strategy is one of addition to the language repertoire while retaining L1, individuals in the market-place score very low in every scale except that of action, while their positioning on the motivational process, as with A above, lies at the point of evaluation of their existing skill with that required by their environment. In terms of the four scales, while those aiming to adopt a lingua franca might sometimes feel that the target language has superior characteristics this is by no means always the case. Similarly, the language lacks vitality almost by definition since the intended use is almost always in one domain only: airline pilots need to acquire sufficient English to cope with the requirements of flying, but have no need for the language of the law or of poetry. They neither know whether L2 is appropriate for these domains nor care. Although the target language may be attractive for some this is again by no means always the case. Only the desire for action is strong: strong enough for individuals to be in effect obliged to learn and use the target means of expression. The motivational pattern is similar to the cases of individuals A and, to a certain extent, E above.

Motivation of individuals (Individuals in the present volume)									
Identity sequence	Attitudinal structure								Ideals/objectives
	Exc'ence		Vitality		Attract		Action		
	L1	L2	L1	L2	L1	L2	L1	L2	
Identity (personal)									
Identity (social)									
Ideology									
Image									
Insecurity									
Maintain identity									
Defend identity									
Maintain inequality									
Correct inequality									
Integrate B	3	3	3	3	3	2	1	3	cooperate/repertoire (L1 + L2)
C	2	3	2	3	2	3	1	3	cooperate/repertoire (L1 + L2)
D	3	2	3	2	3	3	1	3	cooperate/repertoire (L1 + L2); create favourable image
Improve instrument A		1		1		1		3	coherence/add L2
E	3	3	3	1	3	1	1	3	coherence/add L2 in limited domain
Despair									

Motivation of individuals (Lingua franca)									
Identity sequence	Attitudinal structure								Ideal/objective
	Exc'ence		Vitality		Attract		Action		
	L1	L2	L1	L2	L1	L2	L1	L2	
Identity (personal)									
Identity (social)									
Ideology									
Image									
Insecurity									
Maintain identity									
Defend identity									
Maintain inequality									
Correct inequality									
Integrate									
Improve instrument		1		1		1		3	coherence/repertoire (L1 + L2 in limited domain)
Despair									

Immigrants

Although it is immensely difficult to generalise the situation of immigrants, most would be likely to show a mixed pattern of scores. Recognition of the vitality and attractiveness of the host community and language rises as integration increases, although which is the consequence and which the origin is unclear. Depending on their particular position in the immigration process itself, and on how they perceive their economic future, immigrants might in effect score as low as 1 on every attitudinal scale in relation to L2, the host language, and intend to maintain indifference to both the host language and the host community. Such an extreme position is almost unknown today, as we have seen, although it is more likely to occur in the early stages of immigration and in conditions in which immigration from this particular source is rare and newly occurring. It arises particularly in the case of political refugees whose principal concern is to leave rather than to arrive: often, they have not specifically chosen the country to which they go but are most concerned to leave danger behind. It arose of course also in the cases of the first colonialists and imperialists, and still occurs in economic migration intended by the migrants to be temporary. L1 remains paramount and the intention is to retain the coherence of both language and identity. The more likely distribution of scores for later stages and generations, and in conditions in which there is an established immigrant flow, would indicate a fairly high score for the superiority of L2, necessarily a high score for its vitality, with the attractiveness and action indicators increasing as integration seems more desirable, as cooperation becomes a more acceptable goal and as language shift becomes a likely strategy. We are still at this point in the discussion concerned principally with the motivational structures of individuals forming part of the migrant flow rather than with those of the migrant community itself, when it is established and located within the host community. The relative importance of the motivational stages will also differ according to the point in the migratory sequence that the particular situation relates to. The importance of the evaluation stage does not seem necessarily very high, particularly at early points in the migratory flow, while even the importance of the identity stage for those rejecting the host language might be questioned, particularly in cases where the migrants themselves have a prestigious language and issues of identity have not really been posed in any significant way before.

Motives, attitudes and goals of individuals

So far then, a number of motives or points in the identity sequence, such as instrumentality, integration, insecurity or the maintenance of identity, can be related to patterns of scores or potential scores on the four attitudinal scales we have identified and to different language behaviour strategies, different goals. The attitudinal structures seem to bear little consistent relationships to these or to the consequential goals and strategies followed. We feel however that although the motives are undeniably present in all the examples we have reviewed, we need further examination of the degree of motivation. There must be some reason why the attitudinal structure should differ as it does from individual to individual. The most likely explanation is that the scale score differences relate to the perceived contrasts between the individual's situation and that of the individual or group he or she targets. One consequence of such a finding is the relatively higher importance to be attached to the stage in the motivational process at which the social identity of the individual is assessed against that of others, and we shall return to this point also when considering communities and states below. The greater the perceived contrasts between one's own situation and that of the reference group, the clearer the goal towards which the individual is striving, the greater the motivation to action. These contrasts seem to fall into four categories. The first is a contrast of social status; the second a contrast between the perceived status of the subject's native language and associated community and that of a surrounding community; the third that of contrast between the subject's economic circumstances and the subject's goal of success; and finally the age contrast which particularly affects adolescents.

Motivation of individuals (Non-established flow of immigrants)									
Identity sequence	Attitudinal structure								Ideal/objective
	Exc'ence		Vitality		Attract		Action		
	L1	L2	L1	L2	L1	L2	L1	L2	
Identity (personal)									
Identity (social)									
Ideology									
Image									
Insecurity									
Maintain identity	3	1	3	1	3	1	1	1	coherence/no action
Defend identity									
Maintain inequality									
Correct inequality									
Integrate									
Improve instrument									
Despair									

Motivation of individuals (Established flow of immigrants)									
Identity sequence	Attitudinal structure								Ideal/objective
	Exc'ence		Vitality		Attract		Action		
	L1	L2	L1	L2	L1	L2	L1	L2	
Identity (personal)									
Identity (social)									
Ideology									
Image									
Insecurity									
Maintain identity									
Defend identity									
Maintain inequality									
Correct inequality									
Integrate	2	3	1	3	2	3	1	3	shift/reject L1
Improve instrument	3	3	2	3	3	2	1	3	cooperation/repertoire (L1 + L2)
Despair									

The social status of the individual appears to have a strong influence on the 'objective' evaluation accorded to the L1 (the subject's own language). In simple terms, if an individual's social status is high then the objective evaluation of L1 is high, there is little motive for action to improve L1 or to obtain any other language, even if L2 (or others) have high status. The example is that of the standard language as spoken by society's powerful, who historically feel no need to protect their own language since it seems unassailable, nor indeed any need to bother with other languages or varieties. Contrast between the subject's community's status and that of the surrounding environment can affect such indifference. It will strengthen motivation to act in defence of the subject's language or might provoke the opposite in a desire to assimilate to the superior surrounding environment. Contrast in economic circumstances leads to instrumental motivation, sometimes to language shift but certainly to a desire to improve language, acquire another one or otherwise affect the individual's language ability. The final contrast is that of age, where young people normally start to acquire greater social expertise and a greater range of varieties at about adolescence. Motivation here is normally towards integration with the adult community.

The Powerless Community

The language behaviour of individuals, although a fascinating study, is immensely difficult to track. It is hardly surprising therefore that language planning has been mainly examined in relation to human groups, and particularly such secondary groups as those united by kinship or by ethnic origin. The ability of such groups to deploy political power in relation to others is a key element in their behaviour. We make a fundamental division here between communities in society which are in control of their own political destinies ('the state') and are hence by definition powerful, usually majority communities in self-governing states, and those minority communities which do not enjoy such political autonomy. Another distinction of importance is that between 'inclusive' societies like France or Japan, with a strong tradition of linguistic unification, and 'mosaic' societies like India or even the UK, where regional and social languages and dialects are to an extent more tolerated. Mosaic states contain many communities by definition, and although it can occur that political control is not necessarily exercised continually by one of them, in most cases it is safe to assume that political power is normally exercised by one group, whether the social elite, an ethnic group or a language community. This community is the powerful one, and others lack power. Because of their majority or minority status, many communities within the state are vociferous in support of their own identity and desire to ensure that their language, customs and traditions are not lost. Others, particularly dispersed groups and those resulting from sporadic immigration, are less organised or less enthusiastic about preserving their language. Language is an almost inevitable point of contention between communities, and this is particularly the case in mosaic states.

It is practically inevitable that the communities whose language situation has become widely known have progressed beyond the stage in which they are completely without political power. In our first chapter we discussed many: the French regions, linguistic groups in Algeria, Catalan speakers in Spain, the many Indian language groups and Welsh speakers in the UK. But none of these is really politically powerless: the very fact that their situations form the bulk of the research literature on community languages indicates the degree of political consciousness they have aroused, while they have either thrown off the yoke of political control or have come to some accommodation with the state in which they live. Only the Gypsies among the groups which are widely discussed in the research literature have remained really powerless, although there are many examples in the world of oppressed groups and those without the same rights or resources as other groups in the state.

Communities are defined as such by stressing one or more of the many social characteristics of the individuals who form them. Individuals may well belong to different communities, while communities are by no means all-inclusive groups of individuals. Muslims in Bradford, England participate in the British immigrant community, in the British Muslim community, (often) in the Pakistan community-in-exile, (often) in the Urdu-speaking community, in various social communities related to their situation as workers, entrepreneurs, financiers or civil servants and (often) in the social community of the economically deprived. The vast majority of established immigrants speak English, sometimes as monolinguals. The community religions, traditions and myths to which they owe allegiance are many and varied. Community leaders no longer command obedience in all aspects of life, as may have happened at earlier stages in immigration, and it is often difficult to achieve consensus on the views and opinions to present to authorities.

Language communities, groups of people whose uniting factor is the language they use, obviously form a special case when it comes to language behaviour. Even more so than ethnic or social communities, they are unorganised, unsystematic and although politicians in some states would have us believe that they possess some form of collective awareness and are able to act collectively, are in fact quite unable to express an opinion or to consciously plan and enforce the language behaviour of all their members. Nonetheless language communities often modify the language behaviour of their members. They do this the more effectively the more their members are in face-to-face communication. To a certain extent, the smaller the community and the more its members are in face-to-face contact the greater the degree of potential political awareness and thus power it possesses.

Larger language communities now cover the world as 'international' languages like English, French and Spanish are adopted or at least used by many people. 'National' languages like Chinese or Malay often remain the prerogative of ethnic communities, although this generalisation is less and less true as languages like Japanese spread outside ethnic Japanese groups. The boundaries of a language community are immensely difficult to define, as a moment's consideration of the world-wide English-language community will illustrate. There is little doubt that there are linguistic differences between English speakers normally living in different states. Australian, English, American, New Zealand and Indian forms of English present differences which can be as easily recognised as can regional dialects within each state. There remains a world-wide English-language community which shares both the language and at least some of the culture (in the widest sense) it conveys. But it has no political power deriving from the fact that it unites English-speaking countries,   despite the existence of the Commonwealth and suspicions that military and political cooperation has extended to such fields as international email interception and surveillance. The Commonwealth, using English, is a political group but it contains by no means all the world's English speakers and its power over its members does not extend to language policy. The group of fifty-plus Francophone states which form an avowedly political 'Francophonie' now carefully avoids any attempt to dictate language policy, and is still developing approaches towards political influence among its members. Specifically linguistic groupings of countries like those of the   German-speaking countries in Europe, the Hispanophones and the Lusophones world-wide, and others also have not sought direct political influence, although their main aim is to harmonise linguistic policies, particularly on corpus policy, for their respective languages.

The ideals and objectives of politically powerless communities

What types of language behaviour goals are open to politically powerless communities, whether these be distinguished by their ethnic, religious, linguistic or social characteristics? As regards their own language, there are two extremes of the range: either the community loses its language and possibly its separate identity, or maintains its separate existence, together, most usually, with a sense of pride, of innate difference from its neighbours and often with a degree of antagonism towards these and particularly towards the language of the powerful majority. Between these two extremes lies a range of possible strategies.

So at one extreme, the powerless group (also here frequently termed the minority group, even though it may not be in a numerical minority) can integrate or assimilate with another community, usually the powerful, host or majority one. In the process it loses its own identity and language. Such compromise is not necessarily to be condemned, although the most usual reaction is to deplore it as at the very least a loss of human diversity, and at most a crime against humanity. On the face of it, losing one's language is hardly a goal for the powerless community. But abandoning a language and the associated separate identity could avoid possible social conflict; it can work to the advantage of all members of society, including the minority community. In some cases, particularly that of the United States of America in the early part of the twentieth century, submerging individual differences within the accepted common identity was the expected way in which a new country was to be created. Generally speaking, however, policies of assimilation have been carried out as top-down actions by the powerful without the approval of the powerless community and have often been carried out with a degree of political, social or economic brutality and force, as in the case of the French regions. Sometimes, by contrast, members of powerless minorities are refused integration for a long period even though this may be their ideal, as in the case of some Indian castes, or women in many societies, East and West. The goal of loss of distinctiveness and loss of language may be both positive and negative.

At the other extreme the powerless community has the objective of retaining its own identity. If they do not wish or are not forced to assimilate, minority communities can either openly defend their distinctiveness, entering into often political conflict with their dominant neighbours, or do so covertly, avoiding the extremes of conflict. Open conflict has been well documented in many cases; covert opposition perhaps less so. As has often been the case with Jews and other religious minorities in the past, communities might go underground, holding religious services in secret and retaining their language as a symbol. It is often surprising that 'hidden groups' can retain their language use, even when the community is small, incapable of adequate economic progress and located in the midst of a vibrant host community. For this to occur, a strong unifying link must be present over time: religion perhaps is the strongest, but the key to successful retention of separate identity is the existence of numerous links including family, neighbourhood, and occupation as well as the religious or other structure of belief and values, together perhaps with outward symbols of difference. In defending a separate destiny, the strategy can often be to strengthen such diverse and numerous links, and communities can erect exclusion barriers such as religion, skin colour, ethnic origin, custom and language to the extent of making them impregnable. One of the methods by which this can be done is to reinforce, or indeed create, a community myth or set of myths to act as a unifying force justifying separation. Even language revival has occurred, in the case of communities which have practically disappeared. The case of Cornwall comes to mind, where although the last native Cornish speaker died in 1802, revivalist groups try to identify a tradition of separate development for 'real' Cornish people. In Wales there have occasionally been movements aimed at protecting the 'original' way of life by preventing inward immigration, on the argument that incoming visitors dilute the 'original' community. Such incomers are ipso facto not Welsh and hence should be excluded to maintain the separate identity of the 'original' community. Linguistic strategies aimed at the defence of separate identity include those based on the purist motives outlined by Thomas (1991), in particular those related to the archaic purist reaction. The xenophobic, elitist and ethnographic motivations are often also pressed into service with resultant strategies for preserving a community language free from foreign imports, from decadence supposedly related to use by inferior social classes or from contamination by urban dialects.

There is a mid-point between the two extremes. Communities retain difference without necessarily involving themselves in major battles or being crushed. A variety of cooperative strategies is open to communities. Some are linguistic, some political. Political objectives include attempts to ensure their own political control of territory and a de-facto separation from those who hold power, or at the very least political recognition of the right to be different and nonetheless to obtain at least as great political, economic and social advantage for themselves as for any other community within the state. Depending on their situation, the objective might be to press for separate physical location as in Belgium, for political control within a defined territory as in Wales, for legal definition within the state according to the state's definition of identity, as with 'Asians' or 'Afro-Caribbeans' within the UK, or for a looser, self-defining status wherein an individual might simply declare himself or herself to be a member of the relevant community (Aborigines in Australia). Linguistically, objectives include deliberate educational efforts to maintain the language, often against strong pressure towards uniformity on the part of the powerful groups within society. Planning effort on the linguistic front includes the full range of maintenance strategies, including status, corpus and acquisition policies of varying types, so that language planning between the two extremes covers behaviour towards language-as-instrument as well as that towards language-as-object. Much work on the corpus of the language which took place in Quebec in the 1970s and 1980s and still continues today thus reflects behaviour towards the instrument which Quebec French had become by that point in time, while the Quebec language laws have been the more open and widely known aspect of the general aim of language planning.

The motives, goals and attitudes of powerless communities

Wardhaugh (1987) was concerned with the outcomes that communities seeking nationhood could aspire to. In terms of their language behaviour he suggested that there were probably three possible outcomes for powerless communities: they could enter into conflict with their more powerful neighbours or with those in political control of their territory, trying to maintain their own separate identity; they could cooperate with them, attempting to maintain as much of their separate existence as they could; or they could compromise, eventually, possibly, losing the battle and their language. This view, in different forms, has been adopted in many analyses of how powerless communities act. Translating such outcomes to our tabular presentation gives the picture of the powerless community defending its identity fiercely; more or less integrating with others; or being condemned to despairingly finish its separate existence.

Our case studies tend to show that although these three are significant, modifications to the somewhat stark picture are possible. It is hardly surprising that there is little statistically satisfactory data revealing the actual attitudes of powerless language communities in relation to their own language. The problems of identifying attitude are of course no greater than those facing any social scientist attempting to obtain reliable opinions, but the vagueness of the community's boundaries means that the statistical population is difficult to define accurately. Each community, of course, contains a range of opinions. In each case therefore we have used the sources referenced in each of the studies of Chapters 1 to 5 as they occur to help us fix our attitudinal scales. Although imprecise, this procedure seems acceptable given the generality of the points we are making here. It gives great weight to activists and militants and hence to the conflict ideal, but that is inevitable except where accurate and unbiased surveys have taken place, which is in practice nowhere. Motives and goals at whatever level   are less difficult to pin down, and again are sourced from the references given.

Motivation of powerless communities (Wardhaugh)									
Identity sequence	Attitudinal structure								Ideal/objective
	Exc'ence		Vitality		Attract		Action		
	L1	L2	L1	L2	L1	L2	L1	L2	
Identity (personal)									
Identity (social)									
Ideology									
Image									
Insecurity									
Maintain identity									
Defend identity	3		3		3		3		conflict/fight for rights
Maintain inequality									
Correct inequality									
Integrate	3	3	3	3	3	3	3	3	cooperate/use both L1 and L2
Improve instrument									
Despair	1	3	1	3	1	3	1	3	compromise/shift from L1 to L2

Powerless communities: maintaining and defending identity

Almost inevitably, and as we have seen from our case studies, the motives of powerless language communities must be first and foremost those concerned with their own identity. This identity is itself that of the language, as for our purposes the community is linked because it finds its own identity in and through the language. This can paradoxically have the effect that the link becomes transparent: the language community does not recognise that it is the language that forms its only link, and is constantly in search of other links such as the political, managing its own affairs and controlling its own territory, or the social such as kinship, neighbourhood or religion. It is from this confusion for example that attempts stem to unite French-speaking communities in the Aosta Valley or in Belgium with France itself. Nonetheless, the more common situation seems to be that the community's aim of maintaining its social identity is coloured as much by opposition to another language as by any recognition of the inherent qualities of its own language.

Motivation of powerless communities (identity)									
Identity sequence	Attitudinal structure								Ideal/objective
	Exc'ence		Vitality		Attract		Action		
	L1	L2	L1	L2	L1	L2	L1	L2	
Identity (personal)									
Identity (social)									
Ideology									
Image									
Insecurity									
Maintain identity									
French regional languages	2	2	1	3	2	2	2	1	conflict/covert maintenance of L1
Welsh	3	3	1	3	3	2	2	1	conflict/seek equal rights with English; archaic purism
Defend identity									
Catalan	3	1	3	2	3	1	3	1	conflict/defend L1 by attacking L2
Maithili	3	3	3	3	3	3	3	1	cooperate/accept multilingualism but require rights
Poignant report	3	3	3	2	3	3	3	3	cooperate/advocate rights for all
Breton after 1951	3	2	1	3	3	2	3	1	conflict/open defence
Maintain inequality									
Correct inequality									
Integrate									
Improve instrument									
Despair									

Of the communities we have examined here, these scores fairly clearly represent strong Catalan views advocating the open defence of Catalan identity. To a large extent they seem appropriate in the case of the various Indian language groups and the Welsh activists, if not necessarily the whole of the Welsh population. Although some regional language communities like Breton, particularly after 1951, may share the Catalan position this is not the case for all French regional languages which have mostly succeeded in maintaining their identity rather than openly defending it.. Traditionally, too, French regional languages have been little prized by the majority of their speakers and militant action in relation to their maintenance has been the preserve of the few. But the languages have been maintained, more or less, more by covertly continuing to use them in private situations than as a result of vociferous advocacy by the militants.

Powerless communities: correcting inequality

The motive of correcting social inequality, injustice or inequity is a strong force for powerless communities whose identity is important to them. It is close to the idea of actively defending identity. Indeed, a main motive for the language planning of minority communities, and one widely discussed in the research literature, seems to be to correct or at least reduce the inequality, inequity or injustice from which they suffer within the state. Minority languages, whether regional or social, and whether they have long been present within the territory or are the result of more recent migration or border change, are almost by definition   subject to domination by a numerically larger majority. Domination can also occur, as in ex-colonial societies, when the 'minority' is actually numerically in the majority but suffers from a lack of prestige by comparison with the 'majority' language. Minority communities as language planners for their own language behaviour however do not necessarily interact directly with policy-makers at the state level. Awareness of a regional, localised or group language or variety is obviously heightened if the relevant community is close-knit, its members in frequent communication with each other and if the links between members are numerous and varied (marriage, kinship, religion, sport, customs, physical contact). For long, two communities in Belfast have preserved their different manners of speech for such reasons. External threats to the community strengthen such links, but some language varieties persist even without such tight contact or external threat. If minority communities do relate to superior state authorities, demands and pressures for change in policy of any type arise in the social, and particularly the political, environment surrounding government. These pressures are mediated by individuals, groups and organisations of various types, particularly by those who gain access to the policy community, and who thus channel and modify the issue so that it reaches the agenda of the policy-makers. Minority communities are by definition powerless when faced with the majority community or with groups holding power at the state level. A minority community thus has a motive to correct inequality within the state in defence of its own identity, while a majority community might have a motive for oppressing such a minority in defence of its own majority identity as we shall see below when discussing states. Whether communities are powerful or powerless, these motives for action on language seem to concentrate on the identity issue, but from the point of view of social equality and justice for potentially divisive groups, rather than of integration and the possible, eventual, consequential social harmony.

Catalan language planning, again, at certain points reflects such a motive and such an attitudinal structure. Belgium, in both language communities, sees inequality as a fundamental motive requiring action on the political front. Welsh strategy here has been to stress the educational process as important as a policy answer to perceived inequality, although the strategy of according Welsh equal status with English indicates the origin of much of the concern and stresses the cooperative nature of the eventual policy decisions. Algeria, like Wales, and although the language is that of an autonomous political entity, clearly has retained the concept of inequality and paradoxically imposes similar inequality on its indigenous languages. It is precisely in order to gain equality in resource terms that the majority of Indian language groups other than those recognised in the Schedule attempt to gain such recognition. Much of the inspiration behind the European Charter for Regional and Minority languages derives from concepts of inequality and the need to correct this by symbolic declarations as well as by practical action. Both American feminism, in its plans to ensure the use of appropriate terminology, and the Australian Federation of Ethnic Community Councils and Associations, demonstrate attitudinal structures of these types associated with identity issues and sets of goals and strategies which underline the desire to retain difference. They have adopted different goals and strategies: conflict in the one case, cooperation in the other. Indeed, as is becoming obvious, the attitudes of powerless communities might relate to a number of different motives and a range of strategies. Conversely, the motives of different communities relate to fairly different attitudinal structures, even though the motive is the same or very similar.

Motivation of powerless communities (correcting inequality)									
Identity sequence	Attitudinal structure								Ideal/objective
	Exc'ence		Vitality		Attract		Action		
	L1	L2	L1	L2	L1	L2	L1	L2	
Identity (personal)									
Identity (social)									
Ideology									
Image									
Insecurity									
Maintain identity									
Defend identity									
Maintain inequality									
Correct inequality									
Belgium, Assam, Tamil	3	3	1	3	3	1	3	3	conflict/seek rights by territory
Catalan	3	1	3	2	3	1	3	1	conflict/political rights for L1
Welsh	3	3	2	3	3	3	3	1	cooperation/education in L1
European Charter	3	3	3	3	3	3	3	3	cooperation/(some) rights for minorities
Feminism	3	1	3	1	3	3	3	3	conflict/appropriate use of language
FECCA	3	3	2	3	3	3	3	3	cooperation/education in L2 as mainstream provision
Integrate									
Improve instrument									
Despair									

Powerless communities: Insecurity

Insecurity might seem to be almost the fundamental motive of powerless communities. Almost by definition, their political situation gives them less control over their destiny than powerful groups, while the status of their language means that it is constantly less prized than that of the powerful. But this motive is not the same as the desire for correction of inequality. The insecurity involved is a feeling that language is inadequate to the task. Almost inevitably it will be little used in many domains, particularly those of high prestige. In some cases the language community may feel insecure in the excellence as well as the vitality of its own language: some commentators feel that a language may lack mechanisms for expressing particular ideas, its writing or spelling system may be unnecessarily complex. Individuals may feel unsure of their own abilities in the language, particularly if there are few credible authorities and cultural history relates to conditions which have long changed.

Motivation of powerless communities (insecurity)								
Identity sequence	Attitudinal structure							Ideal/objective
	Exc'ence		Vitality		Attract		Action	
	L1	L2	L1	L2	L1	L2	L1	L2
Identity (personal)								
Identity (social)								
Ideology								
Image								
Insecurity								
Neologism in French	1	3	1	3	3	3	1	2	conflict/reformist purism
Maintain identity								
Defend identity								
Maintain inequality								
Correct inequality								
Integrate								
Improve instrument								

Scores such as these do not seem likely in the Catalan case, nor, indeed in any of the others we have discussed in Chapter 1. They seem more likely among some Gypsy groups and possibly some Aboriginals in Australia, although in both cases the separation between the community and the host or majority groups is either deliberately fostered or forms part of the community culture, and judgments about the value of the majority language have not led to the sort of language change one would expect of such an attitude. The example we have inserted is that of French or Quebec reformist purism and the attempts by this means to improve the French language in order to enable it to be used in 'modern', technological, economic or scientific domains.

Powerless communities: instrumentality

Instrumentality, in the sense of ensuring a good fit between the language and the environment of its use, is very close to this motive. This motive arises from the negative evaluation, not of the community's language in relation to that of the majority or of a powerful neighbour such as American English, but of the use of the community's language in the full range of domains. There is hence an associated determination that the community's language could be just as good as that of the majority if something were done about it. It provokes attempts to control, adapt or improve neology and the adaptation of the language's ability to present new social phenomena. The final aim might be economic, but the plans and strategies involved are directed towards improving the language to make it a better instrument for achieving success.

As with the identity motive, Catalan language groups would perhaps also recognise such a motivational picture. It is precisely this belief that Catalan is not being used in all domains of public life which has provoked the two strategies of insisting on its use everywhere and of adding to its capacities. The strategy of ensuring that the language is used in as many domains of public life as possible is followed also by such groups as Welsh speakers and, in a somewhat different way, it is a main motive for support for the European Charter for Regional and Minority Languages. The main example of the instrumental motive and consequential reformist zeal is the Quebec approach to modification of both spoken and written French, and particularly the major effort at improving technical and scientific vocabulary in order to render it unnecessary to have constant recourse to American English.

Motivation of powerless communities (improve instrument)									
Identity sequence	Attitudinal structure								Ideal/objective
	Exc'ence		Vitality		Attract		Action		
	L1	L2	L1	L2	L1	L2	L1	L2	
Identity (personal)									
Identity (social)									
Ideology									
Image									
Insecurity									
Maintain identity									
Defend identity									
Maintain inequality									
Correct inequality									
Integrate									
Improve instrument									
Québec	3	1	1	3	3	3	1	1	conflict/reformist purism
Despair									

Powerless communities: the integrative motive

The integrative motive nonetheless exists, and although it may eventually derive from despair on the part of the minority community that any outcome other than full assimilation is likely, its attitudinal patterns would show that action on language is necessary. Almost inevitably, L2 is regarded as superior, attractive and its vitality in all domains is acknowledged, by contrast with the poor showing of L1 in all these counts. Since the examples we have discussed are mostly those which have demonstrated their willingness not to integrate, it is hardly surprising that none of those in Chapter 1 would recognise this motivational picture and that we have to look to strong centralising and assimilating societies like France and Japan to find examples. Integration with another language community is for some powerless communities a counsel of despair. If all else fails, if the personal and social identity of the group cannot be maintained and there is no other alternative, language loss and language shift ensues, as we have noted in the case of Koreans and, even more despairingly, the Ainu in Japan. There are of course other reasons for language shift and it can be a positive experience, as we have noted. But if a language community declines sufficiently in numbers or self-confidence the end result will be the same. We have no data here on which to base an accurate estimate of attitudinal structure, but one must suspect a pattern of negative scores in relation to L1. In regard to L2, although it is to be expected that the community will find the language superior and vital almost by definition, the pattern could be equally negative if the motive is despair: the community simply sees no way out. L1 is destined to disappear.

Motivation of powerless communities (integration or despair)									
Identity sequence	Attitudinal structure								Ideal/objective
	Exc'ence		Vitality		Attract		Action		
	L1	L2	L1	L2	L1	L2	L1	L2	
Identity (personal)									
Identity (social)									
Ideology									
Image									
Insecurity									
Maintain identity									
Defend identity									
Maintain inequality									
Correct inequality									
Integrate									
Koreans in Japan	1	3	1	3	1	3	1	3	compromise/shift from L1 to L2
Improve instrument									
Despair									
Ainu	1	3	1	3	1	3	1	3	compromise/shift from L1 to L2

Powerless communities: Summary and conclusion

There is one further comment which should be made at this point, and which derives from the experience of some mosaic societies. The word 'community' is convenient shorthand and an extremely useful device in political rhetoric when interest groups present their case. Many so-called communities however exist only in the mind of the observer. The blind community, the left-handed community, the farming community and many similar social subdivisions have a somewhat dubious collective identity. Re-categorising society by such features as religion, ethnicity, language and skin colour results in many cross-cutting groupings in which the same individuals appear in many communities, some with conflicting aims. Which is the more important of these to the individual and to the relevant society varies according to many factors, as does the nature of intergroup relations (e.g. Hewstone et al. (1993) in relation to India). Generally it is the activists in a language community whose views are represented in the research literature, so that we often have no indication of what the 'real' community attitudes might be apart from the eventual outcome in terms of the strategy adopted.

In summary, the motives minority and powerless communities display, the attitudes they seem to demonstrate, and the goals and strategies they follow, are many and varied. The relationship between attitudes, motives and consequential strategies, and the ways these are realised in the individual cases we have examined in earlier chapters, show that many communities have mixed motives. Similarly the attitudes communities record do not always lead to the same outcome, nor is a common attitude a guarantee of similarity of motive, even when the consequential strategy is the same. Finally, the majority of the language behaviour of powerless communities is directed towards L1. In most cases L2, the language of the dominant other, is inevitably regarded as superior and more vital than the language of the powerless. It is less often attractive, even when the eventual strategy is one of integration. But action towards it, other than simply adopting it, is rarely possible.

Although in this section we have limited the examples to those discussed in this book, all these motives seem to be present in community language behaviour, and as we have seen, the relationship between motive, attitude and strategy is by no means obvious. It is when we come to consider the relationships between the motives that the sequential nature of motivation and its relationship to identity construction seems to be relevant. The creation of the social identity clearly precedes any of the other motives, and it is only after evaluation of the exact situation of the community that pressures can be detected towards integration or instrumentality. The correction of inequality, too, depends on both knowledge of the group's identity and a realisation that it is this identity which is receiving inadequate resources, is lacking the rights others enjoy or is unjustly treated. Despair and consequential language loss, too, depend on the realisation that the powerful language must prevail, and on acceptance of this. One might conclude that the primacy of the identity motive and the essential nature of the evaluation stage means that the other motives are simply alternatives, chosen according to the particular situation of the powerless community. Motivation, like identity construction, is dynamic; it is based on social identity; and seems to relate to a range of language attitudes and strategies.

Chapter 9

Language Policy: the Language Behaviour of those in Power

States, Governments and the Elite

Policy-makers

Policy, as opposed to planning, is a term which, as we have defined it, represents the actions of those who hold power in society. Those who are able to implement their opinions and world view are those who are in political charge of autonomous states as members of government, or as government employees. Having said this, there remains a good deal of confusion about the development, implementation and change of policy which actually takes place in states, and particularly about the identity of the policy-makers. These seem to fall into three categories. The first is made up of individuals: politicians, rulers and opinion-formers who have a major role, but whose policies may depend on who they are, on their own ideology, preferences and likings, and sometimes even on their quirks. Powerful individuals sometimes seem to make and implement policy almost single-handedly. The power exercised by Mrs Thatcher, Adolf Hitler, Josef Stalin or Jacques Chirac enabled each to make changes in the language policies of their respective countries which seem to reflect a quite personal view of what should be done, even though each must have been influenced by their associates and the supporting systems and groups. At a less extreme level a minister with particular interests in such questions can exercise considerable influence, like George Walden in the UK in language training.

The second category of policy-maker is the ruling group or community. Some communities, whether regional, ethnic, or religious seem to be consistently in power in some states. Some social classes or social strata, particularly the economic elite, often seem to run things even when presidents and prime ministers fall, when governments change or regimes topple. The state's policy seems to change little.

Different communities or social strata do of course, in plural democracies, alternate power and implement policy which reflects the interests of their supporters. In Britain the Labour Party, in the USA the Democrats, in other countries Socialist Parties traditionally represent a different social group from that supporting the Conservatives, the Republicans, or various Christian Democratic parties. While the structure of the state, and many policies, change little, changes do occur reflecting the priorities of the different groups. Often, political ideologies are the outward expression of the vested interests of particular social groups, so a right-wing ideology is often representative of the interests of the wealthy, of industry or of large-scale farmers, while the left has traditionally externalised the interests of workers, urban as opposed to rural groups, or of the poor. It is not surprising that the change of UK government in 1997 should mean that equality issues in social welfare policies should have been more to the fore, nor that the issue of UK identity within the European Union issue should have taken a different course from that followed by the Major government.

The third type of policy-maker is the state itself. At this level, the long-term characteristics and interests of the state are paramount, and it may well be that policies last considerable periods, surviving changes of government and even quite drastic developments in the environment. At this third level, the unchanging nature of the French bureaucracy's interest in territorial unity and social cohesion has inspired policy, including language policy, over a period of more than two centuries, through monarchies, empires and republics and innumerable changes in government. Madrid's oppression of Catalonia had its origins in fifteenth-century unification of the peninsula against Arab domination and the consequent power of the Church. The imposition of a standard language in Britain as a state requirement has its roots in the Norman conquest of 1066 and the replacement of Anglo-Saxon leaders by Norman ones, even though the language involved is no longer Norman French nor even Latin, and the first textual implementation of the policy is the 1362 Statute of Pleading. One major question here is to discover who exactly represents the state, and where such unchanging principles are rooted. Sometimes they derive from territorial imperatives and the ease of transport up to natural frontiers; elsewhere they derive from administrative traditions. An established bureaucracy, regarding itself as enshrining the State and its eternal values because it is divorced from the hurly-burly of everyday political life, can originate and implement policy whatever the politicians of the day may say.

Goals

In this chapter we shall discuss language policy as it is exercised by those in power, whatever the category. As in the case of powerless communities and individuals, the identity sequence seems to be reflected in the cases we have examined in earlier chapters. As far as motivation is concerned, again as with individuals and the powerless, the identity sequence by itself does not seem to fully account for everything, and the total motivational structure seems to rely in addition on both attitudinal structure and the goals pursued by the organism. It should be remembered also that three approaches to language policy are widespread among the politically autonomous: language is regarded as a right, a resource or a problem. Access to (a particular variety or domain of) language can be one of the fundamental human rights, to be protected and jealously guarded by the gatekeepers of the powerful. Language, and particularly the ability to use many languages, can on the other hand represent a major economic and competitive resource for the state and for individuals. Or language use can be a problem, usually based on or implying social division and fragmentation, that the state has to solve. Policies following one or other of these approaches are themselves many and varied.

The obvious ideal is stability, the unity of the state, and the preservation of territory from internal 'fragmentation'. Such a goal is based on social cohesion, which in some nation-states implies that citizens themselves hold sovereignty which they then, theoretically at least, delegate to authority, while in others sovereignty resides with a monarch, a president or a parliament. As with individuals or powerless communities, there are then at least two different objectives which serve this overriding goal. One extreme is to insist on the use of one language or language variety for all citizens, usually the L1 of the powerful which is declared to be the official language. This will be used within appropriate official institutions like parliament and the Courts, in education and in all public domains. The bureaucracy will be prepared to use it, and it alone, in relationships with the citizen. Declarations of official status can lead to formal, legal attempts to ensure it is always used, and to a whole range of measures to defend it from enemies real and imagined. Particularly, the state will aim to repress diversity within its own borders, whether this derives from the existence of regional languages or from varieties characteristic of social categories other than the elite. On occasion, objectives of this type may fly in the face of reality: Algeria may declare Classical Arabic to be its official language, but the differences between the Classical and the spoken language are enormous, and the policy simply prevents those who cannot master this from gaining power within the state. At other times, it is this strategy that maintains the unequal treatment of internal minorities such as the Roma.

A second goal of the powerful within states is power itself. This usually means that the elite has the aim of possessing and retaining power, however that is defined, and the ideal is in effect the elitist state. The objective most often adopted is that of simply ignoring social diversity and any expression thereof, including any languages other than that of the elite itself. This solution is sometimes thought of as the English one, and is certainly characteristic of British history from 1066 to about 1750. Indeed, the same approach to language policy probably characterises the history of Britain and many other countries after 1750, when the social elite was more and more replaced by an economic one. At one extreme therefore, the state - in this context we shall use the word as shorthand for the elite - has one working language which it uses for all purposes. Its language policy, sometimes openly, sometimes not, associates this language with the state.   The state will not legislate for the language use of its citizens and while there will apparently be complete freedom for them to use any language they wish, the state and its bureaucracy will always use the state language to them. This strategy has been that of kings and dictators in regimes where sovereignty lies with the ruler: provided the King's language was used in dealings with authority, citizens could do what they pleased. The aim is not necessarily social cohesion: it is, rather, the efficient management of the state.

Between the two extremes lies the goal of the plural state, with its acceptance of an ideal mosaic of different groups and, often, at the level of an objective, of a multicultural or even multilingual state again existing in harmony. It has to be stated that harmony in the mosaic state, while it may be an ideal, is rarely achieved in practice and the state conducts a balancing act between fragmentary tendencies. The opposite goal, of social division and the maintenance of social inequality, is rarely openly stated. It has perhaps been most clearly seen in recent years in the case of ideologically motivated objectives and targets. These are inevitably of great importance within states. In pluralist political entities it is inevitable that a variety of political theories, ideals and objectives will be pursued. Some political ideologies tend to support social cohesion; others insist that social division is not merely to be accepted but to be actively encouraged. Ideologies may apply to many domains of life, too, although over the last century they have fundamentally depended on views of the economy and on resource distribution. It is in this context that issues of access to language become important: who has the right to use the language which will enable education, economic improvement, social advantage?

The state also has goals at all three levels of ideals, objectives and targets which are turned towards the exterior, less concerned with internal stability. Aware of languages used outside its borders and the potential of competition, the state can foster a positive image of its language(s) inside and outside the state. This is most often done through a strong cultural policy including linguistic elements and fostering language teaching abroad. The objective of language spread, as in the case of Germany, reflects an innate pride in language and society. But similarly, the desire to ensure the state's language is used abroad may derive from objectives of colonialism, political or economic, or from the desire to foster a favourable image in order to ensure greater power for the state in international relations. Japan's desire to foster a favourable image may be partly an attempt to offset the negative effect of past domination of the Pacific region, or a desire to gain greater influence in political fields.

As a political entity in a world of other such organisms the state may find itself in conflict with other states. Its objectives for survival, for defence and for offence in international relations relate to the degree of insecurity or of self-confidence it feels. Supreme self-confidence can lead to declarations that its ambassadors and representatives will use its own language only. In other cases, the appropriate strategy may approximate to the integrative motive we have noticed in the case of individuals, and the state may try to join such organisations as the Commonwealth or Francophonie. It is very unlikely that the state will voluntarily abandon a language it no longer finds appropriate or adequate or is unable to use in ways which represent its political power. Nonetheless Japan nearly abandoned its complex writing scheme in 1946; both Indian and Pakistani officials use English when they wish to contact a large audience; most countries negotiate diplomacy in English or French.

Motives, attitudes and goals of the powerful

Chapters 1 to 5 above have identified the sources from which we have summarised attitudes and motivations in each case in the discussions that follow, with a degree of generality similar to that we have used in the cases of individuals and powerless communities. As with individuals and powerless communities, a particular policy relates to a particular point within the motivational/identity sequence.

Individual powerful states, governments and people can reveal their thinking at a particular stage by the point they have reached along the process, and although there is no one particular point which seems to characterise all powerful states, some motives seem more frequent than others. Ideology, Image, the defence of Identity and the maintenance (rather than the correction) of Inequality, together with a number of Instrumental motives, seem rather more prevalent than feelings of Insecurity, motives of maintaining Identity, correcting Inequality or Despair. Given the powerful nature of states and of the groups in authority within them this is to be expected.

Grillo, Kallen, Kaplan and Baldauf

Very little has been written in studies of language policy about the actions of powerful states apart from widespread condemnation of what is often seen as their intention to forcibly insist on the use of one language or language variety. Dominance (or domination: both terms are used) is widely seen as the only intention behind state actions, from purism to fascism. The state's aim seems to be cohesion and social unity; its ideal outcome is Hitler's ideal of one nation, one territory, one language. In terms of our presentation, attitudes towards L1 are uniformly strongly supported, while L2 is in effect disregarded. The state has stayed at the point of (social) identity creation, even when it is forced by circumstances to defend itself. Grillo applies this approach to the creation of the French nation after 1789:

> language was seen as a serious object of civil concern...linguistic unification was an egalitarian measure...the Revolutionary premise that a nation must have a single, common, national language...the concept of the nation as unified, homogeneous, socially, culturally, linguistically. (Grillo, 1989: 42-3)

There have been many attempts to achieve such an ideal since the Revolution. At least one of these closed the second millennium in Europe itself as Serbia tried to remove ethnic, religious and language groups from its territory, succeeding only in reducing that territory. The creation of a coherent political identity and its maintenance is thus undeniably a main motive for states, as is the attempt to ensure that this identity covers as many other uniting links as possible. A crucial objective is often a single language, rather than the more achievable one of a multilingual state. The aim is stability and cohesiveness, and all else is sacrificed to this overriding requirement. The attitude structure towards language (L1) which best seems to represent identity as a motive gives priority to the concept of excellence, superiority and attraction, and the state language will score highly in all these characteristics. The vitality, too, of the single language will appear complete as it aims to function in every domain for every citizen. Grillo's analysis of national construction in Britain gave a different ideal, however. It prioritised elitism and the retention of power as the fundamental goal, tracing the development of this from aristocratic control until about 1750 to economic elitism thereafter. He noted how the ruling groups simply ignored diversity including linguistic diversity, absorbing local elites into the national one by linguistic means as well as by force or economic domination. Following the identity motive, Grillo's two overall goals at the level of an ideal in our terminology were hence social cohesion and elitism.

The theory of nationalism, or at least of state construction, as applied to the creation of the USA, shows a third ideal for social identity construction. Most American political analysts accept that pluralism has been fundamental to the country as mass immigration took place in the nineteenth century and afterwards, and that theoretically at least, it is possible for groups to alternate in power. Similarly, the contemporary nation has been constructed from a variety of groups and each has the same set of rights and duties. While the basic approach was that individual identities should be lost in the melting pot and that a new, cohesive nation would be formed, voices have been raised in favour of a different approach accepting a mosaic of different identities (Kallen, 1915). While such an approach has led to the objective of multiculturalism at significant times in recent years it has not led to multilingualism: indeed the opposite is true. The full logic of the mosaic approach has found more favour in countries like Canada.

The Kaplan and Baldauf list of goals or ends of language policy, which include neither attitudes nor underlying motives, (see page 11) cannot readily be reformulated to our motivational structure like the Grillo and Kallen ones. Their list does seem to include mention of the ideals of social cohesion, elitism and mosaicity, but since they go farther than Grillo or Kallen, they pay attention to the state's concerns with other states, and with the world outside its own borders. We shall return to this later, but it is worth noting at this point that the objectives and targets Kaplan and Baldauf indicate as relevant to such matters include, as ideals, both competition and conflict with other states.

Motivation of the powerful (Grillo, Kallen)								
Identity sequence	Attitudinal structure							Ideal/objective
	Exc'ence		Vitality		Attract		Action	
	L1	L2	L1	L2	L1	L2	L1	L2	
Identity (personal)									
Identity (social)									
Grillo (France)	3	1	3	1	3	1	3	1	cohesion/repression
Grillo (GB)	3		3		3		3		elitism/ignore diversity
Kallen (USA)	3	3	3	3	3	3	3	3	mosaic/ multiculturalism
Ideology									
Image									
Insecurity									
Maintain identity									
Defend identity									
Maintain inequality									
Correct inequality									
Integrate									
Improve instrument									
Despair									

Algeria and India

Chapters 1 to 5 allow us to add to the motivational picture for states that Grillo, Kallen, Kaplan and Baldauf have outlined. Algeria faces two contrasts: between the prestigious role of Classical Arabic in relation to the language actually spoken in the streets, and the role of Arabic in relation to the many languages, Arabic and other, spoken in the state. While the main ideal is social cohesion, the strategy of ignoring linguistic reality is closer to that of elitist societies. The consequence is the objective of ignoring Berber languages and promoting Classical Arabic, while tacitly accepting spoken Algerian Arabic as the de facto language. Different again is the case of national identity creation in India, where again neither the French nor the British nationality concepts are appropriate. Multilingualism and multiculturalism, the adaptation of the identity motive often adopted in multilingual states in an attempt to achieve the ideal of political stability, has had a chequered history elsewhere during the final 25 years of the 20th century in countries such as Australia, the UK and USA. Support for one language as the language of the State has there remained the principal component. The attitudinal structure reveals subtle differences in multilingual states where several languages have achieved official status. It generally reveals a much stronger tendency for supportive action in favour of a variety of languages, while the whole language issue will have a higher profile. Nonetheless, official policy rarely supports languages equally, and the excellence score for example is likely to be greater for one language than for another. Nonetheless, the traditional Indian approach has been to accept multilingualism and to adopt a policy of three plus or minus one languages, as we have seen.

Motivation of the powerful (Algeria and India)								
Identity sequence	Attitudinal structure							Ideal/objective
	Exc'ence		Vitality		Attract		Action	
	L1	L2	L1	L2	L1	L2	L1	L2	
Identity (personal)									
Identity (social)									
Algeria (Arabic/ Berber)	1	1	1	1	1	1	1	3	cohesion/accept L1 spoken Arabic, reject L2 Berber
Algeria (spoken/ Classical Arabic)	1	3	1	1	1	3	1	3	cohesion/accept L1 spoken, promote L2 Classical
India	3	3	3	3	3	3	3	3	mosaic/ multiculturalism
Ideology									
Image									
Insecurity									
Maintain identity									
Defend identity									
Maintain inequality									
Correct inequality									
Integrate									
Improve instrument									
Despair									

Ideology

Political ideology, as we have noted, is an important element in the motivational structure of language policy. We examined in Chapter 2 above the opposition of attitudes between politicians following a political ideology and linguists and teachers who quickly became politically involved in the issue of the status of the standard language in Britain between 1988 and 1995. If we represent the British politicians by P and the linguists and teachers by L, the contrasts between the ideologically based attitudes of the two groups could be represented as in Figure 9.1 The ideological convictions of the Conservative politicians involved are well documented, as is the conflict between the ideology of this group and the reactions of others. In general, the ideological motive in this example reveals an attitudinal structure with strong contrasts. As with powerless communities, there is a division to be made in the question of ideological motives between inclusive and mosaic societies. Japan and France both find it ideologically very difficult to accept community difference within the overarching state. In both societies there is strong pressure to adopt the overall social norm and to surrender what they regard as divisive community allegiance. Japan does this by suppression of the individual, while French Republicanism is based on the idea that the individual is all important: he or she voluntarily surrenders his or her inalienable right to control the state to its representatives, but can at any time, theoretically, take this power back. From such differences might stem the difference in crime levels and the nature of crime in the two societies. While in France the individual often feels justified in demonstrating his or her personal power by simply refusing social norms, violently opposing authority as in 1968, in Japan the individual is closer to self-sacrifice and indeed sometimes takes his own life as Mishima did in 1974 when society rejected his view of the future. France is much more worried by fragmentary tendencies than is Japan, because, theoretically at any rate, French citizens have the right to approve fragmentation if they so wish. The policy reaction in both countries is the same: to repress the individual and their language. Certainly the identity motive is strong in inclusive societies and the prevailing political ideology supporting the greater unit provides a way in which the minorities can sink their differences in loyalty to it. The superordinate motive of identity in a society like France or Japan can become so hegemonic that it overcomes the motive supporting the separate identity of the Breton or the Korean minority, even among those of Breton and Korean origin.

	Excellence scale	
COGNITIVE	Inferior	Superior
a) Attributes of standard language		
aesthetic value		P L
richness		P L
communicative value		P L
Attributes of other social dialects		
aesthetic value	P	L
richness	P	L
communicative value	P	L

Politicians generally ascribed high scores to the standard language, while linguists gave high scores also to some regional or social varieties.

b) Language-society relationship   P L

Both politicians and linguists believed in a strong relationship between language, variety and setting. The interpretation of what this means was quite different. For politicians the standard language should represent a common identity for all, while linguists believed that the standard language did not reflect the identity of minority communities. Politicians based their views on the desirability of social cohesion; linguists on the facts of human diversity. The contrast is one of ideology.

	Vitality scale		
c) Number and level of domains	Low	Medium	High
in which language or variety			
is used			
Formal variety	L		P
Informal variety	P		L

Politicians generally believed that the formal variety should be used in most domains while linguists believed each variety should be reserved for the relevant setting and some that less prestigious varieties could be used in public and prestigious settings.

AFFECTIVE	Attractiveness scale		
	Dislike	Midpoint	Like
Archaic variety		L	P
Elitist variety		L	P
Regional varieties	P		
Written variety		L	P
Informal variety	P	L	

Politicians generally expressed approval of formal varieties and disapproval of regional or informal ones, while linguists and teachers showed a neutral attitude. Politicians' purist motives were generally strong.

CONATIVE	Action scale	
	Lax	Prescriptive
Desire for oneself to act, or		
support for intervention on		
status	L	P
corpus	L	P
acquisition	L	P

Politicians and linguists simply disagree.

Figure 9.1 Attitudes of British politicians (P) and linguists (L) to standard English.

Ideology however means different things to different people. Although the term is almost one of abuse in political debate, the general political motive is to gain access to power in society and then to keep it. In a democracy, this involves gaining electoral support within a political environment. It may be that structured social inequalities ensure or prevent access to power in society, as Marxian thinkers have always claimed, and that the language policy of those who hold power is designed to confirm social control. In this way, conflictual ideologies assume that social inequalities will be strengthened by insistence on controlling the means of communication and on giving low status to the language(s) of the underprivileged. The framework of discussion is set through such inequality: what is talked about, how it is presented, the contextual reference to which it points, the language in which politics is conducted is modified by structural inequality. There will be in essence two possible ideologies: that of the powerful and that of those who oppose them. Believers in pluralism as an alternative model of society, however, usually prefer to identify a range of ideologies, seeing language not as an element of domination but as an essential key to freedom. The political motive for action on language behaviour in this analysis is to somehow take control of political discourse in order to ensure that society is conceptualised in a particular way. It is no accident that the connotation of phrases such as social justice, privatisation, taxation, varies as political parties succeed each other in power in plural societies.

'Political ideologies are a kind of 'world view', made up of a collection of doctrines, theories and principles which claim to interpret the present and offer a view of the desired future' (Heywood, 1994: 7). Heywood, in his introduction to the study of politics, identifies three main perspectives: those of liberalism, with its stress on the individual and on laissez-faire economics; of socialism, 'standing for the principles of community, co-operation and social equality'; and of conservatism, resistant to social change and with its recent variant of the New Right justifying the domination of economic interests. The commonest form of political ideology among elites is that which justifies the domination of one political group, social class or category, or economic community, over another. What seems to be common to majority political communities, and indeed to minority communities if they aspire to become ruling political entities, is a sense of internal cohesiveness and a desire to maintain this. Interestingly, the ideological attitudinal structure in the case of both Japan and French nationalism is closer to the conservative than to the liberal or socialist structures.

In this volume we have limited our case studies to conservatism in the UK. The following table indicates however the picture for the range of ideologies we have described here. The contrast between the two French ideological structures is so significant for that society that it is this contrast between the traditional, 'Republican' view and that demonstrated in the Poignant report that brought about the resignation of the Interior Minister, Jean-Pierre Chevènement in August 2000, over the Corsican question.

Motivation of the powerful (UK, France & Japan)									
Identity sequence	Attitudinal structure								Ideal/objective
	Exc'ence		Vitality		Attract		Action		
	L1	L2	L1	L2	L1	L2	L1	L2	
Identity (personal)									
Identity (social)									
Ideology									
conservatism (GB politicians)	3	1	3	1	3	1	3	1	elitism/ignore diversity
liberalism (GB linguists)	3	3	3	3	3	3	3	3	mosaic/ multiculturalism
socialism (Poignant)	3	3	3	1	3	3	1	3	mosaic/ multiculturalism
nationalism (France)	3	1	3	1	3	1	3	3	cohesion/repress diversity
nationalism (Japan)	3	1	3	1	3	1	3	1	cohesion/repress diversity
Image									
Insecurity									
Maintain identity									
Defend identity									
Maintain inequality									
Correct inequality									
Integrate									
Improve instrument									
Despair									

Image projection

The projection of an image to other groups, both inside and outside the relevant country, can mean simply a programme such as the cultural diplomacy of the British Council, the Japan Foundation or the Goethe Institut; it can equally mean a programme of cultural indoctrination such as that which prevents Parisians giving credibility to the cultural productions of French-speaking Swiss or Canadians. The attitudinal structure which relates to the motive of image projection seems to be a mixture of the identity and the insecurity patterns. But fundamentally, if the image motive has any chance of leading to successful policy, it must reflect the identity motive almost in every particular. Japanese views of their own language have given an attitudinal structure similar to that motivated by the identity theme, although it should be emphasised that this does not reveal other aspects of Japanese motivation such as the desire to countenance negative views of resurgent Japanese nationalism. The overriding goal of external actions such as these must be to allow the state to compete on the international stage.

Motivation of the powerful (Germany, Japan)									
Identity sequence	Attitudinal structure								Ideal/objective
	Exc'ence		Vitality		Attract		Action		
	L1	L2	L1	L2	L1	L2	L1	L2	
Identity (personal)									
Identity (social)									
Ideology									
Image									
Germany	3	1	3	1	3	1	3	1	competition/foster German
Japan	3	1	3	1	3	1	3	1	competition/seek favourable image
Insecurity									
Maintain identity									
Defend identity									
Maintain inequality									
Correct inequality									
Integrate									
Improve instrument									
Despair									

Insecurity

The reverse of pride in one's group's identity is fear of the identity of others. It will be a rare society in which the majority community recognises the value or even sometimes the right to existence of the minority community and its language. When the insecurity is that of the majority community in relation to such minority communities then the motive will be that of maintaining inequality, or indeed as we have seen in the cases of Algeria and France, of creating social identity. If the insecurity relates to the position of the state in relation to the outside world, however, action is much more necessary and defensive policies to impose the use of the state's language or to erect barriers to the penetration of an 'enemy' language within the frontiers will be set up. Insecure attitudes seem to have partly inspired both the traditional French state policy on regional languages, and the many declarations opposing the fragmentation and Balkanisation of the French state which might result from any weakening of the pre-1951 centralisation of linguistic control, and which led to the Toubon Law of 1994 opposing Anglicisms. This latter, discussed here in the case study of neologism in French, is a classic example of mixed motives, combining motives of insecurity and the defence of identity.

Motivation of the powerful (France: Toubon Law)								
Identity sequence	Attitudinal structure							Ideal/objective
	Exc'ence		Vitality		Attract		Action	
	L1	L2	L1	L2	L1	L2	L1	L2	
Identity (personal)									
Identity (social)									
Ideology									
Image									
Insecurity									
Neologism in French	1	3	1	3	2	1	3	3	conflict/xenophobia
Maintain identity									
Defend identity									
Maintain inequality									
Correct inequality									
Integrate									
Improve instrument									
Despair									

Defending identity and maintaining inequality

The vast majority of the published literature on states and their language policies is written from the point of view of minority communities whose concern is that states, governments, the elite and established social categories have a poor record of internal tolerance. As a motive for language policy, the defence of state identity and language can generate a number of approaches. The most obvious is that it can lead majority communities simply to ignore or repress others. The cases of both Britain and France can show how such defence has been differently interpreted. The overall attitudinal picture for Britain and France, shown on page 191, also shows up contrasts in attitudes which illustrate how it is that the two countries have developed strikingly different policies in relation to status and corpus policy for the official language, although they are fairly similar in regards to their acquisition policies. Overall, one of the differences is clear in attitudes towards language varieties other than the standard: while the French generally dislike them, British views tend to be more positive.

But it is when inequality, inequity or injustice have been shown to exist within the state that the official attitudinal structure in relation to either the correction or the maintenance of that inequality can be demonstrated. The two sides of the Australian debate on language policy in the late 1980s and early 1990s give examples of both these attitudinal structures, although at that time, the mosaic approach was the one that was adopted and the National Language Policy was instituted. Attitudes in Slovakia, and in the policy actions over Roma, show also how the aspect of state identity involved in ensuring that inequality continues combines with goals of xenophobia responding to internal situations, and the general goal of conflict remains.

COGNITIVE	Excellence Scale		
	Low	Medium	High
Knowledge of			
- one's own language's	GB		F
aesthetic value		GB F	
literary value			GB F
richness		GB	
precision			F
clarity			F
communicative value	F		GB
- the differences between			
language varieties:			
archaic and present-day		GB F	
social varieties	F		GB
regional varieties		GB F	
urban and rural variety	F		GB
functional varieties			
(public and private varieties)	GB		F
written and spoken varieties	GB		F
normal and informal varieties	GB		F
- relationship between			
language and culture	GB		F

AFFECTIVE	Attractiveness Scale		
	Dislike		Like
Attractiveness of			
- one's own language			
(insecurity to pride)			GB F
- other languages			
(xenophobia if disliked)	GB	F	
- non-prestigious			
language varieties (as in the			
list above)	F		GB

CONATIVE	Action Scale		
	Lax		Prescriptive
Desire for oneself to			
- obtain or improve			
linguistic instrument		GB	F
- integrate by adding language			
or language variety	GB	F	
- integrate by language shift	GB F		
Support for intervention on			
status	GB		F
corpus	GB		F
acquisition		GB	F

Figure 9.2. British and French attitudinal space   Source: Ager, 1996b

Motivation of the powerful (UK, France, Central Europe and Australia)									
Identity sequence	Attitudinal structure								Ideal/objective
	Exc'ence		Vitality		Attract		Action		
	L1	L2	L1	L2	L1	L2	L1	L2	
Identity (personal)									
Identity (social)									
Ideology									
Image									
Insecurity									
Maintain identity									
Defend identity									
standard English	3	1	3	1	3	1	3	1	conflict/ethnographic and elitist purism
standard French	3	3	3	3	3	3	3	1	conflict/xenophobic purism
Maintain inequality									
anti-Roma	3	1	3	1	3	1	3	1	conflict/repress Roma
Slovakia	3	3	3	1	3	3	3	3	mosaic/ multilingualism
Correct inequality									
Australia	3	3	3	1	3	3	3	3	mosaic/multiculturalism
Integrate									
Improve instrument									
Despair									

Integration and instrumentality

Integration with another community is not a major motive for state language policy, as we have suggested. There is some evidence to suggest that integration with the English-speaking community is a relevant motive in some parts of the Algerian scientific community, in pursuance of a state-inspired policy of gradual disengagement from French-speaking Francophonie and its associated intent to use only French in science, and the attitudinal structure underpinning this can be seen in the statements and actions of those involved (Chapters 1 and 6). Elsewhere, integrative motives similar to those of the individual seeking acceptance in a different social community might be found among applicants to join international Francophonie itself, such as Vietnam,

Romania and Bulgaria where policy is currently supporting greater teaching of French (Ager, 1996a). Here, as in many areas where state policy turns towards the outside world, the overriding goal is one of competition or indeed conflict with other languages. The aim of joining Francophonie is to gain advantage for Vietnam, not to selflessly support advantage for France or other mainly French-speaking countries. Similar attempts to join the Commonwealth or other international language groups are based on a search for help and support, and certainly not on fellow-feeling and international good-will.

Instrumentality, as far as states are concerned, is the motive which, in the light of the general ideal of oppositional conflict with English, has given birth to such objectives as corpus policy aimed at modernising terminology in Quebec and France. How far the instrumentality motive is itself related to insecurity is a matter of some debate, and there are certainly records of speeches and Parliamentary debates in both countries where both motives have been displayed. Insofar as the instrumentality motive is concerned, the public statements of French experts are relevant (Chapter 4).

Motivation of the powerful (Vietnam and Quebec)								
Identity sequence	Attitudinal structure							Ideal/objective
	Exc'ence		Vitality		Attract		Action	
	L1	L2	L1	L2	L1	L2	L1	L2	
Identity (personal)									
Identity (social)									
Ideology									
Image									
Insecurity									
Maintain identity									
Defend identity									
Maintain inequality									
Correct inequality									
Integrate									
Vietnam	3	3	1	3	1	3	1	3	conflict/internationalisation
Improve instrument									
Quebec	1	3	1	3	3	3	3	1	conflict/reformist purism
Despair									

Chapter 10
Conclusion

Summary

We have considered that motivation for the planning of language behaviour is best analysed as a three-part psychological and social phenomenon. A particular planning or policy decision depends on the structure of motives, on attitudinal structure and on the goals pursued. Motivation is most often discussed as dependent on attitudes as presented within social psychology, or as dependent on needs hierarchies and goal theory. We have prioritised instead the idea of dynamic identity construction, with its phases of identity, ideology, image, insecurity, the defence or maintenance of identity, the maintenance or correction of social inequality, integration, instrumentalism or despair. This list of basic motives seems applicable to all three levels of 'actor': the individual, powerless communities, and states, even though it has normally been applied to groups and has given rise to social identity theory. Our development of social identity theory takes into account its major axioms: that identity develops through stages of social categorisation, identity creation, social comparison and psychological distinctiveness; it is created by awareness of membership of an ingroup and non-membership of an outgroup; the concomitant distinctiveness of such groups; that social comparison is a prime factor in attitudes towards others; that those creating their social identity move towards the positive and high status rather than towards the negative, low status groups. It also responds to the main criticism of social identity theory, that it is static, by stressing the dynamic nature of creating group identity (Chambers, 1995: 250-3). In accordance with Trudgill (1983) we rather question whether moves always take place towards high status groups. We have included the main points of ethnolinguistic identity theory, and particularly focussed realisation of this type of identity and the associated concept of vitality on the issue of language use in public, high status domains (Allard and Landry, 1992).

In order to understand motivation fully the picture needs to be added to by examining the attitudinal structure of the actors with reference to both their L1 and any relevant L2 or other language, and the whole picture then needs to be further clarified by also considering the goals, categorised as ideals, objectives or targets, relevant to the policy or planning behaviour actually pursued. We have been particularly interested to measure language attitudes in such a way that they can be summarised meaningfully. We have done this by establishing four measurement scales, of excellence, vitality, attractiveness and readiness for action, and allocating markers of strength to each. We have also been concerned to distinguish levels of goals, and in particular to distinguish utopian ideals from the actual objectives planners pursue. For individuals, this has meant identifying superordinate ideals of coherence of identity, or of cooperation, sometimes leading to compromise. For powerless communities, we have noted ideals of conflict, cooperation and compromise. For states, ideals of social cohesion, elitism or social mosaicity, on the internal level, are matched by competition or even conflict on the external. Such superordinate goals have often been labelled social mobility, affiliation or assimilation when weak or soft group boundaries are involved, or, at the other extreme, social competition, vitality, rejection or autonomy when rigid or hard group boundaries are noted. Neither for motives nor for goals, however, have we felt it possible to provide markers of strength: rather, our measurement process is limited to one of categorisation.

Although it is perfectly conceivable to measure the strength of policies or planning decisions by assuming that declared and overt policies are stronger than undeclared and covert ones, we have not pursued this idea here. Declared and overt policies are visible because they are enshrined in legal texts, formal decisions or court judgements; covert ones are represented simply by what people do or the attitudes they adopt. It is on this basis that British government sources can claim that 'Britain has no language policy'. But a policy of rejection or discrimination is nonetheless real for not being openly stated, and language shift or the adoption of a new communicative mechanism is likewise a fact. Here, we have simply described language behaviour in relation to our three goal levels, and the commonest level of actual planning or policy, the target level of detailed and precise decisions in education or behaviour, has not been our main concern.

We have assessed how far how our analytical structure matches the opinions on motivation of Hall (1974), Ryan and Giles (1982) for individuals, of Wardhaugh (1987) for powerless communities and of

Grillo (1989) and Kallen (1915) for states, and found that indeed this structure both follows their approaches and also enables us to represent motivation fairly comprehensively.

Motivation (Hall, Ryan and Giles, Wardhaugh, Grillo, Kallen)									
Identity sequence	Attitudinal structure								Ideals/objectives
	Exc'ence		Vitality		Attract		Action		
	L1	L2	L1	L2	L1	L2	L1	L2	
Identity (personal)									
Identity (social) (Grillo 1989 France)	3	1	3	1	3	1	3	1	cohesion/repression
Grillo 1989 UK	3		3		3		3		elitism/ ignore diversity
Kallen 1915 USA	3	3	3	3	3	3	3	3	mosaic/ multiculturalism
Ideology									
Image									
Insecurity (Hall, 1974)	1		1		1-3			3	a)coherence/strengthen identity b) shift/reject L1
Maintain identity (Ryan and Giles, 1982)	2		2		3			3	coherence/improve status of L1 coherence/attract others
Defend identity (Wardhaugh, 1987)	3		3		3			3	conflict/fight for rights
Maintain inequality									
Correct inequality									
Integrate (Wardhaugh, 1987)	3	3	3	3	3	3	3	3	cooperate/use both L1 and L2
Improve instrument									
Despair (Wardhaugh, 1987)	1	3	1	3	1	3	1	3	compromise/shift from L1 to L2

The Motives, Attitudes and Goals of Individuals, Communities and States

Figure 7.5 can now be completed for our three categories of actors, for L1 and L2 in each case, and the relevant goals, with the information derived from the case studies in Chapters 1 to 6 (Fig 10.1, pages 199 to 201). This representation of motives provides a gross over-simplification of the relationships, of course, but the general message holds true as a picture of the complexities of the motivational structure. We have limited Figure 10.1 to the case studies dealt with in this volume, and of course it could be greatly expanded with further case studies which might throw further light on its as yet uncompleted parts.

It is inevitable that some motives, some stages of the identity sequence, are more important for one category of actor than for another. Decisions on instrumentality - what to do about one's own language skills in pursuing career and social opportunities - are particularly important for individuals. They are particularly important in relation to the other language: which language(s) to acquire, which skills to improve. It is at this point that the notion of repertoire, at the level of the personal objective, is important in combating one of the main criticisms levelled at social identity theory and ethnolinguistic vitality theory: that neither copes adequately with issues of stable multiculturalism and multilingualism. In many societies membership of different communities within the state is both possible and indeed normal. Such multiple group membership is represented, linguistically, by the existence of the individual's language/language variety repertoire and his or her ability to move easily from one to another. The notion of repertoire also helps us to avoid the misinterpretations sometimes made of such approaches as accommodation theory or convergence/divergence strategies (Giles and Smith, 1979), that language behaviour necessarily implies upward convergence and 'giving way' to dominant groups.

For communities and states, the instrumentality motive is of less immediate importance, and corpus policy and the reform of the linguistic instrument, of undeniably great importance to states, seem to be associated more with the insecurity motive or with issues of the maintenance of identity. Issues of the correction of inequality are important to powerless communities. The defence of identity, and the creation of a favourable image among possible competitors abroad, are concerns of the state. This is not to say that all the motives cannot be important to all three categories of actor, nor that motives are necessarily 'pure': they are often mixed.

The independence of the three measures of motivation - the identity sequence, the attitudinal structure, and the categorisation of goals - is immediately apparent from Figure 10.1. One cannot predict from any one attitudinal structure what the goals might be, nor is a particular goal immediately and obviously related to a particular attitudinal structure. Furthermore, any one particular stage in the identity sequence can be accompanied by quite different attitudinal structures, quite different goals and quite different policies. In addition to this, a particular policy might derive from mixed motives, a range of attitudes among its supporters, and a diversity of goals.

Figure 10.1 also shows how environments affect motivation and policies. Powerless communities faced with decisions on language do not all adopt similar policies. Individuals do not all shift from their L1 to a higher status L2. States do not all react in the same way to international competition, nor to challenges posed by a diversity of languages and cultures within their borders.

The general conclusion must be that the examples we have explored appear to support other instances within social psychology that indicate the lack of predictive force of attitudinal structure. Attitudes, particularly where these are based on the affective component, do not necessarily predict the actions and strategies actors will implement. Nor do the motives leading directly to the actions undertaken by organisms correlate directly with the expressed attitudes of the actors. Such a conclusion may be cynical, but is hardly unknown in political science. Not all situations are completely Machiavellian, of course, but it is important that the total motivational structure of individuals, communities and states be taken into consideration rather than simply expressed attitudes, expressed goals, or expressed motives.

To take the point further and to return to the views of Terry et al. (1999) outlined in Chapter 7, the strategies and policies implemented by states, communities and individuals represent planned behaviour and reasoned action by these actors, taking account of attitudinal structure but also of environmental conditions, likely outcomes and available means. The creation and constant recreation of identity and particularly of social identity, which we have called dynamic identity construction, followed by willingness to act in conformity with expectations of action, are the key elements in language policy motivation.

Motivation of individuals									
Identity sequence	Attitudinal structure								Ideals/objectives
	Exc'ence		Vitality		Attract		Action		
	L1	L2	L1	L2	L1	L2	L1	L2	
Identity (personal)									
Identity (social)									
Ideology									
Image									
Insecurity									
Maintain identity immigrants (non-establ ished)	3	1	3	1	3	1	1	1	coherence/no action
Defend identity									
Maintain inequality									
Correct inequality									
Integrate B	3	3	3	3	3	2	1	3	cooperate/repertoire (L1 + L2)
C	2	3	2	3	2	3	1	3	cooperate/repertoire (L1 + L2)
D	3	2	3	2	3	3	1	3	cooperate/repertoire (L1 + L2); create favourable image
immigrants (establish'd	2	3	1	3	2	3	1	3	shift/reject L1
Improve instrument A		1		1		1		3	coherence/add L2
E	3	3	3	1	3	1	1	3	coherence/add L2 in limited domain
Lingua franca		1		1		1		3	coherence/repertoire (L1 and L2 in limited domain)
immigrants (establish'd	3	3	2	3	3	2	1	3	cooperation/repertoire (L1+L2)
Despair									

Figure 10.1 (part) Motivation of individuals, communities and states

Motivation of powerless communities									
Identity sequence	Attitudinal structure								Ideal/objective
	Exc'ence		Vitality		Attract		Action		
	L1	L2	L1	L2	L1	L2	L1	L2	
Identity (personal)									
Identity (social)									
Ideology									
Image									
Insecurity Neologism in French	1	3	1	3	3	3	1	2	conflict/reformist purism
Maintain identity									
French regional languages	2	2	1	3	2	2	2	1	conflict/covert maintenance of L1
Welsh	3	3	1	3	3	2	2	1	conflict/seek equal rights with English; archaic purism
Defend identity Catalan	3	1	3	2	3	1	3	1	conflict/defend L1 by attacking L2
Maithili	3	3	3	3	3	3	3	1	cooperate/accept multilingualism but require rights
Maintain inequality									
Correct inequality European Charter	3	3	3	3	3	3	3	3	cooperation/(some) rights for minorities
Feminism	3	1	3	1	3	3	3	3	conflict/appropriate use of language
FECCA	3	3	2	3	3	3	3	3	cooperation/education in L2 as mainstream provision
Integrate									
Koreans in Japan	1	3	1	3	1	3	1	3	compromise/shift from L1 to L2
Improve instrument									
Despair Ainu	1	3	1	3	1	3	1	3	compromise/shift from L1 to L2

Figure 10.1 (part) Motivation of individuals, communities and states

Motivation of powerful states									
Identity sequence	Attitudinal structure								Ideal/objective
	Exc'ence		Vitality		Attract		Action		
	L1	L2	L1	L2	L1	L2	L1	L2	
Identity (personal)									
Identity (social) Algeria (Arabic/ Berber)	1	1	1	1	1	1	1	3	cohesion/accept L1 spoken Arabic, reject L2 Berber
Algeria (spoken/ Classical Arabic)	1	3	1	1	1	3	1	3	cohesion/accept L1 spoken, promote L2 Classical
India	3	3	3	3	3	3	3	3	mosaic/ multiculturalism
Ideology UK	3	1	3	1	3	1	3	1	elitism/ignore diversity
Image Germany	3	1	3	1	3	1	3	1	competition/foster German
Japan	3	1	3	1	3	1	3	1	competition/seek favourable image
Insecurity									
Neologism in French	1	3	1	3	2	1	3	3	conflict/xenophobia
Maintain identity									
Defend identity									
Maintain inequality anti-Roma	3	1	3	1	3	1	3	1	conflict/repress Roma
Correct inequality Australia	3	3	3	1	3	3	3	3	mosaic/multilingualism
Integrate									
Improve instrument									
Despair									

Figure 10.1 (part) Motivation of individuals, communities and states

References

Adams, L. L. and Brink, D. T. (eds.) (1990) *Perspectives on Official English. The Campaign for English as the Official Language of the USA.* Berlin: Mouton de Gruyter.

Ager, D. E. (1996a) *Francophonie in the 1990s. Problems and Opportunities.* Clevedon: Multilingual Matters

Ager, D. E. (1996b) *Language Policy in Britain and France.* London: Cassells

Ager, D. E. (1999) *Identity, Insecurity and Image. France and Language.* Clevedon: Multilingual Matters. Multilingual Matters Series 112.

Allard, R. and Landry, R. (1992) Ethnolinguistic vitality beliefs and language maintenance and loss. In W. Fase, K. Jaspaert and S. Kroon (eds) *Maintenance and Loss of Minority Languages.* Amsterdam/Philadelphia: John Benjamins Publishing Company. pp. 171-95

Ammon, U. (1995) German as an international language. In P. Stevenson. *The German Language and the Real World.* Oxford: Clarendon Press . pp. 25 - 53

Anderson, B. (1983, 1991) *Imagined Communities.* London: Verso

Argemi, A. (1996) Universal declaration of linguistic rights: responding to a need. *Contact Bulletin*, 13, 3, 4

Ashford, S. and Timms, N. (1992) *What Europe Thinks.* Aldershot: Dartmouth

Ayres-Bennet, W. (1996) *A History of the French Language through Texts.* London: Routledge

Baetens Beardsmore, H. (ed) (1992) *European Models of Bilingual Education.* Clevedon: Multilingual Matters.

Bailey, R. W. (1991) *Images of English. A Cultural History of the Language.* Cambridge: Cambridge University Press

Baker, C. (1992) Bilingual Education in Wales. In H. Baetens Beardsmore (ed.) *European Models of Bilingual Education.* Clevedon: Multilingual Matters. pp. 7-29

Baker, K. (1993) *The Turbulent Years: My Life in Politics.* London: Faber

Bamgbose, A. (1994) Pride and prejudice in multilingualism. In R. Fardon and G. Furniss (eds) *African Languages, Development and the State.* London: Routledge. pp. 32-43

Basu, A. (1997) Reflections on community conflicts and the state in India. *The Journal of Asian Studies*, 56, 391-7

Benrabah, M. (1995, La langue perdue. *Esprit*, 208, 1, 35-47

Braselmann, P. (1998) *Sprachpolitik und Sprachbewusstsein in Frankreich heute.* Tübingen: Niemeyer

Brass, P. (1994) (2nd ed) *The Politics of India since Independence.* Cambridge: Cambridge University Press

Bühler, K. (1934) *Sprachtheorie: die Darstellungsfunktion der Sprache*. Jena: Fischer
Calvet, L.-J. (1992) *Les langues des marchés en Afrique*. Paris: Didier Erudition
Chambers, J. K. (1995) *Sociolinguistic Theory*. Oxford: Blackwell
Clyne, M. (1991) *Community Languages: the Australian Experience*. Cambridge: Cambridge University Press
Clyne, M. (1995) *The German Language in a Changing Europe*. Cambridge: Cambridge University Press
Clyne, M. (1997) Managing language diversity and second language programmes in Australia. *Current issues in language and society*, 4, 2, 94-119
Contact Bulletin. Quarterly. Dublin: The European Bureau for Lesser Used Languages
Cortazzi, H. (1993) *The Japanese Achievement*. London: Sidgwick and Jackson
Cooper, R. L. (1989) *Language Planning and Social Change*. Cambridge: Cambridge University Press
Cox, B. (1989) *English from 5 to 16*. London: National Curriculum Council
Croft, K. and Macpherson, R. J. S. (1991) Client demand, policy research and lobbying: major sources of languages administrative policies in NSW 1980-1986. *Australian Review of Applied Linguistics*, Series S, 8, 89-108
Crowley, A. (1989) *The Politics of Discourse. The Standard Language Question in British Cultural Debates*. London: Macmillan
Dawkins, J. (1991) *Australia's Language: the Australian Language and Literacy Policy*. Canberra: Australian Government Publishing Service
de Certeau, M., Julia, D., Revel, J. (1975) *Une politique de la langue*. Paris: Gallimard
DGLF. Annual. *Rapport au Parlement sur l'application de la loi du 4 août 1994*. Paris: Délégation Générale à la langue française. Available: www.culture.fr/dglf/rapport
Dörnyei, Z. and Otto, I. (1998) Motivation in action: a process model of L2 motivation. *Working Papers in Applied Linguistics, Thames Valley University, London*, 4, 43-691
Edwards, J. (1994) *Multilingualism*. London: Routledge
Erasmus, H. (1994) Esperanto as a second language alongside the native tongue. In Jenniges, R. *International Conference 'Nations and languages, and the construction of Europe'. Abstracts*. Leuven
Etat. *Etat de la Francophonie dans le monde*. Annual. Paris: La Documentation Française
Evans, P. B., Reuschmayer, D. and Skocpol, T. (1985) (eds) *Bringing the State back in*. Cambridge: Cambridge University Press
Fairclough, N. (1989) *Language and Power*. London: Longman
Fardon, R. and Furniss, G. (1994) *African Languages, Development and the State*. London: Routledge
Fase, W., Jaspaert, K. and Kroon, S (eds) (1992) *Maintenance and Loss of Minority Languages*. Amsterdam/Philadelphia: John Benjamins Publishing Company
Fasold, R. (1984) *The Sociolinguistics of Society*. Oxford, Basil Blackwell
Fasold, R., Yamada, H, Robinson, D. and Barish, S. (1990) The language-planning effect of newspaper editorial policy: Gender differences in The Washington Post. *Language in society*, 19, 521-39
Fishman, J. A. (1972) *Language and Nationalism*. Rowley, Mass: Newbury House
Fishman, J. A. (1991) *Reversing Language Shift*. Clevedon: Multilingual Matters
Fraser, A. (1995) (2nd ed) *The Gypsies*. Oxford: Blackwell

Fyle, C. B. (1994) Krio as the main lingua franca in Sierra Leone. In R. Fardon and G. Furniss (eds) *African Languages, Development and the State*. London: Routledge. pp. 44-54

Galbally, F. (Chair) (1978) *Migrant Services and Programs*. Canberra: Australian Government Publishing Service

Gardner, R. and Lambert, W. (1959) Motivational variables in second-language acquisition. *Canadian Journal of Psychology*, 13, 266-72

Gellner, E. (1983) *Nations and Nationalism*. Oxford: Blackwell

Giles, H. and St Clair, R. (1979) (eds) *Language and Social Psychology*. Oxford: Basil Blackwell

Giles, H. and Smith, P. (1979) Accommodation theory: optimal levels of convergence. In H. Giles and R. St Clair (eds) *Language and Social Psychology*. Oxford: Basil Blackwell. pp. 45-65

Giordan, H. (ed) (1992) *Les Minorités en Europe*. Paris: Kimé.

Girardet, R. (1983) *Le nationalisme français. Anthologie 1871-1914*. Paris: Seuil

Gottlieb, N. (1995) *Kanji Politics: Language Policy and Japanese Script*. London and New York: Kegan Paul International

Grassby, A. (1973) *A Multi-cultural Society for the Future*. Canberra: Australian Government Publishing Service

Grillo, R. (1989) *Dominant Languages: Language and Hierarchy in Britain and France*. Cambridge: Cambridge University Press

Grosfoguel, R. (1999) Puerto Ricans in the USA: a comparative approach. *Journal of Ethnic and Migration Studies*, 25, 2, 233-49

Guardian. *The Guardian*. Daily. London

Guibernau, M. (1997) Images of Catalonia. *Nations and Nationalism*, 3, 1, 89-111

Hall, R. A. (1974) *External History of the Romance Languages*. New York: Elsevier

Halliday, M. (1978) *Language as Social Semiotic*. London: Edward Arnold

Harding, S., Phillips, D. with Fogarty, M. (1986) *Contrasting Values in Western Europe*. London: Macmillan

Hellinger, M. (1995) Language and gender. In P. Stevenson. *The German Language and the Real World*. Oxford: Clarendon Press. pp. 279-314

Herriman, M. and Burnaby, B. (eds) (1996) *LanguagePolicies in English-dominant Countries*. Clevedon: Multilingual Matters. Language and Education Library 10

Hewstone, M., Islam, M. R. and Judd, C. M. (1993) Models of crossed categorization and intergroup relations. *Journal of Personality and Social Psychology*, 64, 779-93

Hewstone, M., Stroebe, W. and Stephenson, G. M. (eds) (1996) 2nd edition. *Introduction to Social Psychology*. Oxford: Blackwell.

Heywood, A. (1994) *Political Ideas and Concepts*. London: Macmillan

Hoffmann, C. (1995) Monolingualism, bilingualism, cultural pluralism and national identity: twenty years of language planning in contemporary Spain. *Current Issues in Language and Society*, 2, 1, 59-90

Honey, J. (1997) *Language is Power: the Story of Standard English*. London: Faber and Faber

Hornberger, N. H. (1998) Language policy, language education, language rights: indigenous, immigrant, and international perspectives. *Language in Society*, 27, 439-58

Hudson, R. (1980) *Sociolinguistics*. Cambridge: Cambridge University Press

Japan Foundation. *Newsletter*. Available: www.jpf.go.jp. Consulted 14 June 1999

Jenniges, R. (1994) *International Conference 'Nations and languages, and the construction of Europe'. Abstracts.* Leuven

Kallen, H. (1915) Democracy versus the melting pot. *The Nation,* 18 and 25 February 1915.

Kaplan, R. B. and Baldauf, R. (1997) *Language Planning. From Practice to Theory.* Clevedon: Multilingual Matters. Multilingual Matters Series 108.

Kedourie, E. (1961) *Nationalism.* London: Hutchinson

Kellas, J. (1991) *The Politics of Nationalism and Ethnicity.* London: Macmillan

Kingman, J. (1988) *Report of the Committee of Enquiry into the Teaching of English Language.* London: Her Majesty's Stationery Office

Knight, C. (1990) *The Making of Tory Education Policy, 1950-1986.* London: Falmer Press

Kohli, A. (1997) Can democracies accommodate ethnic nationalism: the rise and decline of self-determination movements. *The Journal of Asian Studies,* 56, 2, 325-43

Laitin, D. D. (1997) The cultural identities of a European state. *Politics and Society,* 25, 3, 277-302

Lakoff, R. (1975) *Language and Woman's Place.* New York: Harper and Row

Larsen-Freeman, D. and Long, M. H. (1991) *An Introduction to Second Language Acquisition Research.* London: Longman

Lawton, D. (1994) *The Tory Mind on Education 1979-1994.* London: The Falmer Press

Leitner, G. (1991) Europe 1992: a language perspective. *Language Problems and Language Planning,* 15, 3, 282-96

Light, I., Bernard, R. B., and Kim, R. (1999) Immigrant incorporation in the garment industry of Los Angeles. *International Migration Review,* 33, 1, 5-25

Lo Bianco, J. (1987) *National Policy on Languages.* Department of Education, Commonwealth of Australia

Lo Bianco, J. (1990) *The National Policy on Languages. December 1987-March 1990. Report to the Minister for Employment, Education and Training.* Canberra: Australian Advisory Council on Languages and Multicultural Education

Lodge, R. A. (1993) *French. From Dialect to Standard.* London: Routledge

Marenbon, J. (1987) *English, our English: The New 'Orthodoxy' Examined.* London: Centre for Policy Studies

Marsh, D. and Rhodes, R. A. W. (1992) *Policy Networks in British Government.* Oxford: Oxford University Press

Marshall, D. F. (ed) nd. *Language Planning. Festschrift in honour of Joshua A. Fishman.* Amsterdam: John Benjamin

Martyna, W. (1983) Beyond the he/man approach: the case for non-sexist language. In Thorne, B., Kramerae, C. and Henley, N. (eds) *Language, Gender and Society.* Rowley, Mass: Newbury House. pp. 25-37

Maslow, A. (1954) *Motivation and Personality.* New York: Harper and Row

Massana, A. M. (1992) Droits linguistiques et droits fondamentaux en Espagne. In Giordan, H. (ed) *Les Minorités en Europe.* Paris: Kimé. pp. 251-68

Massana, A. M. (1993) The Catalan language in the conflict between centralism and autonomy, 1850-1940. In Vilfan, S (ed) *Ethnic groups and Language Rights.* Aldershot: Dartmouth. pp. 65-88

Milroy, J. and Milroy, L. (1985) *Authority in Language. Investigating Language Prescription and Standardisation.* London: Routledge and Kegan Paul

Ministry of Foreign Affairs of Japan. (1999) *Japan's Contribution to the World.*

Tokyo: Kodansha Ltd.
Miyawaki H. (1992) Some problems of linguistic minorities in Japan. In W. Fase, K. Jaspaert and S. Kroon (eds) *Maintenance and Loss of Minority Languages.* Amsterdam/Philadelphia: John Benjamins Publishing Company. pp. 357-67
Nahir, M. (1984) Language planning goals: a classification. *Language Problems and Language Planning*, 8, 294-327.
NCO. (1994) *National Curriculum Order.* London: Department of Education and Science
Ozolins, U. (1993) *The Politics of Language in Australia.* Cambridge: Cambridge University Press
Parry, M. M., Davies, W. V. and Temple, R. A. M. (eds) (1994) *The Changing Voices of Europe.* Cardiff: University of Wales Press
Perera, K. (1993) Council for Linguistics in Education report on Cox. *British Association for Applied Linguistics Bulletin.*
Phillipson, R. (1992) *Linguistic Imperialism.* Oxford: Oxford University Press
Poignant, B. (1998) *Langues et Cultures Régionales. Rapport au Premier Ministre.* Paris: La Documentation Française
Posner, R. (1994) Romania within a wider Europe: conflict or cohesion? In Parry, M. M., Davies, W. V. and Temple, R. A. M. (eds) *The Changing Voices of Europe.* Cardiff: University of Wales Press. pp. 23-33
Quell, C. (1997) Language choice in multilingual institutions: a case study at the European Commission with particular reference to the role of English, French, and German as working languages. *Multilingua*, 16, 1, 57-76
Reischauer, E. O. and Jansen, M. B. (1995) *The Japanese Today. Change and continuity.* Cambridge, Mass.: Belknap Press of Harvard University Press
Reynolds, H. (1996) *Aboriginal Sovereignty. Three Nations, one Australia?* St Leonard's: Allen and Unwin
Ricento, T. (1996) Language Policy in the United States. In M. Herriman and B. Burnaby (eds) *Language Policies in English-dominant Countries.* Clevedon: Multilingual Matters. Language and Education Library 10. pp. 122-58
Rosenfeld, R. A., Cunningham, D. and Schmidt, K. (1997) American Sociological Association elections, 1975-96: exploring explanations for "feminization'. *American Sociological Review*, October. 62, 746-59
Ruiz, R. (1984) Orientations in language planning. *National Association for Bilingual Education Journal*, 8, 15-34
Ryan, E. B. and Giles, H. (1982) *Attitudes towards Language Variation.* London: Edward Arnold
Salagnac, G. C. (1995) Le latin, langue véhiculaire. *Le Figaro*, 11.9.1995
Sanders, C. (ed) (1993) *French Today. Language in its Social Context.* Cambridge: Cambridge University Press
Siklova, J. and Miklusakova, M. (1998) Denying citizenship to the Czech Roma. *East European Constitutional Review.* Spring 1998, 58-64
Skocpol, T. (1985) Bringing the State back in: Current Eesearch. In P.B.Evans, D. Reuschmayer and T. Skocpol (eds) *Bringing the State back in.* Cambridge: Cambridge University Press
Smith, A. (1991) *National Identity.* Harmondsworth: Penguin
Smith, M. J. (1993) *Pressure, Power and Policy. State Autonomy and Policy Networks in Britain and the United States.* Hemel Hempstead: Harvester Wheatsheaf
Smolicz, J. J. (1992) Minority languages as core values of ethnic cultures - a study of maintenance and erosion of Polish, Welsh and Chinese languages in

Australia. In W. Fase, K. Jaspaert and S. Kroon (eds) _Maintenance and Loss of Minority Languages_. Amsterdam/Philadelphia: John Benjamins Publishing Company. pp. 277-305

Sontag, S. (1973) The third world of women. _The Partisan Review_, 40, 2

Stahlberg, D. and Frey, D. (1996) Attitudes: structure, measurement and functions. In M. Hewstone, W. Stroebe and G. M. Stephenson. _Introduction to Social Psychology_. 2nd edition. Oxford: Blackwell. pp. 205-239

Stevenson, P. (1995) _The German Language and the Real World_. Oxford: Clarendon Press

Stora, B. (1994) _Histoire de l'Algérie depuis l'indépendance_. Paris: La Découverte

Swigart, L. (1995) _Practice and Perception: Language Use and Attitudes in Dakar_. Ph D thesis, University of Washington, 1992. Ann Arbor, Michigan: University Microfilms International

Sydney Morning Herald. Daily. Sydney

Szulmajster-Celnikier, A. (1996) Le français comme affaire d'Etat. _Regards sur l'actualité_, 221, 39-54

Tames, J. (1993) _A Traveller's History of Japan_. Gloucester: Windrush Press

Terry, D. J., Hogg, M. A. and White, K. M. (1999) The theory of planned behaviour: self-identity, social identity and group norms. _British Journal of Social Psychology_, 38, 225-244

Thomas, G. (1991) _Linguistic Purism_. London: Longman

Thomas, A. (1997) Language policy and nationalism in Wales: a comparative analysis. _Nations and Nationalism_, 3, 3, 323-44

Thorne, B., Kramerae, C. and Henley, N. (eds) _Language, Gender and Society_. Rowley, Mass: Newbury House

Times Higher Education Supplement. Weekly. London: The Times

Tollefson, J. W. (1991) _Planning Language, Planning Inequality_. London: Longman

Truchot, C. (1991) Towards a language policy for the European Community. In D. F. Marshall (ed) _Language Planning. Festschrift in honour of Joshua A. Fishman_. Amsterdam: John Benjamin. pp. 87-104

Trudgill, P. (1983) _On Dialect: Social and Geographic Factors_. Oxford: Basil Blackwell

Vasecka, M. (1999) Romanies in Slovakia on the eve of the Millennium - a social or an ethnic problem? _South-East Europe Review for Labour and Social Affairs_, 2, 1 (April 1999), 47-54

Vilfan, S. (ed) (1993) _Ethnic Groups and Language Rights_. Aldershot: Dartmouth

Walter, H. (1988) _Le français dans tous les sens_. Paris: Robert Laffont

Wardhaugh, R. (1987) _Languages in Competition_. Oxford: Blackwell

Welsh Language Act (1993) _Welsh Language Act. c38_. London: Her Majesty's Stationery Office

Williams, C. H. (1994) _Called unto Liberty!_ Clevedon: Multilingual Matters

Williams, C. (ed) (1991) _Linguistic Minorities, Society and Identity_. Clevedon: Multilingual Matters

Wynne-Jones, A. (1993) New Welsh Language Bill in 1993? _Contact Bulletin_, 10, 2, 1-3

Young, A. S. (1994) _Motivational State and Process within the Sociolinguistic Context. An Anglo-French Comparative Study of School Pupils learning Foreign Languages_. Aston University, Birmingham: Unpublished PhD thesis

Zentella, A. C. (1997) The Hispanophobia of the Official English movement in the US. _International Journal of the Sociology of Language_, 127, 71-86

Index